THE STATE OF FOOD AND AGRICULTURE 2002

ISSN 0081-4539

M-PER

THE STATE OF FOOD AND AGRICULTURE 2002

FOOD AND AGRICULTURE ORGANIZATION OF THE UNITED NATIONS

Rome, 2002

Editing, design and desktop publishing:
Editorial Group
FAO Information Division

ISBN 92-5-104762-6

Foreword

It is impossible to look back over the last year without remembering the tragic attacks of 11 September and the ensuing events, which have opened our eyes to the fragility of the security of us all. They have underlined that, in an era of rapidly advancing globalization, security also can only be global. It is hoped they have strengthened our awareness that the future of humanity is truly a shared future and that many of the challenges humanity faces require common solutions.

This is indeed a period when many of these major challenges seem to be coming to the forefront of attention, thus giving us new hope for the future. Not least among them is the eradication of hunger and poverty – two phenomena and scourges of humanity that are closely interlinked.

In 1996, world leaders met in Rome at the World Food Summit and pledged to eradicate hunger. As a first, but essential, step they agreed to halve the number of undernourished people by 2015. Unfortunately, the latest data available to us suggest that progress over recent years has not been fast enough. It was to accelerate progress that I decided to invite world leaders to meet again in Rome in June this year. Indeed, if we are to meet the objectives that we set ourselves five years ago, it will be necessary to strengthen the political will and to mobilize the necessary financial resources. Much remains to be done, in spite of some striking examples of progress in individual countries and communities. On the other hand, these very examples of success confirm our conviction that the objectives set in Rome in 1996 are achievable.

Other major international events have also taken place recently, or are planned for the near future, with significant implications for our common future. In Monterrey from 18 to 22 March 2002, Mexico hosted the International Conference on Financing for Development to discuss the challenge of ensuring adequate financial resources for meeting internationally agreed development goals, including those contained in the United Nations Millennium Declaration. To this conference, the three Rome-based UN agencies (FAO, the International Fund for Agricultural Development [IFAD] and the World Food Programme [WFP]) brought a joint message calling for increased resources for hunger reduction and for agricultural and rural development. There are encouraging signs that the conference may mark a turning point – a reversal of the past declining trends in development assistance, including that for hunger and agriculture.

Ten years after the United Nations Conference on Environment and Development – the Earth Summit – held in Rio de Janeiro, South Africa is hosting the World Summit on Sustainable Development in Johannesburg in August–September 2002. Here, attention will focus on many of the key challenges in implementing the objectives of sustainable development agreed in Rio in 1992.

No less important may be the agreement reached at the Fourth World Trade Organization Ministerial Conference in Doha, Qatar, in November 2001 to launch a new round of comprehensive multilateral trade negotiations. A particularly encouraging outcome was the strong focus in the Doha Ministerial Declaration on the need to ensure that the development and food security needs of its most vulnerable members are not compromised. Let us hope that the new round of trade negotiations will continue to emphasize the problems and needs of developing countries and lead to a fairer and more equitable international trading system with true benefits for all.

Amid this flurry of important international events, I would particularly like to underline the central role of food, agriculture and rural development in our shared efforts to ensure sustainable development and eradicate poverty and hunger. Three-quarters of the poor live in rural areas and derive their livelihoods from agriculture or from rural activities that depend on agriculture. Much urban poverty is a consequence of rural deprivation and rural economic decline, which lead to distress migration to urban areas. The strengthening of agriculture and rural development is fundamental to achieving overall economic growth and poverty reduction for most developing countries. The decline in financial resources for agricultural and rural development must be reversed. At the same time, we must stress the significance for developing countries of trade opportunities. Developed countries can provide a major impetus to poverty eradication and economic advancement in developing countries by opening their markets to developing country products – particularly agricultural products – and helping these countries take advantage of expanded trade opportunities.

The centrality of food, agriculture and rural development to poverty alleviation and the eradication of hunger underlies most of *The State of Food and Agriculture 2002*. However, I would like to highlight one particular aspect that is strongly featured in the report. This is the recognition that agriculture, fisheries and forestry have an importance beyond that of providing us with the food and raw materials necessary for our survival and well-being and ensuring the livelihoods of farmers, fishermen and foresters worldwide; people employed in these sectors play a role in managing resources the benefits of which accrue far beyond their own individual livelihoods. Through the proper management of these resources, farmers, fishermen and foresters provide a range of benefits to others, such as landscape conservation, watershed protection, biodiversity conservation, ecosystem stability and maintenance of fish stocks. These are so-called public goods, goods that benefit large sections of people – locally, regionally or globally – but that cannot be expected to be provided for free. Some public goods are even global in nature; they benefit all of humanity. Obvious examples are biodiversity conservation and carbon sequestration provided by forests and agriculture through the adoption of more sustainable land-use practices.

These facts are widely recognized, but I would like to stress their implications in terms of financial flows to agriculture, fisheries and forestry. Indeed, there is a strong rationale for providing adequate international flows of finance to these sectors to encourage sustainable practices that ensure the provision of these important global public goods. A further challenge is to develop financing mechanisms that can at the same time compensate for the provision of global public goods and contribute to poverty alleviation. *The State of Food and Agriculture 2002* calls for an increase in international flows of finance towards agriculture and rural areas with a view to promoting the provision of global public goods. Also discussed is one of the possible new mechanisms for financing the provision of global public goods: the Clean Development Mechanism (CDM), deriving from the Kyoto Protocol to the United Nations Framework Convention on Climate Change. Particular attention is paid to the potential use of the CDM as an instrument for both enhancing carbon sequestration through land-use changes and for reducing rural poverty.

As has been the tradition in past editions, *The State of Food and Agriculture 2002* attempts both to provide an overview of the current situation and to reflect on some of the major challenges faced in eliminating world hunger and poverty and ensuring the sustainable use of our natural resources. In view of the growing awareness worldwide of many of these challenges, I am convinced that we have reason to be optimistic about the future. But we must avoid complacency and stay firmly committed to the objectives we have set ourselves. In this respect, FAO, for its part, will continue to play the role that our members and the international community expect of us.

Jacques Diouf
FAO DIRECTOR-GENERAL

Contents

Boxes

Tables

Figures

Map

Acknowledgements

The State of Food and Agriculture 2002 was prepared by a team from the Agriculture and Economic Development Analysis Division, led by Jakob Skoet and comprising André Croppenstedt, Annelies Deuss, Fulvia Fiorenzi and Slobodanka Teodosijevic. Secretarial support was provided by Stella Di Lorenzo and Paola Di Santo. General supervision was provided by Kunio Tsubota.

Contributions and background papers for the World Review were prepared by Adrian Whiteman, Forestry Department (Production and trade of forest products); Adele Crispoldi, Rebecca Metzner and Stefania Vannuccini, Fisheries Department (Fisheries: production, disposition and trade); Pratap Narain and Mohammed Barre, Statistics Division (External assistance to agriculture); Terri Raney, Commodities and Trade Division (Implications of the Fourth World Trade Organization Ministerial Conference for Agriculture, Fisheries and Forestry). The sections on Food shortages and emergencies, World cereal supply situation and Food aid flows were based on contributions prepared by staff of the Commodities and Trade Division, supervised by Ali Gürkan and Mwita Rukandema.

Contributions and background papers for the Regional review were prepared by Floribert Ngaruko (Africa), Jikun Huang and Scott Rozelle (Asia and the Pacific), Fernando Zegarra (Latin America and the Caribbean), Tayeb Ameziane (Near East and North Africa), David Sedik (Central and Eastern Europe and the Commonwealth of Independent States). The section on Developed market economies is based on information provided by the Agriculture, Food and Fisheries Directorate of the Organisation for Economic Co-operation and Development.

The text on The role of agriculture and land in the provision of global public goods is based on a background paper prepared by Dirgha Tiwari, while the section on Harvesting carbon sequestration through land-use change: a way out of rural poverty? was prepared by Leslie Lipper and Romina Cavatassi, Agriculture and Economic Development Analysis Division.

Glossary

AAT	African animal trypanosomiasis
AMS	Aggregate measure of support
BSE	bovine spongiform encephelopathy
CBD	Convention on Biological Diversity
CDM	Clean Development Mechanism
CGIAR	Consultative Group on International Agricultural Research
CIS	Commonwealth of Independent States
COSCA	Collaborative Study of Cassava in Africa
DFID	Department for International Development
EC	European Communities (also called European Union)
ECLAC	Economic Commission for Latin America and the Caribbean
EMBRAPA	Empresa Brasileira de Pesquisa Agropecuaria
ESCAP	Economic and Social Commission for Asia and the Pacific
EU	European Union (also called European Communities)
FDI	foreign direct investment
FRA	Forest Resources Assessment
GCC	Gulf Cooperation Council
GDP	gross domestic product
GCPRT	Coarse Grains, Pulses, Roots and Tubers Centre
GEF	Global Environment Facility
GHG	greenhouse gas
GIEWS	Global Information and Early Warning System on Food and Agriculture

GNP	gross national product
GPG	global public good
IAEA	International Atomic Energy Agency
IBAR	Interafrican Bureau for Animal Resources
IBRD	International Bank for Reconstruction and Development
ICCO	International Cocoa Organization
ICO	International Coffee Organization
IDA	International Development Association
IFAD	International Fund for Agricultural Development
ILCS	International Livestock Centre for Africa
IMF	International Monetary Fund
IPCC	Intergovernmental Panel on Climate Change
IPM	integrated pest management
ISA	International Sugar Agreement
IT	information technology
LIFDC	low-income food-deficit country
MEA	multilateral environmental agreement
MERCOSUR	Southern Common Market
MFN	Most favoured nation
NAFTA	North American Free Trade Agreement
NGO	non-governmental organization
NPR	nominal protection rate
OAU	Organization of African Unity
ODA	official development assistance

OECD	Organisation for Economic Co-operation and Development
PAAT	Programme Against African Trypanosomiasis
PATTEC	Pan African Tsetse and Trypanosomosis Eradication Campaign
PSE	producer support estimate
SAT	sequential aerosol technique
SIT	sterile insect technique
TCOR	Special Relief Operations Service
TRIPS	Trade Related Aspects of Intellectual Property Rights
TRQ	tariff-rate quota
TSE	total support estimate
UNCCD	Convention to Combat Desertification and Drought in those Countries Experiencing Serious Drought and/or Desertification, particularly in Africa
UNCED	United Nations Conference on Environment and Development
UNCTAD	United Nations Conference on Trade and Development
UNDP	United Nations Development Programme
UNEP	United Nations Environment Programme
UNFCCC	United Nations Framework Convention on Climate Change
UPOV	International Union for the Protection of New Varieties of Plants
WFP	World Food Programme
WHO	World Health Organization
WTO	World Trade Organization

Explanatory note

The statistical information in this issue of *The State of Food and Agriculture* has been prepared from information available to FAO up to April 2002.

Symbols
The following symbols are used:

- – = none or negligible (in tables)
- ... = not available (in tables)
- $ = US dollars

Dates and units
The following forms are used to denote years or groups of years:

1996/97 = a crop, marketing or fiscal year running from one calendar year to the next

1996-97 = the average for the two calendar years

Unless otherwise indicated, the metric system is used in this publication.
"Billion" = 1 000 million.

Statistics
Figures in statistical tables may not add up because of rounding. Annual changes and rates of change have been calculated from unrounded figures.

Production indices
The FAO indices of agricultural production show the relative level of the aggregate volume of agricultural production for each year in comparison with the base period 1989–91. They are based on the sum of price-weighted quantities of different agricultural commodities after the quantities used as seed and feed (similarly weighted) have been deducted. The resulting aggregate therefore represents disposable production for any use except seed and feed.

All the indices, whether at the country, regional or world level, are calculated by the Laspeyres formula. Production quantities of each commodity are weighted by 1989–91 average international commodity prices and summed for each year. To obtain the index, the aggregate for a given year is divided by the average aggregate for the base period 1989–91.

Trade indices

The indices of trade in agricultural products are also based on the base period 1989–91. They include all the commodities and countries shown in the *FAO Trade Yearbook*. Indices of total food products include those edible products generally classified as "food".

All indices represent changes in current values of exports (free on board [f.o.b.]), and imports (cost, insurance, freight [c.i.f.]), expressed in US dollars. When countries report imports valued at f.o.b., these are adjusted to approximate c.i.f. values.

Volumes and unit value indices represent the changes in the price-weighted sum of quantities and of the quantity-weighted unit values of products traded between countries. The weights are, respectively, the price and quantity averages of 1989–91 which is the base reference period used for all the index number series currently computed by FAO. The Laspeyres formula is used to construct the index numbers.

PART I

WORLD REVIEW

I. Current agricultural situation – facts and figures

I. TRENDS IN UNDERNOURISHMENT

• According to FAO's latest estimate, there were 815 million undernourished people in the world in 1997–99: 777 million in the developing countries, 27 million in the countries in transition and 11 million in the developed market economies.

• More than half of the undernourished people (61 percent) are found in Asia, while sub-Saharan Africa accounts for almost a quarter (24 percent).

• In terms of the percentage of undernourished people in the total population, the highest incidence is found in sub-Saharan Africa, where it was estimated that one-third of the population (34 percent) were undernourished in 1997–99. Sub-Saharan Africa is followed by Asia and the Pacific, where 16 percent of the population are undernourished.

• Significant progress has been made over the last two decades: the incidence of undernourishment in the developing countries has decreased from 29 percent in 1979–81 to 17 percent in 1997–99.

• However, progress has been very uneven. In Asia and the Pacific, the percentage has been halved since 1979–81. In sub-Saharan Africa, by contrast, the incidence of undernourishment has declined only marginally over the same period. Considering the rapid population growth in this region, this means that the total number of undernourished people in sub-Saharan Africa has increased significantly. In Latin America and the Caribbean, the incidence of undernourishment is lower than in Asia, but progress over the last two decades has been slower. The Near East and North Africa region has the lowest incidence of undernourishment, but has seen no reduction over the last two decades.

• At the World Food Summit in 1996, heads of state and government made a commitment to cut by half the *number* of undernourished people in developing countries by 2015 (with 1990–92 as the benchmark period). Since the benchmark period, the number of undernourished people has declined by a total of 39 million, corresponding to an average annual decline of 6 million. To achieve the World Food Summit goal, the number of undernourished people would have to decrease by an annual rate of 22 million for the remaining period – well above the current level of performance.

Figure 1
UNDERNOURISHED POPULATION BY REGION, 1997–99

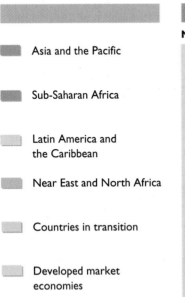

Asia and the Pacific

Sub-Saharan Africa

Latin America and the Caribbean

Near East and North Africa

Countries in transition

Developed market economies

Millions

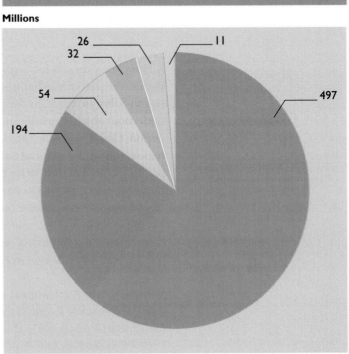

Source: FAO

Figure 2

PROPORTION OF POPULATION UNDERNOURISHED IN DEVELOPING COUNTRIES, BY REGION

1979–81

1990–92

1997–99

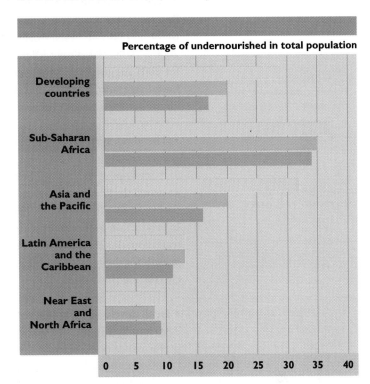

Source: FAO

Figure 3

NUMBER OF UNDERNOURISHED PEOPLE IN THE DEVELOPING COUNTRIES RELATIVE TO THE WORLD FOOD SUMMIT TARGET

Trend

Outcome if current trends continue

Path to the World Food Summit target

Revised point estimates prepared in 2001

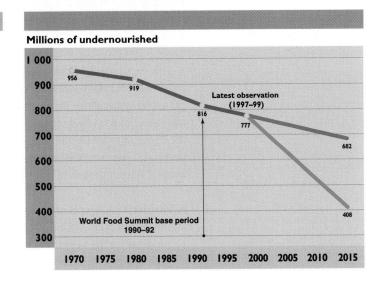

Source: FAO

5

2. CROP AND LIVESTOCK PRODUCTION

• World agricultural (crop and livestock) production over the past two years increased at rates below the average of the preceding periods. Total world agricultural output growth in 2000 is estimated at only 1.2 percent. The preliminary estimates for 2001 suggest even lower output growth, of 0.6 percent, the lowest rate since 1993. In both years, this implies a decline in global per capita production.

• The lower agricultural output growth achieved in the last two years is the result of slowdowns in production in both developed and developing countries. The developed countries experienced an actual decline in production in 2001 as the net result of a decline in the developed market economies and a strong recovery in production in the countries in transition. For the countries in transition, this constitutes the first year of significant output growth for the region as a whole after a decade of mostly contracting production.

• In all developing country regions, output growth was lower in 2000 and 2001 than in 1999, with the most favourable output performance being recorded in Latin America and the Caribbean, the only developing country region not to experience a decline in per capita production in 2001.

• Viewed in the longer-term context, annual agricultural production growth over the last five years averaged 1.7 percent, compared with 2.1 percent over the preceding five-year period and 2.5 percent in the 1980s, suggesting a trend towards declining rates of output growth for the world as a whole.

• This trend towards lower agricultural output growth emerges particularly for the developing countries, although their output growth remains above the level achieved in the developed countries. This is largely attributable to output trends in Asia and the Pacific, where the rate of agricultural output growth has been declining systematically over the last five years, and to lower average output growth in sub-Saharan Africa over the same period.

• The declining trend in agricultural output growth in Asia is largely attributable to China, where the very high rates of growth recorded since the beginning of the economic reform process in the late 1970s have been tapering off in recent years.

Figure 4

CHANGES IN CROP AND LIVESTOCK PRODUCTION

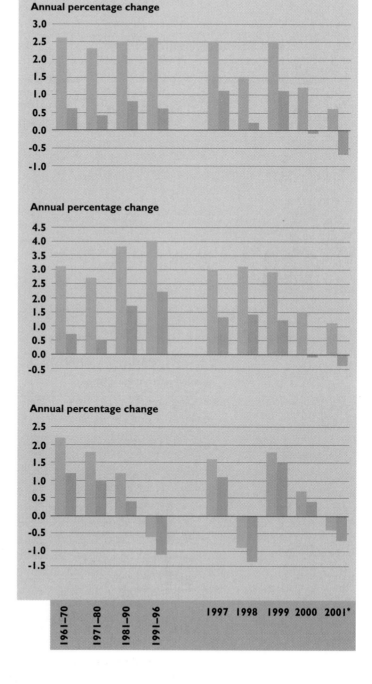

WORLD

 Crop and livestock production

Per capita crop and livestock production

DEVELOPING COUNTRIES

Crop and livestock production

Per capita crop and livestock production

DEVELOPED COUNTRIES

Crop and livestock production

Per capita crop and livestock production

*Preliminary

Source: FAO

Figure 5
CHANGES IN CROP AND LIVESTOCK PRODUCTION, BY REGION

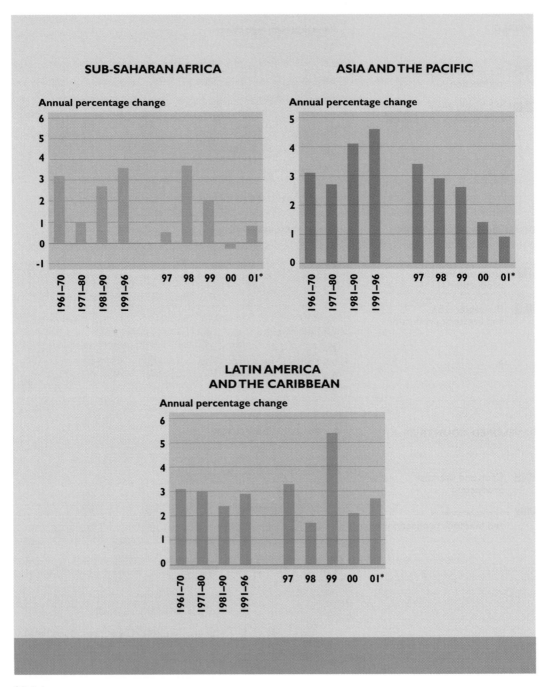

* Preliminary

CHANGES IN CROP AND LIVESTOCK PRODUCTION, BY REGION

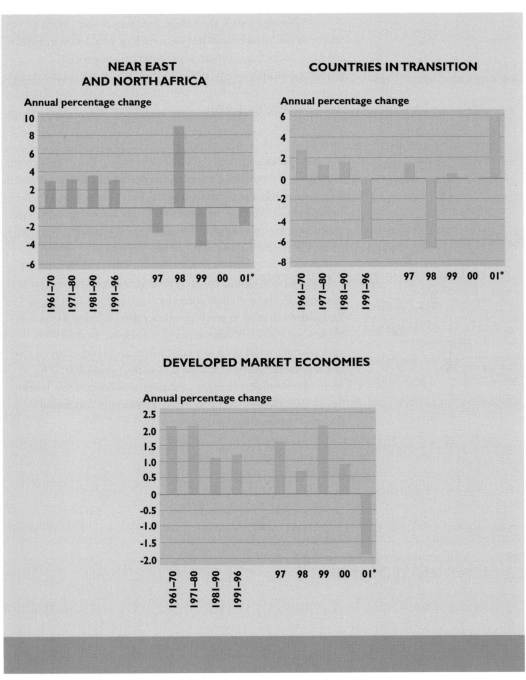

* Preliminary

Source: FAO

Nevertheless, a similar pattern of lower growth in the last five years relative to the preceding five-year period and the 1980s is discernible, although less pronounced, for the rest of Asia as a whole.

• Sub-Saharan Africa is the only developing country region where agricultural output has been trailing population growth for most of the last three decades. Following improved performance in the early 1990s, leading to sustained gains in per capita terms for the first time since the 1960s, agricultural output has reverted in the last five years to a pattern of declining per capita output.

• Latin America and the Caribbean experienced average growth in agricultural output of 3.0 percent over the last five years and of 2.9 percent over the period 1991–96. This represents an improvement over the 2.4 percent average annual growth of the 1980s and a return to the levels of 3.1 and 3.0 percent recorded in the 1960s and 1970s.

• In the Near East and North Africa, agricultural performance has generally been characterized by more pronounced fluctuations than in most of the other regions, owing to the climatic conditions of large parts of the region. In the 1980s, agricultural output grew at a relatively high average annual rate of 3.6 percent, falling to 3.1 percent in the period 1991–96. Successive droughts in many countries over the past few years have adversely affected production, resulting in a marginal decline in production during this period.

3. FOOD SHORTAGES AND EMERGENCIES[1]

• Millions of people in developing countries still need emergency food assistance as a result of natural and human-caused disasters.

• In eastern Africa, food supply difficulties persist in some parts as a consequence of poor rainy seasons and/or civil conflict. In Somalia, where the 2001 main season crops were poor, more than 500 000 people face severe food difficulties. Approximately 5.2 million people in Ethiopia, 1.5 million in Kenya, 2 million in the Sudan and 300 000 in Uganda will depend on food aid in 2002, although the overall food supply situation has improved. In Eritrea, an estimated 1.3 million people will require emergency food assistance through 2002, despite some recovery in cereal production. In the United Republic of Tanzania, nearly 120 000 people are in need of food assistance.

• In West Africa, several countries continue to face food supply difficulties as a result of localized unfavourable weather (Chad, Ghana), or past or ongoing civil strife or population displacements (Guinea, Liberia, Sierra Leone).

• Persistent civil conflict in the Great Lakes region continues to disrupt agricultural production. In the Democratic Republic of the Congo, the prolonged civil war has resulted in over 2 million internally displaced people. In Burundi, despite a good first-season harvest in 2002, production remained reduced in areas affected by insecurity. The food situation is critical for some 432 000 internally displaced people and for vulnerable groups.

• In several parts of southern Africa, the reduced 2001 maize harvest, caused by adverse weather, has led to food shortages. In Malawi, food shortages have emerged in southern parts, where floods affected more than 600 000 people. In Zambia, emergency food aid is required for almost 1.3 million people following the poor 2001 maize harvest. In Zimbabwe, the 2001 maize output declined by 28 percent from the level of the previous year, resulting in food shortages in several areas. In Swaziland, households affected by drought in certain provinces in 2001 are experiencing food difficulties. In Lesotho and Namibia, the food supply situation is tight as a result of poor cereal harvests and commercial imports falling short of requirements. In Mozambique, emergency food aid is being distributed to 172 000 vulnerable people in southern provinces, where the harvest was reduced for the second consecutive year. In Angola, emergency food aid is needed for over 1.3 million internally displaced people.

• In the Near East, the food situation in Afghanistan remains grave. Years of insecurity and war, coupled with three successive years of severe drought, have exposed large numbers of people to extreme hardship. In Iraq, recent years of drought and economic sanctions have left a large number of people in need of assistance. The food situation in the West Bank and the Gaza Strip also gives cause for serious concern.

Map 1

COUNTRIES EXPERIENCING FOOD SUPPLY SHORTFALLS AND REQUIRING EXCEPTIONAL ASSISTANCE*

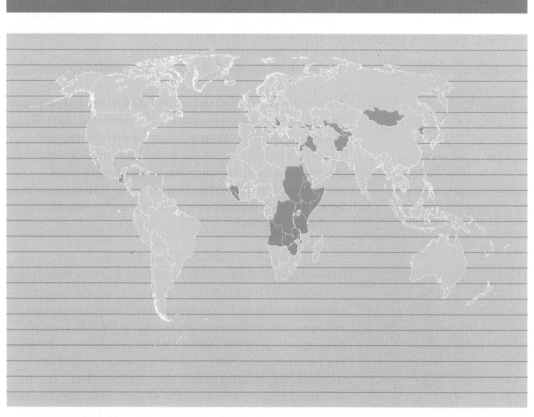

* In current marketing year

Source: FAO/GIEWS, February 2002

• In Asia, a severe winter for the third consecutive year is threatening the already fragile food supply situation of thousands of herder families in Mongolia. In the Democratic People's Republic of Korea, despite a marked recovery in 2001 from the poor harvests of the previous years, food assistance will still be required in 2002. In Pakistan, food assistance continues to be distributed in refugee camps along the border with Afghanistan. In Sri Lanka, more than 1.5 million people have been affected by last year's drought, the worst in 30 years.

• In Latin America and the Caribbean, food assistance continues to be distributed in some Central American countries (El Salvador, Guatemala) affected by earthquakes, drought and storms in 2001, as well as the economic crisis caused by the sharp fall in international coffee prices. There is serious concern over the effects of the coffee crisis on the food security of the poor rural populations, particularly in Honduras and Nicaragua. Food difficulties are being experienced by vulnerable groups in Argentina as a consequence of the severe economic crisis. In Colombia, assistance continues to be provided to large numbers of internally displaced people.

• In the Commonwealth of Independent States (CIS), military operations and civil strife in Chechnya continue to affect food production. Thousands of people have been either internally displaced or have taken refuge in the neighbouring autonomous regions and countries. Elsewhere in the CIS, drought coupled with chronic structural problems and lack of access to sufficient agricultural inputs have led to sharp reductions in crop production for the last three consecutive years. Armenia, Georgia, Tajikistan and Uzbekistan are particularly affected and face severe food shortages.

4. WORLD CEREAL SUPPLY SITUATION[2]

• Since the strong increase achieved in 1996, global cereal production has been stagnating or declining. World cereal output in 2001 was estimated at 1 880 million tonnes (including rice in milled equivalent) – 22 million tonnes, or 1.2 percent, above the previous year's level and representing the first increase since 1997.

• A strong increase of 11 percent was estimated for Europe in 2001, mainly attributable to sharp rises in production in Hungary, Poland, Romania, the Russian Federation and Ukraine. Also in South America, output increased significantly by 8–9 percent thanks to expanded crops in Brazil. On the other hand, cereal output was estimated to have declined by 6–7 percent in North America and, somewhat less, by 1.3 percent in Asia, largely because of a further small reduction in the Chinese crop.

• World coarse grain production in 2001 rose by around 3 percent compared with that of 2000, despite declines in North America. World wheat production in 2001 reached 582 million

Figure 6
WORLD CEREAL PRODUCTION

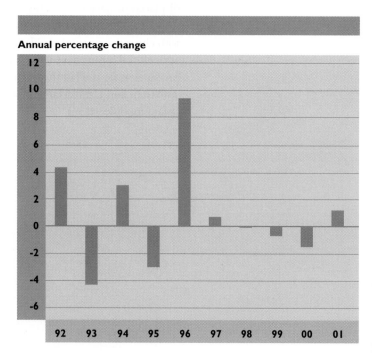

Annual percentage change

Source: FAO

Figure 7

WORLD CEREAL PRODUCTION AND UTILIZATION, 1991/92 TO 2001/02

— Production*

— Utilization

*Production data refer to the calendar year of the first year shown
** Forecast

Source: FAO

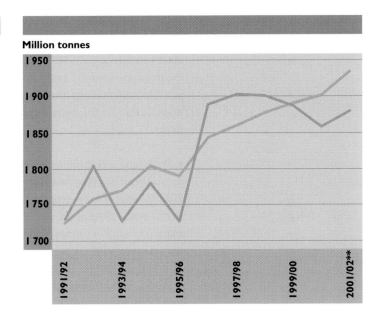

Figure 8

WORLD CEREAL STOCKS AND STOCKS-TO-UTILIZATION RATIO*

■ Cereal stocks

— Ratio

* Stock data are based on the aggregate of national carryover stocks at the end of national crop years

Source: FAO

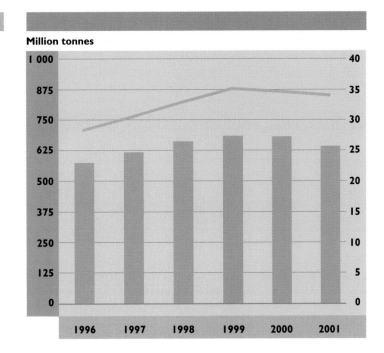

tonnes, close to the level of the previous year. World paddy output in 2001 was estimated at 591 million tonnes (395 million tonnes in milled equivalent), 7 million tonnes less than in 2000. Much of this contraction was concentrated in China.

• World cereal utilization by the close of the seasons ending in 2002 was forecast at 1 935 million tonnes, up 1.7 percent from the previous season. Continuing weak cereal prices in international markets and large cereal supplies were among the main factors for the faster expected expansion in overall cereal usage.

• With total cereal utilization exceeding world production for the second year in a row, world cereal reserves by the close of the 2001/02 season were expected to decline sharply. World cereal stocks by the close of the seasons ending in 2002 were forecast to reach 587 million tonnes, down 8 percent from the previous season's level.

• World cereal trade in 2001/02 was forecast to reach 236 million tonnes, 2 million tonnes higher than in the previous season. Overall, aggregate cereal imports by the developing countries were expected to change little compared with the previous season's level, but imports by the low-income food-deficit countries (LIFDCs) were likely to increase by some 1.8 million tonnes, to 74 million tonnes, reflecting higher imports by several countries in Asia.

5. EXTERNAL ASSISTANCE TO AGRICULTURE[3]

• According to provisional data, in 1999 the major bilateral and multilateral donors committed $10 700 million in current prices as external assistance for agricultural development, compared with $12 605 million in 1998. When these figures are converted into constant 1995 prices, this corresponds to a decline of 17 percent, after increases of 14.5 and 4.6 percent in 1997 and 1998, respectively. Partial data available for 2000 suggest that the level of external assistance to agriculture would decline further.

• Both bilateral and multilateral commitments declined in real terms in 1999, bilateral commitments by 12 percent and multilateral commitments by 20 percent. Most of the decline in the latter was a consequence of significantly lower lending by the World Bank and the International Bank for Reconstruction and Development (IBRD), while International Development Association (IDA) lending remained unchanged in real terms.

• The fall in commitments in 1999 affected both the developing countries and the countries in transition, the sharpest drop (–39 percent in constant prices) being in Latin America and the Caribbean, followed by the transition countries (–32 percent) and the developing countries in Asia (–13 percent). Assistance to Africa dropped only marginally (–2 percent) in constant prices and has remained relatively stable over the last four years. Unsurprisingly, it being the largest continent, the largest portion of assistance (46 percent in 1999) was absorbed by Asia, followed by Africa (25 percent) and Latin America (16 percent). The share going to the transition countries declined from close to 7 percent in 1996 to less than 4 percent in 1999.

• The subsectoral composition of external assistance to agriculture saw agriculture, narrowly defined,[4] absorbing 57 percent of the total (2 percent of which was accounted for by the fisheries sector and 2 percent by forestry). In the broader definition of agriculture, the most prominent component in terms of allocations is assistance to rural development and infrastructure, which increased from 13 percent of the total in 1996 to 24 percent in 1999.

• In spite of a continuing decline in its assistance to agriculture over the past few years, Japan remains by far the largest bilateral donor to the sector, contributing $1 644 million and

Figure 9

COMMITMENTS OF EXTERNAL ASSISTANCE TO AGRICULTURE*
(At constant 1995 prices)

Bilateral

Multilateral

Broad definition
*** Provisional*
*** Incomplete information*

Source: FAO

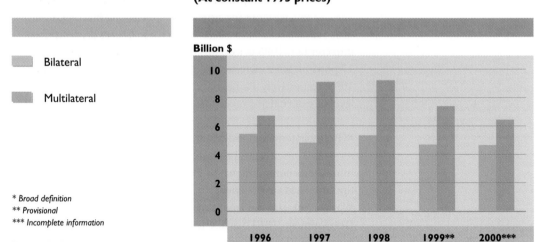

Billion $

Figure 10

COMMITMENTS OF EXTERNAL ASSISTANCE TO AGRICULTURE, BY MAIN RECIPIENT REGIONS
(At constant 1995 prices)

Latin America and the Caribbean

Africa

Asia

Countries in transition

Others*

Including developed countries

Source: FAO

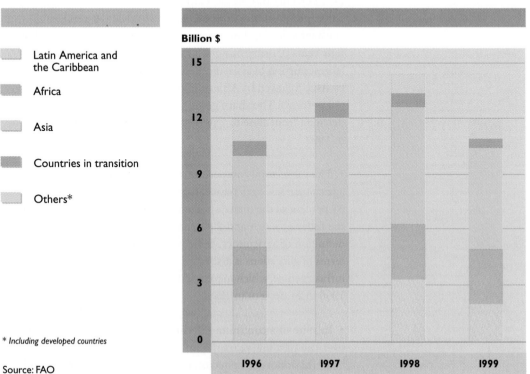

Billion $

$1 265 million, respectively, in 1999 and 2000. After an interval of some years, the United States re-emerged as the second largest donor ($519 million) in 2000, followed by the United Kingdom ($511 million) and Germany ($379 million). The increase in the level of assistance provided by the United Kingdom is particularly marked, having risen sharply over the last few years from a level of only $102 million in 1996.

Figure 11

COMMITMENTS OF EXTERNAL ASSISTANCE TO AGRICULTURE IN 1999, BY MAIN PURPOSE

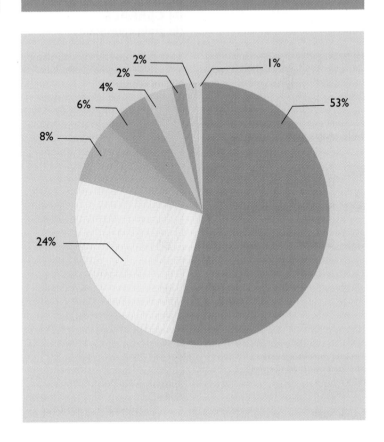

Agriculture –
narrow definition
(excluding Fisheries
and Forestry)

Rural development/
infrastructure

Environmental
protection

Research, training
and extension

Regional and river
development

Fisheries

Forestry

Others (including
agro-industries
and manufacturing of
inputs)

Source: FAO

6. FOOD AID FLOWS[5]

• As of December 2001, according to information from the World Food Programme (WFP), total cereal shipments in 2000/01 (1 July through 30 June) were estimated at 8.5 million tonnes (in grain equivalent), nearly 3 million tonnes, or 24 percent, smaller than in 1999/2000, mainly because of a sharp reduction in shipments to the Russian Federation. Total cereal shipments as food aid to the LIFDCs, as a group, fell slightly to 7.4 million tonnes in 2000/01, or some 160 000 tonnes less than in 1999/2000.

• Cereal food aid from the United States, by far the largest donor, fell by around 2.5 million tonnes in 2000/01 to 4.7 million tonnes, with shipments to the Russian Federation falling from 1.9 million tonnes provided in 1999/2000 to only 127 000 tonnes. Cereal shipments from a number of other major donors, including Canada and the European Communities (EC),

Figure 12
RECIPIENTS OF SHIPMENTS OF FOOD AID IN CEREALS
(In grain equivalent)

Africa

Asia

Latin America and the Caribbean

Russian Federation

Others*

Million tonnes

1996/97   1997/98   1998/99   1999/00   2000/01**

* Including countries in transition
Note: Years refer to the 12-month period July/June
** Provisional

Source: WFP

also registered a sharp decline in 2000/01, while shipments from Japan more than doubled, to 720 000 tonnes.

• For 2001/02 (July/June), total cereal food aid shipments were forecast to reach 9.5 million tonnes (in grain equivalent), 1 million tonnes more than in 2000/01. This increase was likely to be met mainly by larger donations from the United States and Japan, while Pakistan and India, usually among food aid recipient countries, could also emerge as donors this season.

• While the overall global food situation in 2001/02 was generally better than in the previous season, many countries continued to face emergencies and demand for food aid remains strong. Food aid shipments to Afghanistan were expected to increase sharply. Flows to the Democratic People's Republic of Korea and Bangladesh were also expected to remain substantial, although less than in the previous year. In Africa, despite better harvests in several countries, civil strife and localized crop failures in many

Figure 13
RECIPIENTS OF SHIPMENTS OF FOOD AID IN NON-CEREALS
(In grain equivalent)

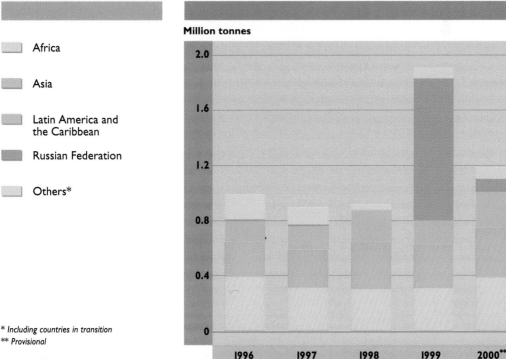

Africa

Asia

Latin America and the Caribbean

Russian Federation

Others*

* Including countries in transition
** Provisional

Source: WFP

areas were expected to maintain food aid needs at high levels. In many parts of Latin America and the Caribbean, the food situation was also precarious, mostly because of natural disasters.

• Following a surge to a near-record volume in 1999, total shipments of non-cereals as food aid in 2000 (January–December)[6] fell to 1.2 million tonnes, representing a decline of 700 000 tonnes, or 38 percent. Most of the decline was due to a sharp reduction in shipments from the United States to the Russian Federation, which more than offset larger aid contributions from Canada and several countries in Europe. Total shipments to the LIFDCs, as a group, exceeded 890 000 tonnes, up 32 percent from 1999.

7. COMMODITY PRICE TRENDS

• Agricultural commodity markets remained depressed in 2001. In spite of some differences in recent price trends among commodities, prices of major agricultural commodities remain well below their peak levels of a few years ago.

• Between May 1996 and January 2000, the FAO total foodstuffs price index declined by some 38 percent. After reaching a highpoint for the 1990s in 1996, by 2000 it had fallen to a record low point for the decade. The index stabilized in 2000 and 2001 but weakened further in January 2002.

• Among the major foodstuffs, the decline in prices has been most pronounced for cereals, for which prices peaked in May 1996, and for oils and fats, which peaked in mid-1998. The average cereals price index for 2001 was more than 40 percent below the average of 1996, but has remained relatively stable over the last three years. The average 2001 index for oils and fats was similarly 45 percent below that of 1998. However, in contrast to the situation for cereals, the price index strengthened significantly in the course of 2001. Price movements over the last few years have been more contained for livestock products, particularly meat.

• Coffee prices in particular have been severely depressed and continued their decline through 2001. Prices in 2001 fell to their lowest level since 1973 in nominal terms and to a record low in real terms. By the end of 2001, coffee prices had dropped to below half the end-1999 level, and average prices for the year were one-third of those of 1998.

• Among the other tropical beverages, cocoa prices had risen steadily over the 1995–98 period but experienced a marked drop in 1999 and 2000. In 2000, the International Cocoa Organization (ICCO) daily price averaged $888 per tonne, the lowest since 1973 in nominal terms. Prices firmed somewhat in 2001 and, overall, cocoa prices increased by 16 percent in 2001. Nevertheless, they remained 38 percent and 12 percent lower than in 1998 and 1999, respectively.

• In contrast to the other tropical beverages, tea prices had remained relatively firm in recent years, but in 2001 they weakened substantially from their relatively high level in 2000. Prices fell in early 2001 but remained steady after April.

Figure 14
COMMODITY PRICE TRENDS

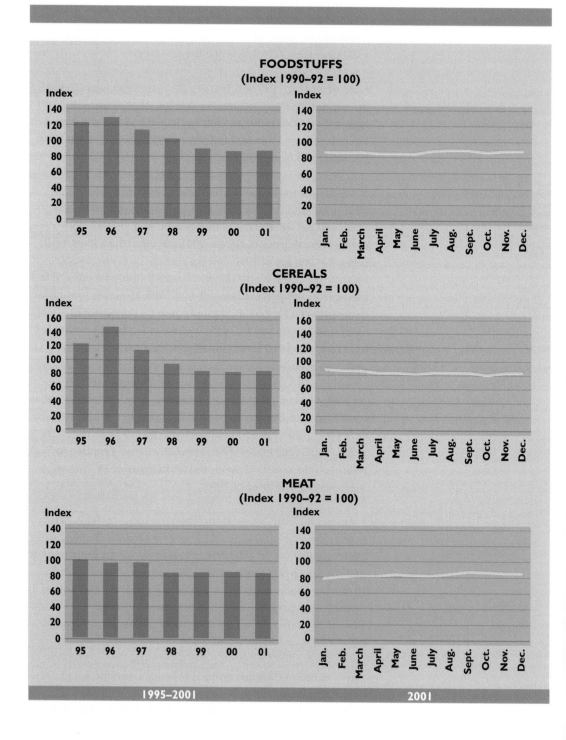

COMMODITY PRICE TRENDS

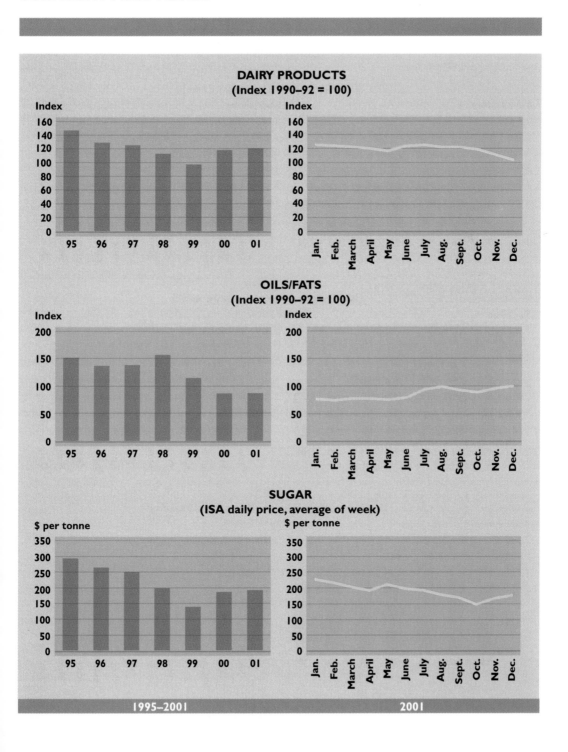

DAIRY PRODUCTS
(Index 1990–92 = 100)

OILS/FATS
(Index 1990–92 = 100)

SUGAR
(ISA daily price, average of week)

1995–2001   2001

COMMODITY PRICE TRENDS

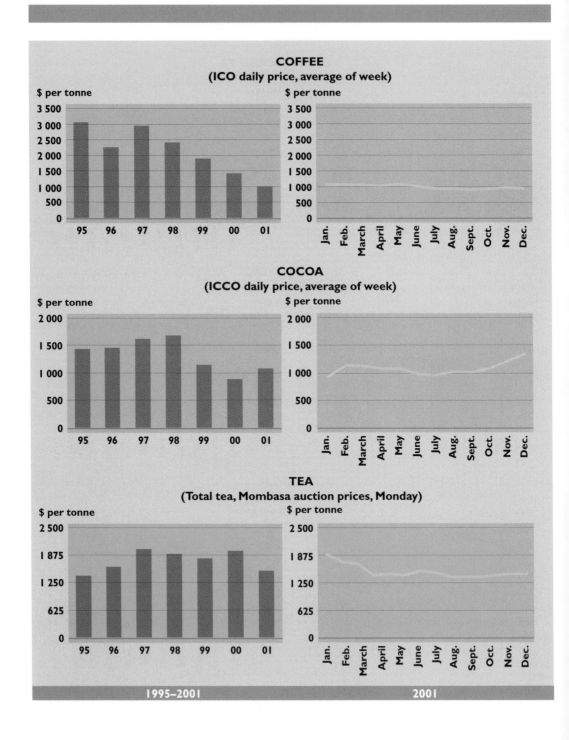

COFFEE
(ICO daily price, average of week)

COCOA
(ICCO daily price, average of week)

TEA
(Total tea, Mombasa auction prices, Monday)

1995–2001   2001

COMMODITY PRICE TRENDS

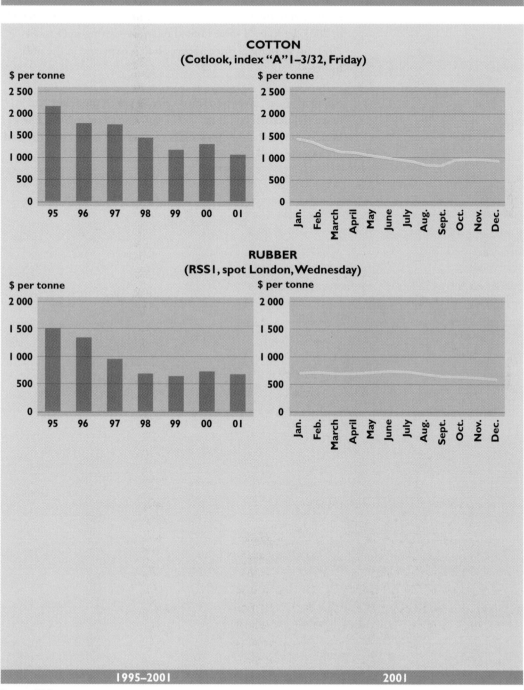

COTTON
(Cotlook, index "A" 1–3/32, Friday)

RUBBER
(RSS1, spot London, Wednesday)

1995–2001   2001

Source: FAO

• After coffee, cotton has suffered the most pronounced decline; average prices in 2001 were down to 50 percent of their level in 1995. Prices have been on a declining trend for the past several years. After reaching a trough in December 1999, they recovered somewhat in the course of 2000, but resumed a downward trend in 2001. In spite of some limited recovery starting in October 2001, no substantial price appreciation is expected in the near future.

• Sugar prices have risen since 1999, at which time they had fallen to less than half their 1995 level. The trend in 2001 has been downward although a slight recovery set in towards the end of the year.

8. FISHERIES: PRODUCTION, DISPOSITION AND TRADE

- Fisheries can provide a key contribution to food security and poverty alleviation. However, productivity gains in fisheries do not always imply long-term increases in supply. In fact, in wild capture fisheries such gains can ultimately lead to the demise of stocks and reduced production.

- Total world commercial fishery production in 2000 – the total of marine and inland aquaculture and capture production – reached a new high of 130.25 million tonnes, an increase of 11.9 percent since 1995,[7] reflecting enormous gains in aquaculture production, particularly in China. Excluding China, world production has remained flat, the 2000 figure of 88.68 million tonnes being only 0.8 percent greater than the 87.95 million tonnes achieved in 1995.

- However, the limited wild fish stocks in both oceans and inland waters place significant constraints on total wild capture production, Total capture production, at 94.65 million tonnes in 2000, was only 3.0 percent higher than the 1995 level of 91.87 million tonnes (excluding China, production decreased by 2.1 percent).

- Aquaculture production is different from wild capture production. Total aquaculture production figures reveal the enormous potential of this source of food towards food security and poverty alleviation if the environmental impacts and other issues of sustainability relating to aquaculture facilities and to aquaculture production receive sufficient attention.

- Increasing by 45.3 percent from 24.5 million tonnes in 1995, total world aquaculture production reached 35.60 million tonnes in 2000, the bulk of it accounted for by China. Excluding Chinese production, world aquaculture production increased by only 27.5 percent between 1995 and 2000, to 11.02 million tonnes.

- These production gains have occurred in both inland and marine environments. Total world inland aquaculture production reached 21.20 million tonnes in 2000, an increase of 50.9 percent over the 1995 level of 14.04 million tonnes. World marine aquaculture production has similarly expanded, increasing by 37.8 percent from 10.45 million tonnes in 1995 to 14.40 million tonnes in 2000.

• In 2000, China alone accounted for 69 percent of total aquaculture production (72 percent of inland production and 65 percent of marine production).

• Total per capita supply of fish for human consumption has increased by 6.9 percent since 1995, from 15.32 kg to 16.38 kg in 2000, but excluding China it decreased from 13.36 kg in 1995 to 12.75 kg in 2000. In 2000, 99 million tonnes of fish supplied were used for food purposes, with 38 million tonnes attributable to China.

• World import and export figures for fish and fishery products reveal the potential of these products for revenue generation. Despite a slump in the late 1990s, exports of fish and fishery products from developing countries or areas have increased by 84.4 percent since 1990, to $28.3 billion in 2000. Imports of fish and fishery products in these countries also increased by 84.3 percent over the same period, and at $9.5 billion represented about one-third of their exports.

• For more than a decade, the developed countries or areas have consistently been net importers of fish and fishery products. In 2000, imports by the developed countries reached $49.9 billion, compared with exports of $27.1 billion.

• At the global level, the composition in terms of commodity groups[8] of international flows of fishery products has changed since 1995. The largest export commodity category of fish (fresh, chilled or frozen) saw exports increase by 17.0 percent in volume (reaching 12 506 430 tonnes) and 13.0 percent in value (to $23.4 billion). The largest increase in exports from 1995 to 2000 occurred in what was, in 1995, the smallest (in terms of absolute tonnage)[9] commodity category – canned crustaceans and molluscs. Indeed, world exports of these increased by 55.8 percent in volume terms, to 574 056 tonnes, and by 27.1 percent in value terms, to $3.91 billion.[10]

Figure 15
WORLD FISH PRODUCTION

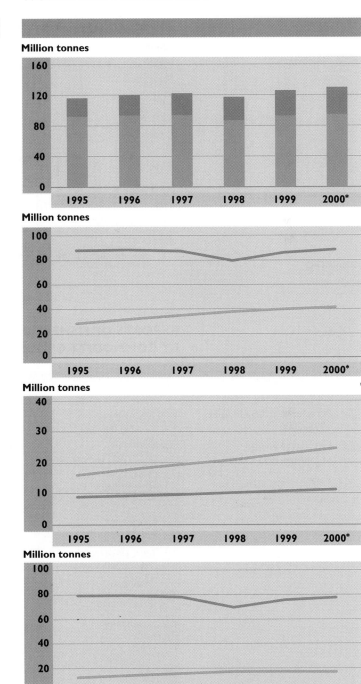

Total world production

Aquaculture
Capture

**Total production,
China and rest of the world**

China
World excluding China

**Aquaculture production,
China and rest of the world**

China
World excluding China

**Capture production,
China and rest of the world**

China
World excluding China

* Provisional

Source: FAO

Figure 16

TRADE IN FISH AND FISHERY PRODUCTS

Imports

Exports

Source: FAO

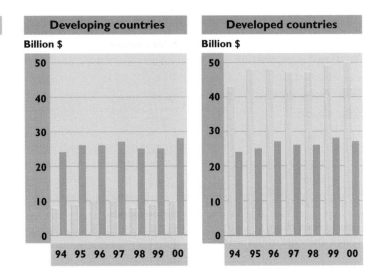

Figure 17

**EXPORTS OF FISHERY PRODUCTS,
BY COMMODITY GROUP**

Percentage change in value,
1995–2000

Percentage change
in tonnage, 1995–2000

Source: FAO

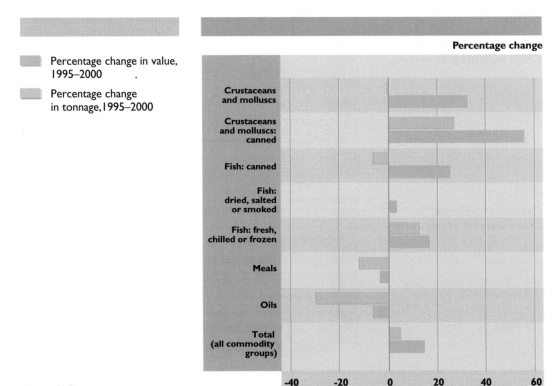

9. PRODUCTION AND TRADE OF FOREST PRODUCTS

• Global markets for forest products continued to recover in 2000, owing to growth in the global economy. Overall, global roundwood production increased by 1.9 percent to 3 352 million m³. In the developing countries, which account for about 60 percent of total roundwood production, production increased by only 0.3 percent, while the developed countries' production increased by 4.3 percent.

• Industrial roundwood production (which excludes the production of wood used for fuel) accounted for about 47 percent of total roundwood production in 2000 and increased by 3.2 percent to 1 587 million m³. The developed countries account for the largest share of industrial roundwood production (about 73 percent), and production in these countries rose by 4.5 percent to 1 154 million m³. Developing countries' production increased marginally from 431 million m³ to 432 million m³.

• Global production of solid wood products (which includes sawnwood and wood-based panels) also increased during 2000, rising by 1.7 percent to a level of 610 million m³. Again, the increase in production was attributable to the developed countries, where production increased by 2.6 percent as opposed to a decline of 1.4 percent in the developing countries.

• Overall, global output of pulp and paper products continued to show strong growth, with an increase of 3.2 percent to 494 million tonnes. As in the previous year, the developing countries led the recovery with an increase in production of 5.7 percent in 2000 to just over 100 million tonnes. In the developed countries, production increased by 2.6 percent to 393 million tonnes.

• Global trade in forest products also continued to grow in 2000. A significant proportion of forest products output is traded on international markets each year, including, in 2000, 30–35 percent of sawnwood, wood-based panel and paper production in the developed countries and 40 percent of wood-based panel and wood pulp production in the developing countries. During 2000, exports increased across all regions in total, but fell slightly in the solid wood products sector. Overall exports of forest products increased by around 6 percent to $140 billion, 83 percent of which was accounted for by the developed countries.

Figure 18
OUTPUT OF MAIN FOREST PRODUCTS

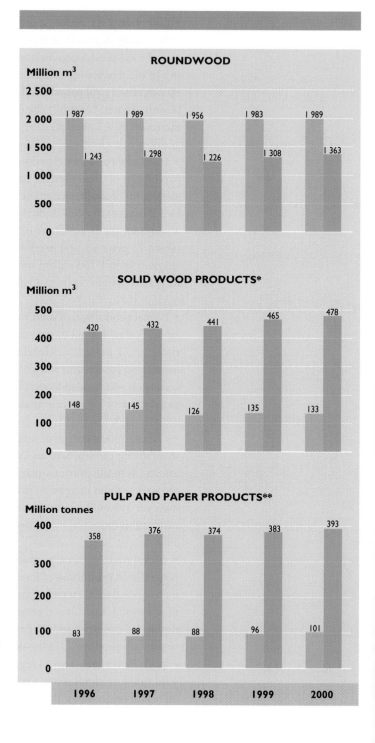

Developing countries

Developed countries

ROUNDWOOD

Million m³

SOLID WOOD PRODUCTS*

Million m³

PULP AND PAPER PRODUCTS**

Million tonnes

1996 1997 1998 1999 2000

* Sawnwood and sleepers and
  wood-based panels
** Wood pulp and paper and paperboard

Source: FAO

Figure 19

EXPORT VALUES OF MAIN FOREST PRODUCTS

Developing countries

Developed countries

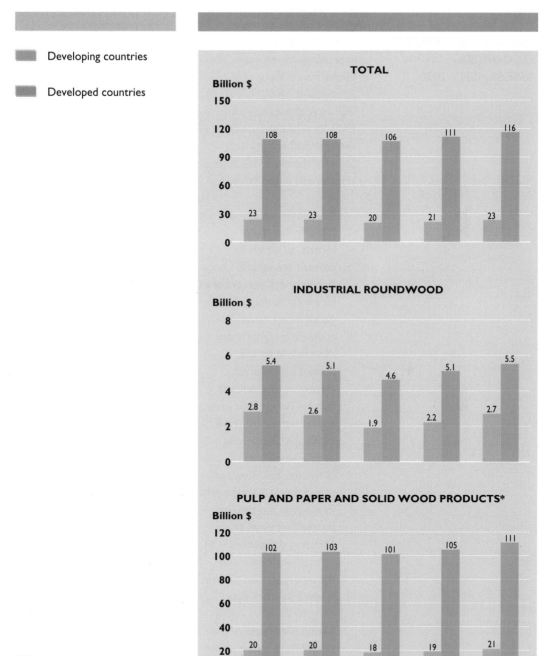

* Wood pulp and paper and paperboard,
  sawnwood and sleepers and
  wood-based panels

Source: FAO

BOX 1

THE GLOBAL FOREST RESOURCES ASSESSMENT 2000[1]

FAO has carried out periodic global forest assessments since 1947, at intervals of approximately ten years. The Global Forest Resources Assessment 2000 (FRA 2000) was a joint endeavour of FAO, its member countries and many other partners. Some of the major results are summarized in the following.

- The world has about 3 870 million ha of forests, of which 95 percent are natural forests and 5 percent are forest plantations. This global forest cover estimate is higher than those made by the previous two forest resources assessments (Global Forest Resources Assessment 1990 [FRA 1990] and the interim 1995 assessment). However, this does not reflect a real increase in forest area but the use, for the first time, of a common definition for all forests worldwide and the incorporation of new forest inventory data.

- About 30 percent of the world's land area is under forests. Of these forests, 47 percent are tropical, 9 percent subtropical, 11 percent temperate and 33 percent boreal.

- The world's natural forests continued to be converted to other land uses at a very high rate during the 1990s. An estimated 16.1 million ha of natural forest were lost each year (14.6 million ha through deforestation and 1.5 million ha through conversion to forest plantations). Around 15.2 million ha of the forest area lost were in the tropics. Against this loss could be offset a gain of 3.6 million ha as a result of natural forest expansion, leading to a net loss of 12.5 million ha. Much of the gain in natural forest area was caused by natural forest succession on abandoned agricultural land. Forest expansion has been occurring for several decades in many developed countries.

- Gains in forest area also occurred through the expansion of forest plantations. Indeed, about half of the 3.1 million ha of new plantation area per year worldwide has been on land recovered from natural forest, i.e. representing reforestation on cleared natural forest land.

- The overall net change in forest area during the 1990s (i.e. the sum of changes in natural forests and forest plantations) was an estimated −9.4 million ha per year, or 0.2 percent of total forests. This was the net result of a deforestation rate of 14.6 million ha per year and forest increase of 5.2 million. Net deforestation rates were highest in Africa and South America. The loss of natural forests in Asia was also high, but was significantly offset (in terms of area) by forest plantation establishment. In contrast, the forest cover in other regions – mainly industrialized countries – increased slightly.

- According to the reported figures, the estimated net loss of forest area was lower in the 1990s than in the 1980s. Indeed, net annual forest change was estimated at −9.4 million ha for the period 1990–2000, −11.3 million ha for 1990–95 and −13.0 million ha for 1980–1990.[2]

- Forest management over the past decade has focused increasingly on sustainable forest management in accordance with the "Forest Principles" agreed at the United Nations Conference on Environment and Development (UNCED) in 1992. As of 2000, 149 countries were involved in international initiatives to develop and implement criteria and indicators for sustainable forest management, although the degree of implementation varies considerably. The area of forests worldwide under formal or informal management has increased. Furthermore, interest in forest certification has increased; a number of forest certification schemes were established during the 1990s, and the total global area of certified forests grew to reach 80 million ha by the end of 2000.

[1] For more detailed information on the Global Forest Resources Assessment, see FAO. 2001. *State of the World's Forests 2001*. Rome.
[2] Although the figures for the two decades are not directly comparable, there is reasonable evidence that the net rate of forest loss has indeed decreased.

II. The global economy and agriculture

WORLD ECONOMIC ENVIRONMENT

World economic output rose strongly by 4.7 percent in 2000 but slowed to 2.4 percent in 2001.

Following the unusually high growth in 2000 of 4.7 percent, world economic output started contracting significantly after late 2000.[11] Prospects for an early recovery in the course of 2001 were shattered by the terrorist attacks of 11 September, which worsened an already difficult situation and led to a further weakening of consumer and business confidence worldwide. As a consequence, world economic growth in 2001 declined to a projected 2.4 percent, the lowest rate since 1993. All major regions participated in the downturn, the high degree of synchronicity being a particularly noteworthy feature of the current global slowdown. The economic slowdown was accompanied by stagnant international trade volumes in 2001.

Growth in the advanced economies declined sharply from 3.9 percent in 2000 to a projected 1.1 percent in 2001. All major countries participated in the slowdown. After several years of strong economic expansion, the United States saw gross domestic product (GDP) growth drop sharply from 4.1 percent in 2000 to only 1.0 percent in 2001. Neither the euro area nor Japan, the other two large economic players among the advanced economies, were in a position to sustain world economic growth in the face of the downturn in the United States. Indeed, GDP growth in 2001 slowed in all the major euro area countries – sharply in Germany and more

Table 1

GROWTH IN WORLD ECONOMIC OUTPUT

	1997	1998	1999	2000	2001[1]
	(Percentage change in real GDP)				
World	4.2	2.8	3.6	4.7	2.4
Advanced economies	3.4	2.7	3.3	3.9	1.1
Countries in transition	1.6	-0.8	3.6	6.3	4.9
Developing countries	5.8	3.6	3.9	5.8	4.0
Africa	3.1	3.5	2.5	2.8	3.5
Asia	6.5	4.0	6.2	6.8	5.6
Latin America and the Caribbean	5.3	2.3	0.1	4.1	1.0
Near East	5.1	4.1	1.1	5.9	1.8

[1] Projections.

Source: IMF. 2001. *World Economic Outlook*, December. Washington, DC.

moderately in France, Italy and the United Kingdom. The economic events in Japan worsened an already difficult economic situation following the tragic attacks of 11 September. After some modest economic recovery in 2000, when GDP expanded by 2.2 percent, GDP declined by 0.4 percent in 2001.

The worldwide slowdown affected developing and transition countries to different degrees, but in most developing country regions growth declined in 2001.

The worldwide slowdown in 2001 affected the transition countries and developing countries to differing degrees and in different ways, according to their economic circumstances and the structure of their economy. Generally, the developing countries were negatively affected by the lower external demand and lower commodity prices. With the exception of Africa, all major developing country regions, as well as the transition countries, saw a decline in their rate of GDP growth in 2001. The most sharply affected regions were the Near East (where oil exporters suffered from lower oil prices and some countries from reduced remittances and tourist revenues) and Latin America (where weak commodity prices and export markets combined with lower domestic confidence have reduced the economic outlook).

In early 2002, prospects for economic recovery still appeared uncertain and were linked to recovery in the United States. However, both the International Monetary Fund (IMF)[12] and the Organisation for Economic Co-operation and Development (OECD)[13] expected low growth rates for 2002, with prospects of recovery in the course of the year and eventually leading to higher rates of economic growth in 2003.

World trade and commodity prices

World trade expanded strongly in 2000 but stagnated in 2001.

The global economic slowdown negatively affected international trade and commodity markets. After expanding strongly in 2000, growth in volumes of world trade came to a halt in 2001 (Table 2). In particular, the export volume growth of developing countries fell to the very low rate of 2.3 percent, while export volumes of the advanced economies declined by about 1 percent.

International commodity prices, which were already weak, suffered further downward pressures caused by the economic downturn and the aftermath of the events of 11 September (Table 3). Oil prices, after collapsing in 1998, had risen strongly in 1999–2000, but saw their sharpest drop in 2001, with average 2001 prices falling 14 percent below those of 2000 and continuing to decline as a result of weak demand and insufficient cutbacks by oil-producing countries.

Non-fuel primary commodities suffered an overall decline of an estimated 5–6 percent in 2001. The decline was particularly sharp for beverages, which in 2001 declined to 19 percent below the 2000 level (Table 4). Prices of agricultural raw materials were reduced overall by 7 percent relative to 2000. Average 2001 prices of foodstuffs increased slightly by some 3 percent in 2001, but were still well below the higher level of several years ago.

Indeed, for all categories of agricultural primary commodities, prices remain well below the peak levels of 1996–97. The steep decline in agricultural commodity prices over the past few years has been most severe for beverages, for which prices have fallen to less than half their 1997 level. The drop has been particularly dramatic for coffee: average annual coffee prices for 2001 were around one-third of those of 1997 and continued to fall through most of the year.

Table 2
VOLUME OF WORLD TRADE IN GOODS

	1997	1998	1999	2000	2001[1]
	(Percentage change)				
World trade	10.5	4.6	5.6	12.8	0.2
Exports					
Advanced economies	10.8	4.3	5.1	11.8	-0.9
Developing countries	12.6	4.8	4.7	15.4	2.3
Imports					
Advanced economies	9.9	5.9	8.5	11.8	-1.0
Developing countries	10.0	0.5	0.8	16.4	3.5

[1] Projections.
Source: IMF. 2001. *World Economic Outlook*, December. Washington, DC.

Table 3
WORLD TRADE PRICES AND TERMS OF TRADE

	1997	1998	1999	2000	2001[1]
	(Percentage change)				
World trade prices[2]					
Manufactures	-8.0	-1.9	-1.8	-5.1	-1.7
Oil	-5.4	-32.1	37.5	56.9	-14.0
Non-fuel primary commodities	-3.0	-14.7	-7.0	1.8	-5.5
Terms of trade					
Advanced economies	-0.6	1.6	-	-2.6	-0.2
Developing countries	-0.9	-6.6	4.7	7.0	-3.0
Fuel exporters	0.2	-26.2	30.4	40.5	-10.9
Non-fuel exporters	-1.1	-1.3	-0.5	-1.3	-0.5

[1] Projections.
[2] In US dollar terms.
Source: IMF. 2001. *World Economic Outlook*, December. Washington, DC.

Declining terms of trade are undermining the economic prospects of many developing countries, although in 2001 lower oil prices helped offset the negative impact on non-fuel exporters of falling commodity prices.

Weakening non-fuel commodity prices had negative implications for the many developing countries that depend heavily on primary commodity exports and had unfavourable consequences for their terms of trade (Table 3). The decline in terms of trade was sharpest for the developing country fuel exporters. For the non-fuel exporters, lower oil prices helped offset the deteriorating terms of trade situation, which nonetheless continued the slow downward trend observed over most of the preceding years. In contrast, for the food-importing developing countries, the lower international prices of foodstuffs reflected positively on their food import bills.

For the developing non-fuel commodity exporters, the negative impact on poverty may be more pronounced than would immediately appear. Indeed, lower agricultural commodity prices negatively affect rural areas, where the majority of poor people live, while the positive impact of lower fuel prices benefits urban areas to a larger extent.

Even with global economic recovery under way in the course of 2002, commodity exporters still appear vulnerable, as market conditions continue to exercise downward pressure on commodity prices. After the decline in 2001, The World Bank projected no rebound in commodity prices in 2002 and some recovery only in 2003.[14] For agricultural commodities, the World Bank projected an increase of 1 percent in 2002 followed by an increase of 9 percent in 2003.

Table 4

PRIMARY COMMODITY PRICE INDICES IN US DOLLAR TERMS[1]

Year/quarter	Non-fuel primary commodities					Petroleum
	All	Food	Beverages	Agricultural raw materials	Metals	
1996	116.7	127.7	124.9	127.1	88.8	88.7
1997	113.2	114.0	165.5	119.4	91.5	83.9
1998	96.6	99.7	140.3	100.0	76.6	56.9
1999	89.8	84.1	110.5	102.2	75.5	78.3
2000	91.4	83.7	92.2	104.2	84.6	122.8
2001[2]	86.4	86.2	74.6	96.7	76.6	105.7
2001 Q1	89.4	86.5	80.7	99.2	83.0	113.4
2001 Q2	88.1	83.9	76.7	101.3	79.7	116.3
2001 Q3	85.7	88.4	70.9	96.1	73.1	109.1
2001 Q4	82.4	86.2	70.1	90.3	70.6	84.1

[1] 1990 = 100.
[2] Provisional data.
Source: IMF.

Implications of the Fourth World Trade Organization Ministerial Conference for agriculture

The value of world agricultural trade, including fishery and forestry products, has more than doubled since 1980, reaching close to $661 billion in 1995–99. The share of farm products in merchandise trade has fallen over time and currently stands at about 12 percent at the world level. However, this average conceals the much greater dependence on agricultural trade of many individual developing countries, both as exporters and as importers. Given the important role of agriculture and trade in agricultural products for many developing countries, the international regulatory framework governing agricultural policies and trade is essential for them and for their efforts to reduce poverty. Indeed, the World Bank points out that developing countries that have experienced more rapid agricultural export growth have also tended to see more rapid growth in agricultural GDP; thus agricultural exports have contributed to increasing agricultural incomes and reducing rural poverty.[15]

New multilateral trade negotiations were launched at the WTO Ministerial Conference in Doha, Qatar, in November 2001.

New multilateral trade negotiations were launched at the Fourth World Trade Organization (WTO) Ministerial Conference, held in Doha, Qatar, from 9 to 14 November 2001. The negotiations, which will be concluded by 1 January 2005, will have important implications for agriculture, fisheries and forestry. In addition to the talks on agriculture and services that have been under way for more than two years,[16] the new negotiations will cover a much broader agenda. The Doha Ministerial Declaration focused considerable attention on the need to ensure that the development and food security needs of its most vulnerable members are not compromised in the drive towards a fair and market-oriented international trading system.

At the Doha Conference, Ministers agreed to undertake comprehensive negotiations on agriculture to improve market access and reduce export subsidies and trade-distorting domestic support.

For agricultural trade, in the Doha Ministerial Declaration the WTO members agreed to undertake "comprehensive negotiations aimed at: substantial improvements in market access; reductions of, with a view of phasing out, all forms of export subsidies; and substantial reductions in trade-distorting domestic support". They committed to providing special and differential treatment for developing countries to enable them to take account effectively of their development needs. Non-trade concerns, such as food security and the need to protect the environment, are also to be taken into account. The Doha Declaration recognized the progress already achieved in the agriculture negotiations that began in March 2000 under Article 20 of the Agreement on Agriculture.

In the first phase of these negotiations, discussed in depth in *The State of Food and Agriculture 2001*, some 44 negotiating proposals were tabled, sponsored by a total of 125 WTO members. A major positive development in the first phase was the broad participation of developing countries in the process. The second phase of the negotiations, which ran from March 2001 to March 2002, focused on more in-depth work on all issues and options for policy reform as set out in members' proposals during the first phase, with further elaboration as appropriate.

Discussions on further agricultural trade liberalization have been under way for some time and will continue.

The third phase of the negotiations, which will last until 31 March 2003, will involve reaching agreement on the "modalities" for further reforms; these will spell out the specific procedures countries must follow in reforming their agricultural trade policies, for example the formula and timing for tariff reduction. The WTO members will then have until the date of the Fifth WTO Ministerial Conference (which must be held before the end of 2003) to prepare their draft "Schedules of Commitments". The final phase of the negotiations will entail debate, verification and acceptance of the final commitments. The negotiations on agriculture will be concluded as part of the broader negotiations, currently scheduled to be finalized by 1 January 2005.

Market access

Different approaches to agricultural tariff reductions are being discussed.

The discussions on market access have dealt primarily with tariff reductions and the administration of tariff-rate quotas (TRQs). On *tariff-cutting*, two basic approaches have received the most support thus far. The first would repeat the Uruguay Round formula, whereby a minimum cut per tariff line is required along with an overall average cut for all tariffs. In the Uruguay Round, the minimum cut was 15 percent (10 percent for developing countries) and the average cut was 36 percent (24 percent). No cuts were required of least developed countries. This approach gives the member countries some flexibility in tariff reductions by commodities.

The second approach, a "cocktail" approach, would combine a flat-rate percentage cut for all tariffs with additional cuts on higher tariffs. The cocktail approach would also include the expansion of tariff quotas and the provision of special treatment for developing countries. This approach could be effective in reducing tariff dispersion both among countries and among product categories, including a reduction in tariff escalation.

On the *administration of TRQs*, no consensus appears to be imminent. The basic concern is that the method by which a

Box 2

SELECTED WTO TERMS

Aggregate measure of support (AMS)
The sum of domestic agricultural support under the amber box measures (see below).

Amber box measures
Domestic agricultural support that is considered to distort trade and is therefore subject to reduction commitments.

Blue box payments
Payments made as part of certain domestic support policies (mainly those of the European Communities [EC] and the United States) that are specifically exempt from reduction commitments.

***De minimis* payments**
Domestic agricultural support payments representing only a small percentage of transfer to producers (less than 5 percent of the production value for developed countries and 10 percent for developing countries). Even if the effects of *de minimis* payments are potentially production- or trade-distorting, such support is exempt from reduction commitments.

Green box measures
Support measures that are considered to have no, or

minimal, trade-distorting or production-related effects. Such payments are therefore exempt from domestic support reduction commitments.

MFN tariff
A tariff applied on a most-favoured-nation (MFN) basis and which, therefore, does not discriminate against individual suppliers.

Special and differential treatment
Exceptional treatment reserved for developing countries, allowing greater flexibility in establishing support and protection measures.

Tariff escalation
Increasing tariff protection on products in line with their stage of processing. Tariff escalation implies protection of the processing industry.

Tariff rate quota
A two-tier tariff system under which a given quota volume of imports is charged an in-quota tariff rate, which is lower than the above-quota MFN tariff.

Measures for "special and differential treatment" for developing countries are being considered in the area of market access.

TRQ is allocated may act more as a barrier than an opportunity for market access. The challenge is how to ensure fair market access for all WTO members while protecting the interests of traditional suppliers.

In the area of market access, measures for *special and differential treatment* are being considered for developing countries, new WTO members and economies in transition. Some developing countries consider that their tariff should be conditional on the reduction by developed countries of trade-distorting domestic support and export subsidies. Small, "single-commodity", exporters are calling for their trade preferences in developed countries to be preserved and strengthened, while some countries find that certain preference schemes unfairly discriminate against other developing countries. Members generally agree that the erosion of preferences is a problem and that appropriate transition measures may be needed.

Domestic support

A wide range of topics has been debated in the area of domestic support to agriculture, with little consensus emerging so far. Some countries have argued that high levels of domestic support – including measures currently exempt from disciplines – are trade-distorting and should be disciplined. Others argue that current exemptions should be continued and broadened to include measures related to a variety of "non-trade concerns" such as animal welfare or the viability of rural areas.

Little consensus has emerged so far on domestic support export subsidies, although many topics have been discussed.

There appears to be a general willingness to reconsider the imbalance between developed and developing countries regarding their commitments on domestic support. Most developing countries are bound by their *de minimis* support levels whereas most developed countries have much higher amber box or blue box limits and no limits for green box policies (developing countries also have the right to use green box policies, but few have the financial capacity to do so). Recent discussions have revolved around the possible need for a "development box" that would provide significant flexibility for developing countries to support their domestic production, particularly of staple food commodities.

Export subsidies

Some countries are proposing the total elimination of export subsidies, with an immediate 50 percent cut. Others are prepared to negotiate further progressive reductions but only if

Box 3

OTHER ASPECTS OF THE WORK PROGRAMME AGREED AT DOHA WITH IMPLICATIONS FOR AGRICULTURE

Market access for non-agricultural products

Negotiations in this area will aim to reduce or eliminate tariffs and non-tariff barriers. Product coverage will be comprehensive and without *a priori* exclusions. The modalities for the tariff reductions must be agreed as part of the negotiations. Fishery and forestry products and agricultural products that were excluded from the Agreement on Agriculture, such as rubber and hard fibres, will be covered under the new negotiations.

Trade Related Aspects of Intellectual Property Rights (TRIPS)

It was agreed to negotiate the establishment of a multilateral system of notification and registration of geographical indications for wine and spirits. The extension of the protection of geographical indications to products other than wine and spirits (e.g. cheeses and hams) will also be addressed in the Council for TRIPS. The WTO Committee for TRIPS was further instructed to examine, *inter alia,* the relationship between the TRIPS Agreement and the Convention on Biological Diversity and the protection of traditional knowledge and folklore.

Subsidies and countervailing measures

Negotiations will aim at clarifying and improving disciplines under the Uruguay Round Agreement on Subsidies and Countervailing Measures. The Conference agreed specifically that the negotiations would "aim to clarify and improve WTO disciplines on fishery subsidies, taking into account the importance of this sector to developing countries".

Trade and the environment

The Doha Ministerial Declaration, for the first time, recognized the right of each country to take measures to protect the environment "at the levels it considers appropriate" on the same basis as measures taken for the protection of human, animal and plant life or health, i.e. provided such measures are not applied in an arbitrary or discriminatory manner or as a disguised restriction on trade and that they are in compliance with other WTO provisions. It was agreed that there would be negotiations on the relationship between existing WTO rules and specific trade obligations set out in multilateral environmental agreements and on the reduction or elimination of tariff and non-tariff barriers to environmental goods and services.

all forms of export subsidies are covered. Net food-importing developing countries fear higher food prices if subsidies are eliminated abruptly. Others argue that their domestic producers are placed at a disadvantage by competition with subsidized products in their home and export markets. Many countries would like to extend and improve the rules for preventing "circumvention" of commitments on export subsidies through the use or misuse of state trading enterprises, food aid and subsidized export credits.

Other agriculture topics

Other important issues, such as state trading, food security, food safety, rural development, safeguards and the environment, are also being discussed.

The agriculture negotiations are addressing a number of other issues, including state trading, food security, food safety, rural development, geographical denominations, safeguards, the environment, trade preferences and food aid. The specific concerns of various groups of countries have also been identified. These groups include small islands, landlocked countries, countries in transition to market economies, new WTO members, net food-importers, and least developed countries. Considerable debate revolves around the need to create special rules and exemptions for vulnerable groups of countries versus the need for a coherent set of international trading rules applying to all countries.

NOTES

1   This report is based on information available as of March 2002. Up-to-date information can be found in FAO's *Foodcrops and Shortages* report, issued every two months.

2   This report is based on information available as of February 2002. Up-to-date information on the cereal market can be found in FAO's *Food Outlook* report, issued every two months.

3   The information in this section is drawn from FAO's databank on commitments made by bilateral and multilateral donors. The analysis is based on data obtained from OECD, the Annual Report of the World Bank and data received from other organizations and regional development banks. The data exclude some donors and regional banks for which data are not available. They do not include food aid or technical cooperation provided in kind.

4   The narrow definition of agriculture includes only agriculture (crops and livestock), agricultural services and input provision, fisheries, forestry and development of land and water resources. The broader definition also includes (in declining order of importance): rural development and infrastructure, environmental protection, research, training and extension, regional and river development, manufacturing of inputs and agro-industries.

5   More detailed statistics on cereal and non-cereal food aid shipments are available at apps.fao.org/page/collections.

6   While cereal shipments are reported on a July/June basis, non-cereal food aid is reported on a calendar year basis.

7   The capture and aquaculture production statistics provided in this section are based on liveweight equivalents and reflect preliminary data available to FAO at time of writing.

8   Crustaceans and molluscs; crustaceans and molluscs – canned; fish – fresh, chilled or frozen; fish – canned; fish – dried, salted or smoked; meals; and oils.

9   Export volumes (tonnes) refer to the net weight of the commodity and are based on product weight.

10   Dollar values provided for exports and imports are free on board (f.o.b.) and cost, insurance, freight (c.i.f.) values, respectively.

11   Unless otherwise indicated, macroeconomic estimates and projections in this section are drawn from IMF. 2001. *World Economic Outlook*, December. Washington, DC.

12   Ibid.

13   OECD. 2001. *OECD Economic Outlook No. 70*, December. Paris.

14   World Bank. 2002. *Global economic prospects and the developing countries*. Washington, DC.

15   Ibid. (pp. 40–41).

16   For an overview, see FAO. 2001. *The State of Food and Agriculture 2001*. Rome.

PART II

REGIONAL REVIEW

I. Africa

REGIONAL OVERVIEW
General economic performance

Economic growth improved slightly in 2000 and 2001.

Economic growth in sub-Saharan Africa stood at 3 percent in 2000, a slight improvement over 1999. Despite the global economic slowdown, real GDP is expected to grow by 3.5 percent in 2001.[1] Growth is estimated to have accelerated in most major economies of the region. International Monetary Fund (IMF) projections for 2002 put economic growth at 4.2 percent. Many countries in sub-Saharan Africa continue to experience large external deficits, driven in part by weak non-fuel commodity prices and still high external debt servicing costs.

With exports accounting for more than one-third of regional GDP, the global slowdown is undermining the traded goods sector, in particular trade with the European Union (EU), which absorbs around 40 percent of the region's exports.[2]

However, local influences still play a dominant role in the economic prospects of most African countries. In particular, the outlook for private investment, economic diversification and longer-term growth is generally brighter in countries that have pursued sound macroeconomic and structural policies (such as Botswana, Cameroon, Mozambique, the United Republic of Tanzania and Uganda). In contrast, poor policy performance, often combined with political uncertainty and/or conflict, has marked adverse effects on prospects for sustained growth and for reductions in poverty in a number of countries.

Table 5

ANNUAL REAL GDP GROWTH RATES IN SUB-SAHARAN AFRICA

Country	1997	1998	1999	2000	2001[1]	2002[1]
			(Percentage)			
Cameroon	5.1	5	4.4	4.2	5.3	4.6
Côte d'Ivoire	6.2	5.8	1.6	-2.3	-1.5	2.8
Ghana	4.2	4.7	4.4	3.7	4.0	4.0
Kenya	2.1	1.6	1.3	-0.2	1.1	1.4
Nigeria	3.1	1.9	1.1	3.8	4.2	1.8
Uganda	5.1	4.6	7.9	4.4	5	5.2
United Republic of Tanzania	3.5	3.7	3.5	5.1	4.6	4.2
South Africa	2.5	0.7	1.9	3.1	2.2	2.3
Sub-Saharan Africa[2]	**3.7**	**2.6**	**2.5**	**3.0**	**3.5**	**4.2**

[1] Projections.
[2] Including South Africa.
Source: IMF.

Figure 20
SUB-SAHARAN AFRICA: SELECTED INDICATORS

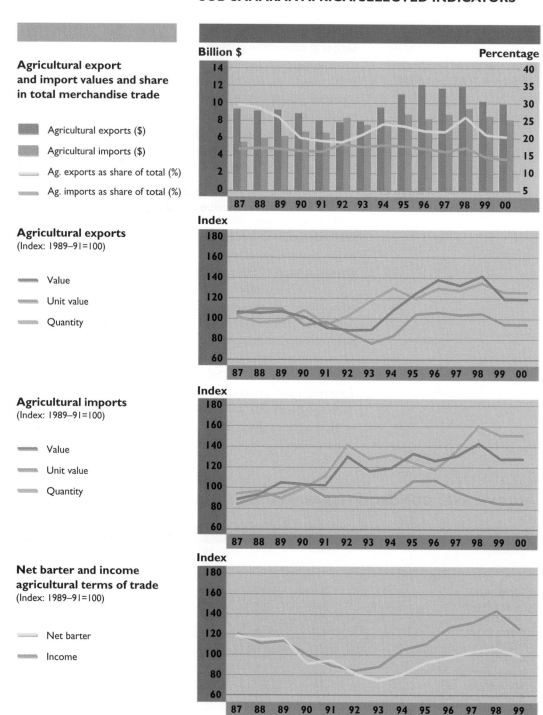

Agricultural export and import values and share in total merchandise trade

- Agricultural exports ($)
- Agricultural imports ($)
- Ag. exports as share of total (%)
- Ag. imports as share of total (%)

Agricultural exports
(Index: 1989–91=100)

- Value
- Unit value
- Quantity

Agricultural imports
(Index: 1989–91=100)

- Value
- Unit value
- Quantity

Net barter and income agricultural terms of trade
(Index: 1989–91=100)

- Net barter
- Income

SUB-SAHARAN AFRICA: SELECTED INDICATORS

Real GDP
(Percentage change from
preceding year)

Percentage

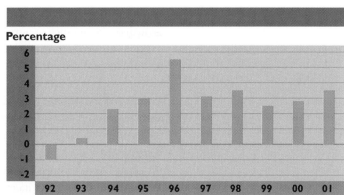

Dietary energy supplies
(kcal per capita per day)

kcal

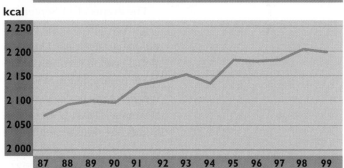

Agricultural production
(Index: 1989–91=100)

▬▬▬ Total agricultural production

▬▬ Per capita food production

Index

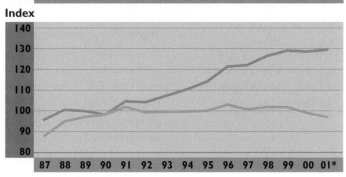

* Preliminary

Source: FAO and IMF

Undoubtedly, in recent years, different sectors of the economy have played an increasing role in sub-Saharan economic growth. Since the 1980s, industrial growth has fallen behind GDP growth and there appears to be a shift towards a higher dependency on growth in sectors such as agriculture and services.

While African countries have in the past experienced surges of investment and growth, they have often not been able to establish a virtuous circle of investment, savings and exports. Both domestic savings and investment ratios dropped significantly in the 1980s and recovered in the latter part of the 1990s. Investment in the 1990s in sub-Saharan Africa reached 18.2 percent of GDP,[3] an increase of 1.2 percentage points compared with the 1980s. On the other hand, savings amounted to 14.5 percent of GDP in the 1990s, only a 0.6 percent increase over the 1980s.[4]

The events of 11 September and their aftermath have negatively affected the outlook for developing countries in sub-Saharan Africa. The consequent further weakening of global economic prospects has pushed down prices of most commodities, many of which were already at depressed levels. World oil prices declined to around $18 per barrel by late November 2001, from over $25 prior to the attacks.[5] These trends have weakened the outlook for many of the poorest countries in the region, causing a substantial revision of prospects for the year 2002.

Agricultural performance

2000 was a year of weak agricultural performance, and only a modest recovery was expected for 2001.

Agricultural performance in sub-Saharan Africa weakened substantially in 2000. Overall agricultural production decreased by 0.3 percent in 2000 after increasing by 3.7 and 1.9 percent in 1998 and 1999, respectively. Crop production fell by 1 percent and food production contracted by 0.3 percent. Cereal production fell by 3.2 percent, the second consecutive drop. Roots and tubers output rose by a mere 0.5 percent, down from the 5.5 and 4.2 percent growth achieved in 1998 and 1999, respectively. Livestock production increased by 1.4 percent, which marks a slowdown over the previous two years. The preliminary estimates for 2001 point to another year of disappointing agricultural performance in the region, with agricultural output expanding by less than 1 percent and with crop and livestock production expected to rise by only 0.9 and 0.5 percent, respectively.

In western Africa, agricultural production stagnated in 2000 after robust growth of 6 and 3 percent in 1998 and 1999, respectively. Several countries, in particular Benin, the Gambia and Liberia, saw agricultural production expand strongly.

However, Burkina Faso, Mali, the Niger, Sierra Leone and
Togo all experienced marked falls in overall net output. Crop
production fell by about 0.3 percent. Cereal output was down
by 3.5 percent in 2000. In the Sahelian countries, in particular,
cereal production fell by 12.7 percent. Production of roots and
tubers rose by 2 percent, a much lower rate of growth than in
the two previous years. Nevertheless, a number of countries,
including Benin, Côte d'Ivoire, Liberia, the Niger and Senegal,
saw large increases in cassava production. Livestock production
grew by 27.4 and 8.4 percent in Côte d'Ivoire and Ghana but
aggregate output rose by only 2 percent.

Preliminary estimates for 2001 suggest that agricultural
production will increase by only 0.5 percent. However, prospects
for cereal production in the Sahelian countries are good
following a favourable rainy season, and record harvests are
forecast for Burkina Faso, the Gambia and the Niger.

In central Africa, agricultural output fell by 1 percent in
2000 after contracting by 1.7 percent in 1999. Crop and
livestock production fell by 4.1 and 0.7 percent, respectively,
both contracting for the second year in a row. Cameroon and
the Central African Republic recorded overall output gains of
2.4 and 3.7 percent, respectively, largely attributable to strong
expansions of cereal output, while Chad and the Democratic
Republic of the Congo saw output fall by 7.6 and 3 percent,
respectively.

Estimates for 2001 suggest a further small contraction in
agricultural output in the region. A moderate expansion of
agricultural output is forecast for Cameroon and Chad. In the
Congo, the food supply situation has yet to recover and
continuing civil strife points to another reduced cereal harvest.

Table 6
NET PRODUCTION GROWTH RATES IN SUB-SAHARAN AFRICA[1]

Year	Agriculture	Crops	Cereals	Roots and tubers	Livestock	Food
			(Percentage)			
1992–96	3.9	4.4	5.8	2.4	2.6	3.7
1997	0.5	0.2	-4.2	2.0	1.4	0.3
1998	3.7	4.1	4.1	5.5	2.6	3.9
1999	1.9	1.8	-0.6	4.2	2.5	2.5
2000	-0.3	-1.0	-3.2	0.5	1.4	-0.3
2001[2]	0.8	0.9	2.4	0.7	0.5	0.6

[1] Excluding South Africa.
[2] Preliminary.
Source: FAOSTAT.

Eastern Africa also saw poor agricultural performance in 2000, with output falling by 0.5 percent after growing by only 1.1 and 1.5 percent in 1998 and 1999, respectively. In particular, Burundi, Eritrea and Mozambique saw large output falls. On the other hand, Rwanda and Zimbabwe recorded strong growth in overall output. Crop output fell by 1 percent, with particularly large contractions recorded in Eritrea, Kenya and Mozambique. Favourable harvests in Rwanda, Somalia and Zimbabwe were offset by large falls in output in Burundi, Eritrea, Kenya, Madagascar, Mozambique and the United Republic of Tanzania, leading to a fall in cereal production of 3.5 percent in 2000. Roots and tubers output increased by only 0.5 percent after increasing by 6.7 and 8.2 percent in 1998 and 1999, respectively. Livestock production rose by only 0.5 percent. Drought in the pastoral areas in Ethiopia, northern Kenya and Somalia led to the deaths of an estimated 3 million head of cattle.[6] In Mozambique, flooding caused the death or serious injury of around 350 000 head of cattle.

Estimates for 2001 indicate that agricultural production has grown only by about 1.3 percent, with crop and livestock output growing by 1.6 and 0.8 percent, respectively. In Somalia, cereal output grew by almost 54 percent in 2000 but prospects for the 2001 food situation are a cause for serious concern. In Eritrea, the food situation remains tight as a result of the war with Ethiopia and the drought in 2000. The 2000 cereal crop was sharply reduced as a result of the displacement of hundreds of thousands of farmers from agriculturally rich regions that normally account for more than 70 percent of cereal production, and the prospects for 2001 cereal production are not favourable. In the Sudan, the overflow of the Nile in the northern regions has displaced tens of thousands of people, destroyed crops and aggravated the already precarious food supply situation. Despite this, overall prospects for coarse grains in 2001 are favourable. Better prospects are also forecast for Uganda due to improved pasture conditions and water availability for livestock in the Kotido and Moroto districts.

In southern Africa (excluding South Africa), agricultural production fell by 3.3 percent in 2000 after increasing by 14.2 percent in 1999. Crop and livestock production fell by 3 and 3.9 percent, respectively. However, cereal production grew by 6.8 percent, with particularly good crops reported for Botswana and Namibia. In South Africa, agricultural output rose by 3.4 percent in 2000 after a 6.5 percent gain in 1999. Crop production rose by 5.2 percent, with cereal output rising by 37.1 percent after three years of declining output.

Projections for 2001 suggest a further fall in agricultural output of about 0.5 percent. A combination of prolonged dry spells, severe floods and disruption of farming activities is expected to lead to production shortfalls in the region. Preliminary estimates for 2001 indicate a reduction in cereal output of more than 8 percent over the previous year. South African net agricultural output is also projected to fall by 5.7 percent with crop production down by 10.5 percent.

WOMEN FARMERS' PRODUCTIVITY IN SUB-SAHARAN AFRICA
Introduction
The need to focus on women farmers' productivity, which can be an effective engine for social change, has become increasingly clear in sub-Saharan Africa. Women have a significant role in farming and post-harvest activities in most countries in the region. Nevertheless, a complex set of rights and obligations reflecting social and religious norms prevail within rural communities; these dictate the division of labour between men and women and act as constraints to women farmers. An understanding of women farmers' role, its importance and these constraints is a prerequisite to devising policies to improve productivity and socio-economic development.

The role and importance of women farmers

In sub-Saharan Africa women contribute most of the labour for food production.

In sub-Saharan Africa women contribute between 60 and 80 percent of the labour for food production, both for household consumption and for sale.[7] Moreover, agriculture is becoming a predominantly female sector as a consequence of faster male out-migration.[8] Women now constitute the majority of smallholder farmers, providing most of the labour and managing a large part of the farming activities on a daily basis.[9]

Traditionally, the roles of men and women in farming differ in Africa. Men clear the land and women undertake most of the remaining farming activities, particularly weeding and processing. Since the colonial period, men have been most active in cash crop production, while women have been mainly concerned with food and horticultural crops, small livestock and agroprocessing. Women's activities have tended to be homestead-based, for biological and cultural reasons. Men and women have also been responsible for their own inputs and have controlled the output. In sub-Saharan Africa, men traditionally owned land, but plots of land have been cultivated or managed jointly or separately by men and women.

Box 4

CASSAVA AND THE ROLE OF WOMEN

Cassava is the most widely cultivated tuber in sub-Saharan Africa and the second most important food staple in terms of per capita food energy consumed.[1] Because of its tolerance to extreme ecological stress conditions and poor soils, cassava plays a major role in reducing food insecurity and rural poverty.

Cassava production in the region has grown sharply over the last two decades. Between 1980 and 2001, total output rose from 48 to almost 94 million tonnes, while the area under cultivation rose from 7 to 10 million hectares. Today, sub-Saharan Africa accounts for more than half of global cassava production.

Although cassava is generally considered as a traditional subsistence crop, the recent introduction of new varieties (such as the TMS[2] varieties of the International Institute of Tropical Agriculture) has transformed its status from that of a low-yielding famine-reserve crop to a high-yielding cash crop. With the aid of mechanical graters to prepare *gari* (roasted granules, a value-added product), cassava is increasingly being produced and processed as a cash crop for urban consumption.

This trend is partly attributable to the fact that cassava has multiple uses. As a food, it can be used for baking, cereals and snacks, soups, beverage emulsifiers, powdered non-dairy creamers and confections.

CASSAVA PRODUCTION, AREA HARVESTED AND YIELDS

Country	Production		Area harvested		Yields	
	1980	2001	1980	2001	1980	2001
	(Million tonnes)		(Million ha)		(Tonnes/ha)	
Nigeria	11	34	1	3	9.6	10.8
Democratic Republic of the Congo	13	16	2	1	7.0	14.5
Ghana	2	8	0.2	0.6	8.1	12.1
United Republic of Tanzania	5	6	0.4	0.9	10.7	6.8
Mozambique	4	5	0.9	0.9	4.1	5.8
Uganda	2	5	0.3	0.4	6.9	13.0
Angola	1	3	0.3	0.5	3.4	6.0
Sub-Saharan Africa	48	94	7	10	6.9	9.1
World	124	176	14	16	9.1	10.7

Source: FAOSTAT.

Cassava starch is also used in various industrial sectors, such as paper manufacturing, cosmetics and pharmaceutics.

Cassava as a "woman's crop" is becoming more evident. Women undertake most processing activities, such as peeling, washing and transporting to grating and milling sites, where cassava meal and grated cassava are stacked in sacks and placed in traditional processors for the starch to drain off. Nowadays, it is mostly women and young girls who undertake the roasting and sieving of *gari*.

A recent study[3] shows that women's labour is becoming increasingly significant in production also. Men still play central roles in land preparation and ploughing but women provide the bulk of the labour for weeding, harvesting, transporting and processing. The later stages of transportation, processing and marketing are also handled mainly by women.

The recent rise in commercial cassava production will accord even greater importance to the role of women, as it is in the post-harvest activities that women's labour predominates (see Figure).

DIVISION OF LABOUR IN CASSAVA PRODUCTION, BY TASK, AVERAGE FOR SIX AFRICAN COUNTRIES

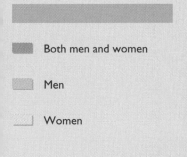

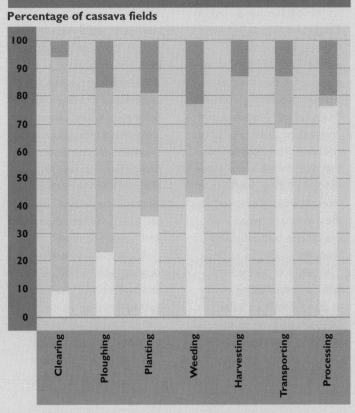

Percentage of cassava fields

Both men and women
Men
Women

Clearing · Ploughing · Planting · Weeding · Harvesting · Transporting · Processing

Source: F.I. Nweke, D.S.C. Spencer and J.K. Lynam. 2002.
The cassava transformation: Africa's best-kept secret.
East Lansing, USA, Michigan State University Press

Ghanaian women peeling cassava roots
Cassava constitutes an important part of the diet of many poor people in Africa.

There are some exceptions, however. For example, grating and pressing are handled largely by men in Ghana and Nigeria, where these tasks have been mechanized.[4] In Nigeria, men and women have a equal share in processing. This may be explained by the fact that women's access to resources is limited. The study found that men own twice as many food-processing machines as women, although the services the machines provide are available to both men and women.

In addition, women still lack decision-making power in many instances. When large proportions of the products are intended for sale, household decisions are mostly taken by the male head, who usually dictates how the cash earned will be used. Women are allowed to control only small cassava sales, the proceeds of which are used to buy necessities for the family such as soap, matches and salt.

Cassava continues to gain importance in many sub-Saharan countries, both as a food staple and a cash crop. Women's labour inputs for production, harvesting, transport and processing are very substantial and increasing. Targeted policies with regard to credit, gender-sensitive extension services and technological and institutional changes geared towards women would further advance productivity in this sector. The empowerment of women is the key to success in the cassava economy.

[1] Cassava provides 286 kilocalories (kcal)/person/day out of a total of 2 198 kcal/person/day.
[2] Tropical Manioc Selection varieties.
[3] The Collaborative Study of Cassava in Africa (COSCA) undertaken by the International Institute of Tropical Agriculture from 1989 to 1997, based on data drawn from 281 villages in six African countries (F.I. Nweke, D.S.C. Spencer and J.K. Lynam. 2002. *The cassava transformation: Africa's best-kept secret*. East Lansing, USA, Michigan State University Press).
[4] Ibid.

These farming patterns are changing over time. Many countries have seen an increasing trend in female-headed households. By the mid-1980s women headed an average of 31 percent of all rural households – a much greater proportion than in other regions. There is much variation within this trend, however, ranging from a proportion of 10 percent in Burkina Faso and the Niger in the early 1990s to 46 percent in Botswana and 72 percent in Lesotho in the late 1980s.[10]

The traditional roles of men and women farmers are changing.

Moreover, population pressure and off-farm employment opportunities for men have led to an increasing proportion of women becoming de facto farm managers. In such households, women's autonomy and authority vary over time. In some cases, male migrants return to work on the farm during the peak agricultural season. Men are often absent from the rural labour force when in their twenties and thirties, and women exceed men in the age group 20–44. For example, in Kenya, about 86 percent of farmers are women, 44 percent of whom work in their own right and 42 percent of whom represent their husbands in their absence.[11] As a result, a higher proportion of women than men are engaged in most phases of the production cycle for food, cash crops and livestock – in addition to their household work and small income-earning activities.

Women are also engaged on a more regular basis than men in all farm activities and phases of the production cycle. They provide most of the labour and manage many farms on a daily basis. As Table 7 suggests, women work much longer hours than men and spend more time on farming activities, even though the figures are far from being homogenous.

Table 7

AVERAGE DAILY HOURS IN FARMING AND NON-FARMING ACTIVITIES BY GENDER, 1994

Country	Farming		Non-farming	
	Men	Women	Men	Women
		(Hours)		
Burkina Faso	7.0	8.3	1.7	6.0
Kenya	4.3	6.2	3.8	6.1
Nigeria	7.0	9.0	1.5	5.0
Zambia	6.4	7.6	0.8	4.6

Source: K.A. Saito, H. Mekonnen and D. Spurling. 1994. *Raising productivity of women farmers in sub-Saharan Africa.* World Bank Discussion Paper 230. Washington, DC.

Gender differentials in agricultural productivity and constraints facing women farmers

While men and women generally face the same external constraints, they have an unequal access to human-controlled factors. They have different endowments, such as land rights and education, and different access to technologies, labour, capital, support services and credit. This disparity results in differentials in productivity to the detriment of women.

Female productivity in agriculture is lower than that of men.

A number of studies have examined the relative productivity of men and women in farming in sub-Saharan Africa. Often, but not always, findings indicate that women farmers have lower productivity for reasons of poor access to resources. Figure 21 also reflects the weaker productivity of women farmers: the average production per farmer[12] tends to be lower in countries in which women represent the larger share of agricultural labour force than men.

Although women are less productive in farming, the general consensus is that they are no less efficient than men in their use of resources.[13] Rather, a lack of complementary inputs leads to a lower labour productivity for female farmers.

Figure 21

SUB-SAHARAN AFRICA: AGRICULTURE SECTOR LABOUR PRODUCTIVITY AND GENDER COMPOSITION OF LABOUR FORCE IN 2000

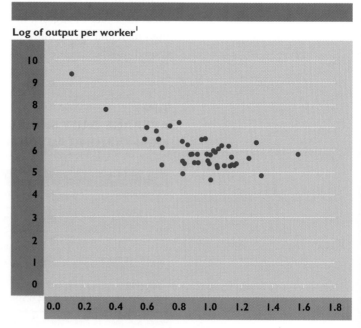

Log of output per worker[1]

Female–male ratio of labour force[1]

[1] For economically active population in agriculture

Source: FAOSTAT

Evidence from Burkina Faso shows that, compared to males from the same household, female cultivators of the same crops in the same year achieved yields 30 percent below average.[14] One reason for this differential was the lower level of male and child labour used on plots controlled by women. Additionally, virtually all fertilizer was concentrated on male-controlled plots. It was estimated that a reallocation of the variable factors of production from male- to female-controlled plots in the same household would raise household output by between 10 and 20 percent. An important conclusion of the findings was that households generally do not act as a single individual and that appropriate modelling of the complexity of the household decision-making process is needed in order to provide better policy guidance.

Lower female productivity seems to derive from unequal access to resources and education.

For a sample of Kenyan farmers, it was found that the gross value of output per hectare from male-managed plots was 8 percent above that of female-managed plots.[15] It was estimated that if women were to use the same resources as men their productivity would increase by about 22 percent. The study also concluded that educating women is more likely to increase the use of new technologies than educating men.

Other research in Kenya indicates that increasing women's levels of physical and human capital (to that of men's in the sample) would increase yields by between 7 and 9 percent.[16] The impact of schooling on farm output was also found to be greater for women than for men because men with more schooling tend to seek off-farm employment and are more likely to be successful in finding and keeping a job. Women, on the other hand, are seldom able to find off-farm work.

Many factors explain the weakness of women's productivity in agriculture. Women farmers have quantitatively and qualitatively less access to information, technology, land, inputs and credit. Policy-makers, managers, agents and participants in agricultural support services are generally males, who are not always sufficiently aware of the specific problems and needs of women farmers. As a result, information and extension services are typically geared towards male farmers, on the assumption that the message will trickle across to women. Evidence shows that, in reality, this is not the case.

Women's access to land is a particular problem.

In sub-Saharan Africa women are particularly disadvantaged compared with men because they farm smaller plots of land with more uncertain tenure.[17] Women's access to land is limited by legal and institutional factors such as legal discriminations against their ownership and inheritance of land. Although legislative changes now permit women to own property, in many countries in the region traditions and customs continue to prevent women from having effective ownership.

In Wadi Kutum, the Sudan, for example, a titling scheme registered most of the land owned by women in men's names, but women did not even protest because, customarily, they do not conduct relations with the state, which has long been considered as men's domain.[18] Without secure title to land, women are often denied membership of cooperatives and other rural organizations. Lack of ownership title also means a lack of collateral and hence access to credit. Many developing countries have legally affirmed women's basic right to own land but actual female control of land is rarely observed.

Women typically receive less than 10 percent of the credit awarded to smallholders and only 1 percent of the total amount of credit directed to agriculture in Kenya, Malawi, Sierra Leone, Zambia and Zimbabwe.[19] In sub-Saharan Africa, more women than men are too poor to buy inputs such as fertilizer, and they are not generally considered as creditworthy by classical financial institutions.

Training and extension services, and in particular the use of female field extension workers, have been identified as a potentially important factor in raising female productivity.[20] However, in a glaring example of "gender blindness", only 7 percent of agricultural extension services in Africa were directed to women farmers in 1988 and only about 11 percent of all extension personnel were women.[21]

Conclusion and policy implications

Women's labour productivity appears to be lower than men's in sub-Saharan Africa. This does not mean that women's potential productivity is low, nor that women's role in agriculture can be neglected. On the contrary, evidence shows that the apparent low productivity of women is a result of the social and economic constraints they face.

To improve women farmers' productivity in the region, much change is required. Less discriminatory laws and policies must replace legislation and customs that constrain women's access to factors of production such as land, credit, inputs, information and technology. The interventions must be situation-specific. Actions must be technically relevant and be suited to the sociocultural and religious precepts of the farming community and the resources of the community.

Yet no quick solutions are likely to guarantee remarkable results, because the success of many of the required remedies depends on changes in attitude on the part of women themselves. Finding ways to increase women farmers' awareness of the gender-related inequities they face and the resulting inefficiencies and to give greater empowerment to women in their public choices are some of the most important challenges currently faced by agriculture in sub-Saharan Africa.

TSETSE AND TRYPANOSOMIASIS CONTROL[22]
Introduction

Tsetse fly and African trypanosomiasis affect 37 African countries.

Tsetse-transmitted African animal trypanosomiasis (AAT)[23] infests between 9 and 10 million km^2, or 37 percent of the continent, and affects 37 countries.[24] Some 45 million head of cattle and many other domestic animals live within or directly at the margin of the tsetse-infested areas. According to the World Health Organization (WHO), many millions of humans are also at risk, with tens of thousands of deaths attributed each year to sleeping sickness, the human form of trypanosomiasis, and an estimated 300–500 thousand people carrying this usually fatal form of the disease.[25]

The disease leads to loss of productivity in animals and, without treatment, is frequently fatal. Large areas of land are today left with relatively few cattle because of the presence of the tsetse fly, and the estimated losses in agricultural output and productivity are very significant.[26] However, the costs of tsetse/trypanosomiasis (T&T) control or eradication are considerable and only relatively limited evidence is available on the cost–benefit relationship of T&T control and/or eradication on a sub-Saharan scale.

The direct impact of trypanosomiasis

The disease directly affects livestock productivity by:
- reducing calving rates by 1–12 percent in trypanotolerant breeds and 11–12 percent in susceptible breeds;
- increasing calf mortality by 0–10 percent for tolerant breeds and 10–20 percent for susceptible breeds;
- reducing milk offtake by 10–26 percent in tolerant breeds.[27]

The disease reduces livestock productivity.

Although there are significant variations among observations, an average reduction of 20 percent in herd meat and milk output in areas of tsetse challenge is considered to be a conservative estimate.[28] Overall, the cattle population is reduced by 30–50 percent because farmers keep their animals away from areas with a high tsetse challenge or trypanosomiasis risk.

Evidence based on actual farmer's practice (as opposed to controlled experiments) from a sample of livestock owners in Burkina Faso indicates that 87 percent of respondents recognized a substantial reduction in the number of cattle dying of AAT following implementation of tsetse control. Livestock owners estimated that the overall mortality rate fell from 63 percent in 1993/94 – prior to control – to 7 percent in 1996/97 – after control.[29]

Using data from the Programme Against African Trypanosomiasis (PAAT) Information System, it has been estimated that a 200 percent increase in cattle numbers in areas at risk might result in the theoretical case of complete and instant tsetse removal.[30]

The indirect impacts of the disease

The disease also has negative implications for crop–livestock production systems.

Even more significant may be the indirect impact on crop production, land use, ecosystem structure and function, and human welfare. Trypanosomiasis prevents, in many places, the development of integrated crop–livestock production systems. That means that tilling must be performed by hand and agricultural productivity is lower than if healthy animals were available to provide draught power.

Evidence from Ethiopia suggests that a team of oxen in a tsetse-infested area is only capable of cultivating 60 percent of the land that can be cultivated in a tsetse-free area.[31] The disease can lead to species well suited for animal traction not being introduced into areas at risk. For example, West African zebus and horses are little used in the wetter semi-arid and drier subhumid regions of West Africa because of the risk of contracting AAT.

The low use of draught animal power in sub-Saharan Africa, even within trypano-free areas, means that additional measures, such as training, credit and infrastructure, are needed to obtain the full benefit of tsetse control.

Further adverse effects of trypanosomiasis include less-efficient nutrient recycling, less diversification of income and

Table 8

CATTLE STOCKS, CATTLE AT RISK AND CATTLE NOT KEPT OWING TO TSETSE INFESTATION[1]

	Total cattle stocks	Cattle at risk	Cattle not kept owing to tsetse infestation
		(Thousands)	
Sub-Saharan Africa	196 196	45 343	90 743

[1] Based on 1997 data.

Source: FAOSTAT; PAAT; M. Gilbert, C. Jenner, J. Pender, D. Rogers, J. Slingenbergh and W. Wint. 1999. *The development and use of the Programme Against African Trypanosomiasis Information System.* Paper prepared for the International Scientific Council for Trypanosomiasis Research and Control (ISCTRC) Conference, 27 September to 1 October 1999. Mombasa, Kenya.

Box 5

THE PROGRAMME AGAINST AFRICAN TRYPANOSOMIASIS

The Programme Against African Trypanosomiasis (PAAT) was endorsed in 1997 by the FAO Conference. By combining the forces of FAO, WHO, the International Atomic Energy Agency (IAEA) and the Organization of African Unity (OAU)/ Interafrican Bureau for Animal Resources (IBAR), the programme seeks to:

- ensure a harmonious, sustainable approach towards improved human health and sustainable socio-economic and agricultural development of tsetse-infested areas;
- promote and coordinate international alliances and efforts assisting in harmonized interventions against T&T;
- achieve integrated trypanosomiasis control in Africa.

PAAT is primarily concerned with the development and application of science-based standards for assessing the economic, social and environmental benefits and costs of T&T management. It studies and analyses the balance between human needs in terms of food security and livelihood sustenance and the preservation of natural resources and prevention of environmental degradation.

Much discussion within PAAT has focused on prioritizing tsetse interventions, integrated into the overall agricultural production scheme, in selected, well-demarcated areas. This principle has become recognized as a prerequisite for success. The integration of T&T intervention into the general process of agricultural development and production provides the opportunity to maximize the benefits for the rural poor while minimizing the negative effects on the environment. It will thus contribute to sustainable pest management in targeted farming systems, and enhance the opportunities for adoption by livestock owners and producers.

In order to deal comprehensively with the magnitude and complexity of the T&T problem within the context of national and regional action plans for poverty alleviation, multidisciplinary efforts are progressively replacing the technology-based approaches of the past.

less access to credit. Moreover, substantial (tenfold) increases in milk production can result from the introduction of dairy cows that are trypano-intolerant.[32]

Cost–benefit ratios for tsetse control

The relationship between the cost of T&T control/eradication and its resulting benefits depends on a number of factors. For example, in areas of low-challenge trypanosomiasis control through trypanocides is possibly more profitable than through other techniques.[33] The appropriate type of T&T control (see Box 6 on page 70) depends on the type of farming landscape, topography, the degree of tsetse challenge, the type of insecticide used, the scale of the operation and the time frame envisaged; it therefore follows that a multitude of different approaches are required in sub-Saharan Africa. Consequently, any effort to assess the cost–benefit ratio of T&T control is a complex undertaking.

A study of cost–benefit ratios for a number of techniques, time periods and degrees of tsetse challenge, using data from Burkina Faso, suggests that at low levels of challenge trypanosomiasis control through trypanocides is the most profitable option unless the time period is very long. A comparison of the use of traps versus insecticide shows that the

Setting up a trap to catch tsetse flies

This trapping technique, in comparison with other catching methods, is appealing for its cheapness, flexibility and environmental compatibility.

FAO/8948/J. VAN ACKER

latter technique produces higher cost–benefit ratios only when the time period is long and the interest rate used for discounting future benefits is low. The sterile insect technique (SIT) is profitable only when applied to areas of relatively high tsetse challenge and over a long time horizon (15 years). Even under such assumptions, SIT does not compare favourably with the trap and insecticide methods.[34]

Studies have shown the favourable cost–benefit ratios of tsetse control.

A further study estimated, on the basis of available evidence for a wide range of techniques and making some simplifying assumptions, cost–benefit ratios of regionwide tsetse control.[35] These estimates, which should be taken as approximations only, range from 1:1.4 to 1:2.6 when considering a 20-year period. The full extent of the benefits is expected to be obtained at the end of the 20 years, when the cost–benefit ratio is estimated to rise to 1:5.

Conclusion

Tsetse control or eradication thus appears to be desirable and feasible in certain sets of circumstances, where the conditions are conducive and long-term agricultural benefits can be secured. Many different methods have been, and are being, applied, including drug therapy, trypanotolerance, vector control or eradication and SIT. However, controversy remains within the scientific community with regard to appropriate products and methods and whether they would be effective in the long run.

It is perhaps relevant here to consider the campaign to eradicate Chagas disease (American trypanosomiasis) from South America. The so-called Southern Cone Initiative against Chagas disease is one of the largest disease-control programmes ever mounted, covering an area of over 6 million km^2 with a time frame of ten years. The aim is to eliminate transmission of the causative agent *Trypanosoma cruzi* in Argentina, Bolivia, Brazil, Chile, Paraguay and Uruguay. Formally launched in 1991, the programme has achieved remarkable success, with transmission interrupted in Uruguay in 1997. Interruption of transmission is expected for the other countries within the next few years. More recently, the Andean and Central American Initiatives have started with the same aim.

This suggests that concerted action on the part of the affected countries and international organizations is indispensable to the eradication of this disease. It is in this spirit that PAAT (see Box 5) is seeking to combine the forces of FAO, WHO, the International Atomic Energy Agency (IAEA) and the Organization of African Unity (OAU)/Interafrican Bureau for Animal Resources (IBAR) to promote integrated trypanosomiasis control within the broader goal of enhancing food security, sustainable agriculture and rural development.

More recently, the OAU Heads of State and Government Summit of July 2000 endorsed the Pan African Tsetse and Trypanosomosis Eradication Campaign (PATTEC), with the

---

Box 6

METHODS OF TSETSE CONTROL

Combating trypanosomiasis is technically and organizationally difficult. First, civil stability is needed for any large-scale vector control programme. Moreover, the sustainability of funding that takes into account the permanent nature of the commitment of maintaining an area's trypanosomiasis-free status is necessary.

Drug therapy

Drug therapy currently protects more cattle than all other artificial techniques combined. At a cost of about $35 million (about $1 per dose), it protects 10–15 million head of cattle living in tsetse-infested areas from the full effects of trypanosomiasis. A drawback to drug therapy is that cattle that have been treated are not as productive as those in a completely disease-free environment.[1] Moreover, there is concern that the level of resistance to the two main drugs (isometamidium and diminazine), which were developed in the 1950s, may be increasing.

Trypanotolerance

Trypanotolerant and partially or semi-trypanotolerant cattle in West Africa account for about 10 million (in 1983) of the 45 million head of cattle living in and in close proximity to tsetse-infested areas.[2] Although these cattle are not immune, they do possess a degree of tolerance that allows them to remain productive while being infected.

Vector control or eradication

Tsetse flies require a tree habitat. Early in the twentieth century, wide areas of land were cleared of trees and game. After the Second World War, insecticide-based control techniques, i.e. ground and aerial spraying, were developed and deployed widely. Ground

ultimate objective being the eradication of tsetse and trypanosomiasis from Africa. With a view to pursuing this objective, PATTEC will undertake the organization and coordination of the campaign and mobilize the necessary human, financial and material resources to do so.

spraying and sequential aerosol technique (SAT) have been tried and proven in field situations, with variable results but general technical success in Nigeria, South Africa and Zimbabwe.

In response to increasing concern about the environmental impact of control measures, and with the advancement of science, different bait systems such as various traps and odour-baited targets impregnated with insecticide were developed. Artificial bait techniques are appealing for their cheapness, flexibility, low pollution factor and relatively larger local input. A drawback that is preventing their widespread use is the recurrent costs of continuous tsetse suppression, which is necessary to keep re-invading flies at bay. The use of herd animals treated with insecticide is a technique that is currently being evaluated on a significant scale. The cost of this control method is difficult to compare with those of other methods as it is proportional to the number of cattle per square kilometre. However, where dipping infrastructure is in place, the use of live animals as bait is invariably the most appropriate method of tsetse control.

The sterile insect technique (SIT) is very sophisticated and, under specific conditions, potentially powerful. It is also relatively expensive and may therefore prove cost-effective only when implemented on a relatively large scale and in an organized manner. This method was successfully applied against New World screwworm in the Libyan Arab Jamahiriya, Mexico and the United States, and in Central America, and against the fruit fly in countries in the Mediterranean basin, the Near East and South America. SIT was successfully applied against the tsetse fly in Zanzibar, where eradication was achieved by the aerial release of sterilized males over Unguja island (1 500 km^2) in 1995–97.

Following successful control or eradication, re-invasion must be controlled in order to sustain livelihoods. Tsetse flies are estimated to be able to regenerate their population from very low levels within four years. In practice, the greatest threat of re-invasion comes from outside the cleared area.

[1] J.C.M. Trail, K. Sones, J.M.C. Jibbo, J. Durkin, D.E. Light and M. Murray. 1985. *Productivity of Boran cattle maintained by chemoprophylaxis under trypanosomiasis risk.* ILCS Research Report No. 9. Addis Ababa, International Livestock Centre for Africa.
[2] FAO. 1987. *Trypanotolerant cattle and livestock development in West and Central Africa.* Vol. 1. *International supply and demand for breeding stock,* by A.P.M. Shaw and C.H. Hoste. FAO Animal Production and Health Paper No. 67/1. Rome.

II. Asia and the Pacific

REGIONAL OVERVIEW
General economic performance

Economic growth in the Asian economies slowed down somewhat in 2001.

Recent economic performance in Asian developing countries confirms their level of integration into the world economy, their post-crisis strength and their heterogeneity. In 2000, economic performance was strong but weakened after mid-year as a result of the global economic slowdown. Continuing weak external demand, especially for electronic goods, contributed to an overall reduction in growth to about 5.6 percent in 2001.[36]

As a consequence of the events of 11 September, projected GDP growth for 2002 was revised down for most countries in the area. The region as a whole is projected to grow by 5.6 percent but the impact of the attacks and their aftermath, transmitted through various channels, will be felt by different countries with varying degrees of intensity.

Within Southeast Asia, Indonesia, Malaysia, the Philippines, Thailand and Viet Nam all saw high rates of growth in 2000, with Malaysia recording a particularly strong performance. However, in 2001 lower growth rates are expected in all the major countries in the subregion, in particular Malaysia and Thailand.

In 2000, economic growth reached 8 percent in China, continuing the strong performance of past years. A considerable slowdown in exports has led to a moderate reduction in the

Table 9

ANNUAL REAL GDP GROWTH RATES IN SELECTED COUNTRIES OF DEVELOPING ASIA

Country/region	1996	1997	1998	1999	2000	2001[1]	2002[1]
				(Percentage)			
Bangladesh	5	5.3	5	5.4	6	4.7	3.2
China	9.6	8.8	7.8	7.1	8	7.3	6.8
India	7.3	4.9	5.8	6.8	6	4.4	5.2
Indonesia	8	4.5	-13.1	0.8	4.8	3.2	3.5
Malaysia	10	7.3	-7.4	6.1	8.3	0.3	2.5
Pakistan	2.9	1.8	3.1	4.1	3.9	3.7	4.4
Philippines	5.7	5.2	-0.6	3.4	4	2.9	3.2
Thailand	5.9	-1.5	-10.8	4.3	4.4	1.5	2
Viet Nam	9.3	8.2	3.5	4.2	5.5	4.7	4.8
Developing Asia	**8.3**	**6.5**	**4**	**6.2**	**6.8**	**5.6**	**5.6**

[1] Projections.
[2] China, excluding Hong Kong Special Administrative Region and Taiwan Province.
Source: IMF. 2001. *World Economic Outlook*, December. Washington, DC.

Table 10

NET PRODUCTION GROWTH RATES IN DEVELOPING ASIA AND THE PACIFIC

Year	Agriculture	Crops	Cereals	Livestock	Food	Non-food
			(Percentage)			
1992–96	4.9	4.1	2.5	7.3	5.3	0.0
1997	4.0	1.6	0.2	7.4	4.0	4.4
1998	2.6	1.5	1.9	5.7	3.3	-8.1
1999	3.3	3.4	3.1	2.1	3.5	-0.1
2000	1.7	0.3	-3.6	4.6	1.7	2.6
2001[1]	1.1	-0.7	-2.3	3.8	0.9	3.6

[1] Preliminary.
Source: FAO.

growth rate for 2001. Strong domestic demand and foreign investment are expected to contribute to sustained strong growth in 2002.

South Asia as a whole has seen lower average growth rates compared with those of Southeast Asia, although still quite respectable in recent years at rates of 5 percent or more, in particular for India and Bangladesh. The region is less exposed, although not completely immune, to the downturn in global trade and economic activity compared with most of the smaller Asian countries. Lower economic growth in 2001 is forecast for Bangladesh, India and Pakistan.

Agricultural performance

Relatively low growth in agricultural output in 2000 seems to have declined further in 2001.

Overall agricultural output growth for the region fell to 1.7 percent in 2000, continuing the trend towards a gradual decline in growth seen over the last few years. The reduced performance was entirely due to lower growth in crop production, which fell to 0.3 percent after the 3.4 percent expansion in 1999. Cereal production fell by 3.6 percent in 2000, with most of the decline linked to the fall in Chinese cereal output. Regional livestock production, on the other hand, expanded by 4.6 percent, compared with 2.1 percent in the previous year.

Preliminary estimates for 2001 point to a further reduction in regional agricultural output growth to about 1 percent, with crop production contracting by almost 1 percent while livestock output is expected to expand by just under 4 percent. Cereal output is forecast to drop by 2.3 percent, reflecting adverse weather conditions in the key grain-producing countries of the region.

The poor performance in 2000 was largely accounted for by South Asia, where agricultural output declined by 0.3 percent

Figure 22

ASIA AND THE PACIFIC: SELECTED INDICATORS

**Agricultural export
and import values and share
in total merchandise trade**

■ Agricultural exports ($)

■ Agricultural imports ($)

━ Ag. exports as share of total (%)

━ Ag. imports as share of total (%)

Agricultural exports
(Index: 1989–91=100)

━ Value

━ Unit value

━ Quantity

Agricultural imports
(Index: 1989–91=100)

━ Value

━ Unit value

━ Quantity

**Net barter and income
agricultural terms of trade**
(Index: 1989–91=100)

━ Net barter

━ Income

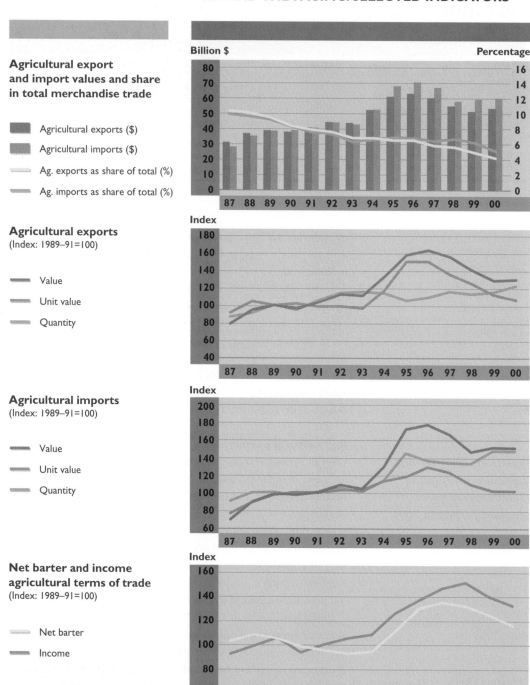

ASIA AND THE PACIFIC: SELECTED INDICATORS

Real GDP
(Percentage change from
preceding year)

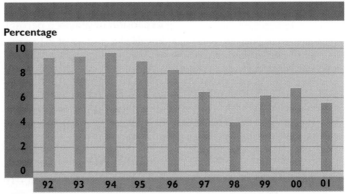

Dietary energy supplies
(kcal per capita per day)

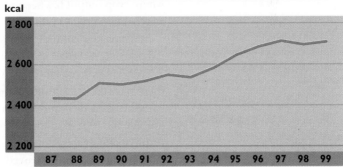

Agricultural production
(Index: 1989–91=100)

Total agricultural production

Per capita food production

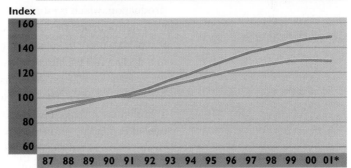

* Preliminary

Source: FAO and IMF

after experiencing strong growth of 4–5 percent in the previous year. Crop production declined by 1.2 percent while livestock output rose by 2.8 percent, in line with its performance in 1999. In India, agricultural output fell by 1.1 percent, following its expansion by almost 5 percent the previous year. This was the net result of a decline of 2.1 percent in crop production and a 3 percent increase in livestock output. While output growth in 2000 was relatively robust, at 6.5 and 3.7 percent in Bangladesh and Nepal, respectively, it was a more modest 1.6 and 0.8 percent in Pakistan and Sri Lanka.

Projections for 2001 indicate a further drop in agricultural output of about 1.5 percent. This would be the result of an estimated decline in crop production in the three largest countries of the subregion – India, Pakistan and Bangladesh – where crop output has been negatively affected by unfavourable weather conditions in the major producing areas.

In China, agricultural production growth in 2000, at 2.6 percent, recorded only a modest improvement over the 2.1 percent achieved in 1999. Although still quite respectable, these rates are significantly lower than the levels of 6.4 and 4.2 percent of 1997 and 1998, respectively, and the 6.6 percent average for 1992–96. The lower performance in 2000 was the result of almost stagnant crop production, increasing by only 0.3 percent, and the improved performance of livestock production, which is estimated to have expanded by 5.8 percent. Cereal production declined by almost 10 percent, largely as a result of changes in government price support policies, which led to a decline in area harvested (see the review of Chinese agriculture and the implications of China's accession to the World Trade Organization [WTO] below).

Preliminary projections for 2001 point to Chinese agricultural output expanding at the same rate as in 2000: around 2.5 percent. Again, livestock production, growing at 4–5 percent, would outperform crop production, which is forecast to rise by only 0.5 percent. Cereal production is expected to continue its decline, owing to a further reduction in area harvested and unfavourable weather. Growth for both crop and livestock production is forecast to remain well below the rates that were prevailing prior to 1997.

In East and Southeast Asia, agricultural production slowed down somewhat in 2000, to an estimated 2.9 percent, from the high growth of 4.8 percent achieved in 1999 – a year of recovery following the poor output performance in 1997 and 1998. Indonesia appears to have experienced only modest growth of 1.5 percent, as a result of weak crop production growth of

0.8 percent as opposed to livestock production growth of 5.9 percent. Cambodia, the Republic of Korea, Malaysia and the Philippines all saw production rise by between 2 and 3 percent. In the Democratic People's Republic of Korea, severe drought in 2000, following the coldest winter in decades, contributed to a contraction in output of 3.8 percent, with cereal production in particular declining sharply for the second year in a row. Vietnamese agriculture, however, continued the strong performance of the preceding years with annual output expanding in the range of 4–5 percent.

Preliminary estimates for 2001 suggest a slowdown in agricultural output growth for the subregion to just under 1 percent, with crop production stagnating but livestock output rising by about 4 percent. Most countries in the subregion are expected to follow this pattern. Output is expected to contract sharply in Cambodia, where heavy flooding caused extensive damage to the paddy crop, and somewhat less in the Philippines and Viet Nam. In the Democratic People's Republic of Korea, cereal production in 2001 witnessed a strong recovery after the very poor harvest of the preceding year.

In the developing countries of the Pacific, agricultural production reached 1.6 percent in 2000 after expanding by 3.7 percent in 1999, while preliminary estimates for 2001 point to unchanged levels of agricultural production. This largely reflects the estimated output performance of Papua New Guinea, the subregion's largest agricultural producer, where agricultural production rose by 1 percent in 2000 after expanding by 5.7 percent in 1999, and output is estimated to have stagnated in 2001.

CHINA'S ACCESSION TO THE WORLD TRADE ORGANIZATION AND IMPLICATIONS FOR CHINESE AGRICULTURAL POLICIES

In January 2002 China became a member of the World Trade Organization.

On 10 November 2001, the Ministerial Conference of the World Trade Organization in Doha approved the agreement for China's entry into the WTO. Agriculture has been at the centre of entry negotiations, and the accession agreement includes numerous commitments concerning agriculture. However, there is disagreement over the likely impact of the accession. Some argue that its impact on China's agriculture will be substantial[37] while others believe that the overall effects on agriculture will be modest.[38] These diverse views can in part be attributed to a general uncertainty about the likely policy changes that may be induced after WTO accession.[39] The following will: briefly review China's current agricultural policies and past performance of the sector; examine the main features of the accession agreement pertaining to agriculture and consider a number of possible ways in which policy-makers may respond.

The changing role of agriculture in the Chinese economy
China's economic liberalization has proceeded for more than two decades. Since economic reforms were initiated in 1978, China's economy has grown substantially. The annual growth rate of GDP was 8.5 percent in 1979–84 and 9.7 percent in 1985–95 (Table 11). Despite the Asian financial crisis, GDP continued growing at 8.2 percent annually between 1996 and 2000. Foreign trade has expanded even more rapidly. The ratio of trade to GDP increased from 13 percent in 1980 to 44 percent in 2000.[40]

China's economy and agriculture have grown rapidly since economic reforms began in the late 1970s.

Although reform has touched the whole economy since the early 1980s, most of the successive transformations began with, and in some way depended on, growth in the agriculture sector.[41] Decollectivization, price increases and the relaxation of local trade restrictions ignited the takeoff of China's agricultural economy after 1978. Grain production increased by 4.7 percent per year in 1978–84 and even higher growth was recorded in horticulture, livestock and aquatic products (Table 11). Although agricultural growth slowed down with the disappearance of the one-off efficiency gains deriving from decollectivization, the country continued to enjoy agricultural growth rates that outpaced the rise in population (Table 11). Even faster growth of the industrial and service sectors followed, leading to a decline in the share of agriculture in GDP from more than 30 percent before 1980 to 16 percent in 2000 (Table 12). At the same time, agriculture's share in total employment fell from 81 percent in 1970 to only 50 percent in 2000.

Rapid economic growth, urbanization and the development of food markets have boosted demand for meat, fruit and other non-staple foods, causing major shifts in the structure of agricultural production.[42] For example, the share of livestock in agricultural output value more than doubled, from 14 percent to 30 percent, between 1970 and 2000 (Table 12). One of the most significant signs of structural change is the much reduced share of crops (from 82 percent to 56 percent), and particularly that of grains.

Major changes have occurred in external trade also. Whereas the share of primary (mainly agricultural) products in total exports was over 50 percent in 1980, it fell to only 10 percent in 2000 (Table 12). Over the same period, the share of food in total exports fell from 17 percent to 5 percent, while the share of food imports fell from 15 percent to 2 percent. The composition of agricultural trade increasingly reflects China's comparative advantage (Table 12 and Figure 23). Indeed, net exports of land-intensive bulk commodities such as grains, oilseeds and sugar crops have fallen, whereas exports of higher-valued labour-intensive products such as horticultural and animal (including aquaculture) products have risen. The proportion of grain exports in the 1990s (about 20 percent) is less than half of what it was in the early 1980s. By the late 1990s horticultural products and animal and aquatic products accounted for about 80 percent of agricultural exports.[43]

These trends seem to indicate that China was already moving towards a pattern of production and trade that is more consistent with its domestic resource endowments and comparative advantage – allowing more land-intensive products into the domestic market and stimulating labour-intensive crops

Table 11

ANNUAL GROWTH RATES OF CHINA'S ECONOMY, 1970–2000

	Pre-reform 1970–78	Reform period		
		1979–84	1985–95	1996–00
		(Percentage)		
Gross domestic product	4.9	8.5	9.7	8.2
Agriculture	2.7	7.1	4.0	3.4
Industry	6.8	8.2	12.8	9.6
Services	n.a.	11.6	9.7	8.2
Foreign trade	20.5	14.3	15.2	9.8
Import	21.7	12.7	13.4	9.5
Export	19.4	15.9	17.2	10.0
Grain production	2.8	4.7	1.7	0.03
Oil crops	2.1	14.9	4.4	5.6
Fruits	6.6	7.2	12.7	8.6
Red meats	4.4	9.1	8.8	6.5
Fishery	5.0	7.9	13.7	10.2
Rural enterprises output value	n.a.	12.3	24.1	14.0
Population	1.80	1.40	1.37	0.90
Per capita GDP	3.1	7.1	8.3	7.1

Note: Figure for GDP in 1970–78 is the growth rate of national income in real terms. Growth rates are computed using the regression method. Growth rates of individual and groups of commodities are based on production data; sectoral growth rates refer to value added in real terms.
Source: National Bureau of Statistics of China. *China Statistical Yearbook*, various issues. Beijing, China Statistical Publishing House; Ministry of Agriculture. *Agricultural Yearbook of China*, various issues. Beijing.

Table 12

CHANGES IN THE STRUCTURE OF CHINA'S ECONOMY, 1970–2000

	1970	1980	1985	1990	1995	2000
			(Percentage)			
Share in GDP						
Agriculture	40	30	28	27	20	16
Industry	46	49	43	42	49	51
Services	13	21	29	31	31	33
Share in employment						
Agriculture	81	69	62	60	52	50
Industry	10	18	21	21	23	22.5
Services	9	13	17	19	25	27.5
Share in exports						
Primary products	...	50	51	26	14	10
Foods	...	17	14	11	7	5
Share in imports						
Primary products	...	35	13	19	18	21
Foods	...	15	4	6	5	2
Share in agricultural output						
Crops	82	76	69	65	58	56
Livestock	14	18	22	26	30	30
Fishery	2	2	3	5	8	11
Forestry	2	4	5	4	3	4
Share of rural population	83	81	76	74	71	64

Source: National Bureau of Statistics of China. *China Statistical Yearbook*, various issues; *China Rural Statistical Yearbook*, various issues. Beijing, China Statistical Publishing House.

for exports. The main impact of the country's entry into the WTO will be to advance these emerging trends.

Agricultural policy in the reform period

Major policy reforms affecting agriculture have been implemented over the last two to three decades.

In spite of these past trends, few can dispute that China's WTO accession poses new challenges to the agriculture sector. However, the nature and depth of the impact will depend on how China's agricultural policy-makers will manage the agriculture sector as the new trade rules take effect. Before examining this in greater detail, a brief review of agricultural policies during the reform era is provided.

Fiscal and financial policies. Although government expenditures in most areas of agriculture have increased gradually during the reform period, the ratio of agricultural investment to agricultural GDP has declined since the late 1970s. In 1978, the government sector invested 7.6 percent of agricultural GDP.[44] By 1995, the share had fallen to 3.6 percent. Moreover, significant capital outflows from agriculture to industry and from rural to urban areas occurred during the last two decades through the financial system and government agricultural procurement.[45]

Foreign exchange and trade policies. China's external economic policies have played a major role in shaping the growth and structure of agriculture for many decades. During the entire pre-reform period (1950–78), China's inward-looking policies and overvalued currency discouraged exports.[46] After the reforms were initiated, the real exchange rate was allowed to depreciate by as much as 400 percent between 1978 and 1994. Adjustments in the exchange rates throughout the reform period have increased export competitiveness and contributed to China's export growth record.

Rural development and labour market policies. Shifting the labour force from the farm to the non-farm sector has been crucial to

Figure 23

CHINA: AGRICULTURAL TRADE BALANCE BY FACTOR INTENSITY OF PRODUCTS

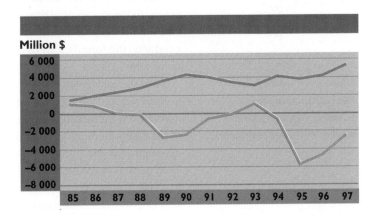

Labour-intensive products[1]

Land-intensive products[2]

Million $

[1] Labour-intensive products include: live animals, fish and crustaceans, and other aquatic invertebrates; dairy produce, birds' eggs, natural honey and other edible products of animal origin; live trees and other plants; bulbs, roots, etc.; cut flowers and ornamental foliage; edible vegetables and certain roots and tubers; edible fruits and nuts, peel of citrus fruits or melons; coffee, tea, maté and spices; products of the milling industry, malt, starches and wheat gluten; plants for industrial and medicinal use; rice straw and forage; lac, gums, resins and other vegetable saps and extracts; vegetable plaiting materials; vegetable products not elsewhere specified or included; animal fats and waxes; raw silk and raw wool.

[2] Land-intensive products include: cereals; vegetable oil seeds and oleaginous fruits; edible vegetable oils; raw cotton and other vegetable textile fibres.

Source: J. Huang and C. Chen. 1999. *Effects of trade liberalization on agriculture in China: institutional and structural aspects.* Bogor, Indonesia, United Nations ESCAP CGPRT Centre

the country's modernization efforts. This has been achieved through the absorption of labour by rural firms and through massive migration to cities. Rural industrialization has played a vital role in generating employment for rural labour, raising agricultural labour productivity and farmers' income. The share of rural enterprises in GDP rose from less than 4 percent in the 1970s to more than 30 percent by 1999. Rural enterprises have dominated the export sector throughout the 1990s.[47] And, most importantly, they employ 35 percent of the rural labour that works off-farm. In addition, a large and increasing proportion of the rural labour force (rising from 8 percent in 1990 to 13 percent in 2000)[48] also works in the self-employed sector. A recent survey suggests that more than 100 million rural workers also found employment in the urban sector in the late 1990s.[49]

Food price and marketing policies. Price and market reforms were key components of China's policy shift from a centrally planned to a market economy. The reforms, however, began slowly and have proceeded gradually. Market liberalization began with commodities considered non-strategic, such as vegetables, fruit, fish, livestock, and oil and sugar crops, while little effort was made regarding the major crops. Most of the significant early reforms were done by administrative measures.[50] However, as the right to private trading was expanded in the early 1980s, and traders were allowed to buy and sell the surplus of almost all categories of agricultural products, the foundations of the state marketing system began to be undermined.

China's agricultural markets increasingly resemble those in more market-oriented economies.

Since the mid-1980s, market reforms have continued intermittently. Despite periodic swings in the reform process, markets have gradually emerged in rural China. The proportion of retail commodities sold at market prices has continued to rise. The share for agriculture was just 6 percent in 1978 but had risen to 40 percent by 1985, 79 percent by 1995 and 83 percent by 1999.[51] Also, the state's intervention was unable to halt the flow of grain across provincial boundaries. A recent study found that agricultural prices for all major commodities, including rice, wheat and, especially, maize and soybean, have moved together across far-reaching localities within China.[52] China's markets are becoming more integrated and efficient, and increasingly resemble those in more market-oriented economies.

What have these policies meant in the international context? Tables 13 and 14 show estimated nominal protection rates (NPRs) for major agricultural commodities since 1985. The NPRs estimate the percentage by which domestic prices of agricultural products differ from the border prices for those same products. A positive NPR indicates that domestic prices are above the border price (and that domestic producers receive a subsidy) and a negative NPR that they are below the border price (and that domestic producers are subject to an implicit taxation). Although further adjustment may be required for quality and other factors, these NPRs roughly illustrate the basic nature of policy changes in the past. The requirement that farmers submit a mandatory delivery quota at below-market prices has represented an implicit tax on farmers and a subsidy to the urban consumers, who were able to get access to sales at below-market value.[53] Between 1990 and 1997, the average price farmers received for compulsorily delivered grains and soybean was between one-eighth and one-third below the border price. Only in recent years have those prices been above the border price. It should be noted that NPRs for rice have been mostly negative throughout this period and for all three sets of prices. On the other hand, wheat and cotton, the nation's main imported farm commodities, received favourable treatment relative to rice. This difference is more acute given the fact that the proportion of production procured at the low quota procurement price is higher for rice. Meat producers, in contrast, still appear to receive less than they would if they could sell their output at international prices (Table 14).

A farmer selling cauliflower and spinach
Today in China the majority of agricultural produce is traded on private markets.

FAO/22265/A. PROTO

China's WTO accession commitments and provisions related to agriculture

In its WTO accession agreement China has committed to further agricultural trade liberalization.

China's commitments affecting the agriculture sector can be classified into three major categories: market access, domestic support and export subsidies. As for market access, China committed itself to lowering tariffs on all agricultural products, increasing access by foreign producers of some commodities through tariff rate quotas (TRQs) and removing quantitative restrictions on others (see Box 2 on page 44). The import

Table 13

NOMINAL PROTECTION RATES FOR GRAIN, CHINA, 1978 TO EARLY 2000

Year	Quota procurement price				Negotiated procurement price				Wholesale market price			
	Rice	Wheat	Maize	Soybean	Rice	Wheat	Maize	Soybean	Rice	Wheat	Maize	Soybean
							(Percentage)					
1978–79	-42	15	12	2	-6	72	65	22	10	89	92	40
1980–84	-43	-3	-15	13	2	50	28	25	9	58	46	44
1985–89	-30	4	-13	-13	-5	34	17	15	-4	52	37	39
1990–94	-37	-14	-35	-32	-16	14	-7	7	-7	30	12	26
1995–97	-23	-12	-14	-22	-4	6	3	8	-1	19	20	19
1998–00	-3	10	22	33	-16	9	19	39	-6	26	32	49
1998	2	16	33	8	-16	5	26	37	-6	22	40	37
1999	-6	22	30	53	-19	12	20	59	-9	30	33	67
2000	-4	-7	2	38	-13	9	11	21	-2	26	23	44

Note: Border prices are average prices of exports (rice and sometimes maize) or imports (wheat, soybean and sometimes maize) for the varieties that are comparable with domestic grains. Data for 2000 are from early 2000. Official exchange rates are used to convert border prices.
Source: J. Huang and S. Rozelle. 2001. *The nature and extent of current distortions to agricultural incentives in China.* Paper presented at the second project meeting on WTO Accession, Policy Reform and Poverty Reduction in China, World Bank Resident Mission, Beijing, 26–27 October 2001.

Table 14

NOMINAL PROTECTION RATES FOR COTTON AND LIVESTOCK PRODUCTS, CHINA, 1997–99

Year	Cotton	Pork	Beef	Chicken
		(Percentage)		
1997	20	-19	-2	-34
1998	11	-25	-10	-37
1999	4	-17	24	-30
1997–99	12	-20	4	-33

Note: Export prices of pork, beef and chicken, and import prices of cotton are used as border prices. Domestic prices are prices at urban wholesale markets. The cotton wholesale price is estimated as the state procurement price multiplied by 1.25. Official exchange rates are used to convert border prices.
Source: J. Huang and S. Rozelle. 2001. *The nature and extent of current distortions to agricultural incentives in China.* Paper presented at the second project meeting on WTO Accession, Policy Reform and Poverty Reduction in China, World Bank Resident Mission, Beijing, 26–27 October 2001.

market access commitments made by China appear to be substantial (Tables 15 and 16). Overall, agricultural import tariffs (in terms of their simple average) will be reduced from about 21 percent in 2001 to 17 percent by 2004 (after having already declined from 42.2 percent in 1992 to 23.6 percent in 1998). Quotas under low tariff will be expanded, while shares of state trading will be reduced significantly.

With a few exceptions (e.g. in the case of some commodities considered "national strategic products"), most agricultural products will come under a tariff-only regime. For this commodity group all non-tariff barriers and licensing and quota procedures will be eliminated and their effective protection will be lowered substantially by January 2002 and fall further by 2004 (Table 15). However, imports will not necessarily grow correspondingly. Indeed, China has a comparative advantage in many of the commodities presented in Table 15. The real challenge for agricultural products with tariff-only protection will be for crops such as barley, and wine and dairy products. The case of soybean, for which China has little comparative advantage, may also be instructive. Before 2000, the import tariff for soybean was as high as 114 percent; importers required licences; and Chinese farmers met most of the nation's soybean demand. However, in anticipation of China's WTO accession,

Table 15

IMPORT TARIFF RATES ON MAJOR AGRICULTURAL PRODUCTS SUBJECT TO TARIFF-ONLY PROTECTION IN CHINA

	Actual tariff rates in 2001	Effective as of 1 January	
		2002	2004
		(Percentage)	
Barley	114 (3)[1]	3	3
Soybean	3[2]	3	3
Citrus	40	20	12
Other fruits	30–40	13–20	10–13
Vegetables	30–50	13–29	10–15
Beef	45	23.2	12
Pork	20	18.4	12
Poultry meat	20	18.4	10
Dairy products	50	20–37	10–12
Wine	65	45	14
Tobacco	34	28	10

[1] Barley was subjected to licence and import quota; the tariff rate was 3 percent for import within the quota and no above-quota barley with 114 percent tariff was imported in 2001.
[2] The tariff rate was as high as 114 percent before 2000 and lowered to 3 percent in early 2000.
Source: China's WTO Protocol of Accession, November 2001.

Table 16

CHINA'S MARKET ACCESS COMMITMENTS ON FARM PRODUCTS SUBJECT TO TARIFF RATE QUOTAS

	Import volume (million tonnes) (State trading share [percent])			Quota growth	In-quota tariff	Out-of-quota tariff		
						2002	2003	2004
	Actual 2000	Quota 2002	Quota 2004					
				(Percentage)		(Percentage)		
Rice	0.24 (100)[1]	3.76 (50)	5.32 (50)	19	1	74	71	65
Wheat	0.87 (100)	8.45 (90)	9.64 (90)	8	1	71	68	65
Maize	0.00 (100)	5.70 (67)	7.20 (60)	13	1	71	68	65
Cotton	0.05 (100)	0.82 (33)	0.89 (33)	5	1	54.4	47.2	40
Wool[2]	0.30	0.34	0.37	5	1	38	38	38
Edible oils[3]	1.79 (100)	5.69 (40)	6.81 (10)	15	9	75	71.7	68.3
Sugar[4]	0.64	1.68	1.95	8	20	90	72	50

[1] Figures in parentheses are the share (in percentage terms) of non-state trading in import quota.
[2] Designated trading in 2002–04 and phased out thereafter.
[3] The tariff rate quota regime will be phased out in 2006. In 2005, import quota will be 7.27 million tonnes with 9 percent in-quota tariff and 65 percent out-of-quota tariff.
[4] Phased out quota for state trade.
Source: China's WTO *Protocol of Accession*, November 2001; National Bureau of Statistics of China. 2001. *China Statistical Yearbook*. Beijing, China Statistical Publishing House.

tariffs were lowered to 3 percent in 2000 and subsequently import quotas were phased out. Prices fell as a consequence and the NPRs declined from 44 percent in early 2000 (Table 13) to less than 15 percent in October 2001. As a result, imports surged from 4.32 million tonnes in 1999 to 10.42 million tonnes in 2000 and are likely to exceed 14 million tonnes in 2001.

Such dramatic movements, however, should be limited for the commodities considered as "national strategic products". Indeed, China's WTO agreement allows the government to manage the trade of rice, wheat, maize, edible oils, sugar, cotton and wool with TRQs.[54] As shown in Table 16, while the in-quota tariff is 20 percent for sugar and 9 percent for edible oils, it is only 1 percent for rice, wheat, maize and wool, but the amount brought in at these tariff levels is restricted. The in-quota volumes, however, are set to grow over a three-year period (2002–04) at annual rates ranging from 4 percent to 19 percent. At the same time, tariffs on out-of-quota sales will drop substantially in the first year of accession and fall further between 2002 and 2005.

China will phase out most state-trading monopolies.

After the first four to five years following accession, a number of other changes will take place. For example, China has agreed to phase out its TRQ for edible oils after 2006. State trading monopolies will also be phased out for wool after 2004 and will gradually disappear for most other agricultural products (Table 16). Although China National Cereals, Oil and Foodstuffs Import

& Export Corporation will continue to play an important role in rice, wheat and maize trade, there will be an increasing degree of competition from private firms in the importing and exporting of grains in the future.

China's WTO accession agreement also contains a number of other commitments, some of which are specific to China. First, unlike other countries, China must phase out all export subsidies.[55] Second, in spite of its status as a developing country, China's *de minimis* exemption (see Box 2 on page 44) is equivalent to only 8.5 percent of the value of production of a basic agricultural product for product-specific support and the same percentage of the value of total agricultural production for non-product-specific support (as compared with 10 percent for other developing countries and 5 percent for developed countries). Third, investment and input subsidies for the low-income and resource-poor farmers who are not subject to reduction commitments must be included as part of its aggregate measure of support (AMS) (see Box 2 on page 44).

China also agreed to a series of specific conditions for anti-dumping and countervailing duties. For a period of 15 years, China will be subject to a different set of rules that will make it easier for countries to bring, prove and enforce dumping cases against the country. However, China will benefit from the same rights in dealing with other countries, as reciprocity.

China's WTO commitments and privileges in other areas of the agreement will also, directly or indirectly, affect its agriculture. For example, for agricultural chemicals, China has committed to replacing quantitative import restrictions on three types of fertilizer (DAP, NPK and urea) by TRQs. Additionally, tariffs will be cut on accession and further cuts will be phased in by 2005 for almost all industrial products (e.g. tractors and pesticides). Furthermore, China will significantly reduce its non-tariff measures and eliminate all quotas, tendering and import licensing on non-farm products by no later than 2005. For textiles and clothing, however, the current "voluntary" export restraints will not be completely phased out until the end of 2008, meaning that exports may not expand as rapidly as they would under a less restrictive regime. Substantial commitments to open up services markets in China have also been made.

Recent policy shifts and likely changes as a result of accession to the WTO

While the agricultural reforms implemented by China since the late 1970s will make it easier for the sector to cope with the changes that will arise in the wake of WTO entry, the country still faces many challenges in meeting its WTO commitments.[56] These may, however, at the same time be seen as opportunities to provide an impetus to the ongoing domestic and trade policy reforms. Policy responses to WTO accession are expected to take one of two forms: one consists of policy responses to meet the WTO commitments; the other is represented by policy reforms aimed at boosting the economy and minimizing the adverse shocks of WTO accession.

Legislative changes

China is introducing major legislative changes to abide by the WTO rules.

Many important changes should occur in the area of legislation. China has been given one year from the date of accession to make economic policy institutions, regulations and legislation consistent with the spirit of non-discrimination and transparency of the WTO. Preparations for this had started already in the late 1990s.

To provide general guidance to ministerial and local government authorities for amending or repealing relevant regulations, laws and policies, two important sets of regulations were promulgated in January 2002: the Regulations on Formulation Process of Laws and the Regulations on Formulation Process of Administrative Laws. Essentially a guide for local governments and ministries, these new regulations were issued in order to ensure the transfer of many government functions to the market and to direct the government to take a more regulatory, indirect role in commerce and trade.

Efforts towards creating and implementing this new regulatory framework are widespread. For example, during the last stage of WTO negotiation, each ministry formed a committee to review all laws and regulations under its jurisdiction and make them consistent with the WTO rules and China's accession commitments. Local governments formed similar committees. Several recent experiences involving the amendment of laws and regulations and the creation of new institutions related to agriculture demonstrate the effectiveness of these committees and China's overall commitment to its WTO obligations. For example, China's Patent Law (which was originally issued in 1984 and then amended in 1992) was re-amended on 1 July 2001. Moreover, a new set of regulations on plant variety protection was put into effect in 1999 when China became the 39th member country of the International Union for the Protection of New Varieties of Plants (UPOV).

The Ministry of Agriculture has also repealed several regulations since 2000 subsidizing certain types of enterprise or discriminating between different economic actors in agricultural input industries. The Regulations on the Development of

Integrated Agricultural, Industrial and Commercial Enterprises under State Farms (issued in 1983 to assist in the development of state-owned farms) and the Regulations on the Development of Rural Township and Village Owned Enterprises (issued in 1979 to assist collectively owned enterprises) have also been eliminated. Seed management regulations that gave monopoly powers to local seed companies and pesticide field trial rules that discriminated against foreign companies have likewise been abolished.

Despite the substantial efforts outlined above, China still requires considerable institutional reform to allow it to fulfil the legal obligations that it is committed to in its Protocol of Accession to the WTO.

Agricultural trade reforms

Agricultural trade will have to be further liberalized.

Reforms and liberalization in China's trade laws and regulations are perhaps the most advanced. Throughout nearly 20 years of reform, China's foreign trade regime has gradually changed from a highly centralized, planned and import substitution regime to a more decentralized and market-oriented one focusing on export promotion.[57] These changes in trade and other policies have progressively transformed China's trade structure in favour of products for which China has a comparative advantage. On the other hand, trade in many agricultural goods will continue to operate under relatively non-transparent state trading arrangements.[58] The next few years will be a critical time for China in terms of advancing its trade reform in the agriculture sector, including both tariff and non-tariff measures.

Changes in tariff policies are more straightforward and simple than non-tariff policy reforms. China followed its tariff reduction schedule as specified in the Protocol. On the first day of 2002, the average tariff rate was reduced from 15.3 percent in 2001 to 12 percent. For agricultural products the tariff reduction was from 21 percent to 15.8 percent. Export subsidies were also to be completely phased out on the first day of 2002.

In the light of the past decade's trend towards tariff reduction, the tariff changes resulting from China's WTO accession should present relatively few problems. Significant reforms will, however, be required in the area of non-tariff measures. State trading is a particularly important area to consider when reforming China's agricultural trade policy. China has agreed to eliminate restrictions on trading rights for all products except those under the TRQ trade regime, for which a more gradual approach will be followed in phasing out the state-trading regime (Table 16). Three years after WTO accession, the private sector is supposed to dominate trade in almost all agricultural products. There are, however, provisions allowing the state to remain involved for three commodities: wheat, maize and tobacco.

Technical barriers to trade, sanitary and phytosanitary measures, and institutional arrangements to fulfil the Agreement on Trade Related Aspects of Intellectual Property Rights (TRIPS), including Trade in Counterfeit Goods, are other important issues that China has to deal with.

Domestic market reform and infrastructure development

After 20 years of reform, China's agriculture has become more market-oriented.[59] Traders have moved products around the country with increasing regularity. By the late 1990s, only grain, cotton and, to some extent, silkworm cocoon and tobacco were subject to price interventions. Even in these cases, their markets, especially those for grain, have become increasingly competitive, integrated and efficient over time.[60]

Domestic agricultural markets must also be reformed further.

Despite this progress, China faces many tasks in the direction of further market reform under the WTO regime. A major challenge will be to improve the efficiency of domestic markets while also minimizing the adverse shocks of trade liberalization. The case of grains can be considered indicative of the direction of market reforms. Over the past two decades state-owned grain traders have chronically underperformed as a consequence of imperfect incentives and a number of taxing policy burdens. In spite of reform efforts, many state-owned grain companies were still losing money in the late 1990s. There has also been international criticism of China's marketing practices. WTO negotiators often pointed out that China's traditional food pricing systems had a market-distorting effect. Others argued that the preferential treatment of state-owned grain-trading enterprises violated the WTO's national treatment principles.

Facing these pressures and concerns, China launched a new set of reforms in 2000. As a first step, government control over lower-quality grain trading (e.g. early *indica* rice and maize in southern China, spring wheat in northern China, and all wheat in southern China) was phased out. Almost immediately, this policy resulted in an adjustment of crop variety patterns in some regions. Producers have begun planting better varieties to improve grain quality. With the successful performance of this grain "varietal" reform in 2000, the government is now officially liberalizing grain markets. This was done first in a subset of grain-deficit, coastal provinces – Zhejiang, Jiangsu, Shanghai, Fujian, Guangdong and Hainan – but it was expected to be extended to all grain-deficit provinces in 2002.

In response to WTO accession, the government has also devised ambitious plans to increase investment in market infrastructure. There is an acknowledged need to establish an effective national marketing information network. The Ministry of Agriculture is attempting to standardize agricultural product quality and promote marketing by farmers. The creation of agricultural technology associations is being examined. All of these moves are part of an effort to shift fiscal resources – which have been used to support China's expensive price subsidization schemes – towards productivity-enhancing investments and improvements in marketing infrastructure. The magnitude of this shift is highlighted by the fact that the total subsidies for price and market interventions reached 40.3 billion yuan renminbi in 2000, representing around 4 percent of the national budget.

Land-use policy, farm organization and farm enterprises

The implications of China's WTO accession on land use and farm organization are also much debated. Many of the concerns centre on the ability of China's small farms to compete after trade liberalization. Every farm household in China is endowed with land but the average farm size is very small and declining (from 0.56 ha in 1980 to 0.45 ha in 2000).[61] Although this structure can be considered positive in terms of social equity and

Chinese women transplanting rice

Recent policy reforms in the grains sector have led farmers to reduce areas sown to grains and to adopt better varieties.

FAO/22495/M. TRAMAGNINI

China's small farm size may constrain productivity increases.

stability, land fragmentation will also constrain the growth of labour productivity and farm income. Some argue that farm size and productivity could be expanded under more secure land-tenure arrangements. Others call for a continuation of policies under which local authorities periodically reallocate land to the farmers to keep land in the hands of all rural residents.

Although many policy-makers currently seem to favour relying on more secure tenure rights, they are still searching for complementary measures that will not forego all of the pro-equity benefits of the current land-management regime. Land in rural areas is, by law, collectively owned by the village (about 300 households on average) or a small group (*cunmin xiaozu*, normally comprising 15–30 households) and is contracted to households.[62] One of the most important changes in recent years is the extension of use-contract duration from 15 to 30 years. By 2000, about 98 percent of villages had amended their contract with farmers to reflect the longer duration of use rights.[63]

The government is now searching for a mechanism that would permit the remaining full-time farmers to gain access to additional cultivated land and increase their income and competitiveness. A new Rural Land Contract Law has recently been prepared for this purpose. Although ownership of land remains with the collective, the law conveys to the contract holders almost all other rights that they would have under a private property system. In particular, the law clearly defines rights to transfer and exchange contracted land. This is an acknowledgement of the ongoing changes; indeed, more and more land in China is being rented.[64] The new legislation also allows farmers to use contracted land for collateral to secure commercial loans and allows family members to inherit the land rights during the contracted period.

In an effort to increase China's agricultural productivity, large farm enterprises are also being encouraged, although this remains a controversial issue. Large farms have been supported with incentives such as tax reductions for infrastructure investments, credit subsidies for inputs and financing for food-processing facilities.

The other major attempt to increase farm productivity is the promotion of farmer organizations. Policy-makers now recognize that, given the small scale of China's farms, the creation of effective rural organizations may prove to be one of the most promising options for raising productivity and incomes. It is on this basis that China's 240 million farms have been allowed to form farmers' organizations. The organizations are encouraged to work closely with the government in the areas of technology extension, marketing information and quality control.[65]

Financial reforms

The financial sector has been reformed more slowly than some other sectors, and the government maintains strong control.[66] China's WTO commitments require it to open up gradually the country's financial markets. After a four-year transition period, all regional restrictions will be removed and foreign banks will receive national non-discriminatory treatment. The implications for agriculture are not clear. The sector, in poor regions in particular, could suffer, but it is not certain that the situation will be worse than before the reforms. The financial sector has systematically shifted funds away from farming.[67] Throughout the entire reform period, there was a net capital outflow. However, the experiences of other countries suggest that in the short run small, poor farmers will be rationed out of financial markets.[68]

Agricultural investment and supporting policies

In one of its most fundamental concessions, China agreed to phase out its export subsidies in the first year of WTO accession. Such subsidies have often promoted exports of maize, cotton and other agricultural products and thus indirectly supported domestic prices.

The WTO also exerts strict control over the types and amounts of certain subsidies that member countries can provide. As is the case with other WTO members, China has to circumscribe with care the rules regarding the amount that can be classified as "amber box" policy (see Box 2 on page 44). China's accession protocol sets the *de minimis* level of subsidies at 8.5 percent of agricultural gross production value. A study on historical government investment in these areas indicates that the *de minimis* limit is not likely to be binding for the time being.[69] The real impact might begin only sometime in the future, when budget constraints would become less tight after years of further economic growth.

In a post-WTO accession environment, China may give more thought to how it can best use its *de minimis* conditions. A recent study has shown that although labour-intensive sectors (such as livestock and horticulture) had negative NPRs in late 2001, many land-intensive products (including maize, wheat, oilseed crops and sugar) had positive NPRs ranging from 5 to 40 percent.[70] The crops with positive NPRs are almost all under TRQ management – a finding that has important implications for how China may most effectively provide support to its agriculture sector. Instead of continuing market support or subsidies, China could promote productivity-enhancing measures such as agricultural research and transportation and communication investments.

China is shifting its agricultural support from price support towards productivity-enhancing investment.

The impact of WTO accession will differ not only among crops, but also among regions according to their comparative advantage in agricultural production and government policies. In redirecting support to the sector, particular attention may be paid to this differentiated regional impact, with priority attention being called for with regard to the poorest rural areas.

Recent shifts in the government's support to enhancing agricultural productivity seem to indicate that policy changes have already begun. For example, real-term government spending on agricultural research grew annually at about 10 percent in the late 1990s, with public investment in plant biotechnology increasing at an even faster rate.[71]

Agricultural structural adjustment and macropolicies

Structural adjustments in agriculture are a policy priority.

Structural adjustments in agriculture were considered a central policy goal of the government in 2000 and were further emphasized in 2001. The adjustments include structural changes among agricultural commodities, quality improvement for major commodities, and the promotion of regional specialization. These new policy directions, in part a consequence of China's efforts to prepare for WTO membership, are referred to as the "Strategic Adjustment of Agricultural Structure".[72] Key policies and measures to support these adjustments include many of the actions discussed above.

The policy direction is to re-initiate grain-marketing reforms and redirect part of the government's resource allocation from cotton and grain staples towards commodities for which China has a comparative advantage, such as horticulture crops, and to promote regional specialization. The intention is to rely more on indirect measures that are WTO compatible: technology improvement, investments in infrastructure and the creation of a favourable institutional and economic environment.

A number of policies can complement the structural transformation of agriculture and serve to make China more competitive in its post-WTO environment, although these policies are not within the control of those who are directly in charge of agriculture. Agricultural producers must increase the scale of their operation. This requires the transfer of massive amounts of labour into the off-farm sector, in general, and into urban areas, in particular. Hence, policies that promote labour movement will also be good for agricultural income and production. Such policies involve the promotion of employment policies leading to greater urbanization, rural township development and labour market development (by removing the constraints to small enterprise expansion in rural areas). Particular emphasis on the poorest rural areas may also be warranted here.

Conclusions

China has already started preparing itself to adjust to the environment of a post-WTO accession regime. Tariff rates have come down; many laws and regulations have been amended; investment priorities have shifted and policy strategies have changed. The government has many options at its disposal. Even though the WTO protocol that China has agreed to imposes restrictions on its actions, China's authorities can still play an active role in assisting its farming sector. Some of the most obvious and important activities will be to increase support through productivity-enhancing investments that are not limited by the WTO, such as expenditures on agricultural research, road construction and the creation of nationwide information networks, as well as enhancing China's capacity to apply technical barriers to trade and to sanitary and phytosanitary measures and standards.

Even after these investments, China will still have some latitude, fiscal resource constraints notwithstanding, to promote certain sectors. Although land-intensive sectors may face difficulties, China has a comparative advantage in many commodities – horticulture, fruit, livestock and aquaculture – that would be able to compete with imported products and even be exported.

Most fundamentally, the government's response to WTO accession involves an entire shift of paradigm – from direct participation in the economy to assuming a more indirect regulatory role. This would involve the setting up of institutions for effectively creating and managing public goods and regulating markets to compensate for natural market failures. An effective and multifaceted government policy can allow China to take maximum advantage of the benefits and minimize the costs of adverse consequences that will definitely arise.

III. Latin America and the Caribbean

REGIONAL OVERVIEW
General economic performance

2001 was a year of economic stagnation for Latin America and the Caribbean.

The year 2001 has been a period of stagnation, if not outright recession, for most economies in the Latin America and Caribbean region. The difficult external environment, characterized by slow economic growth and unstable financial markets, has combined with internal problems linked to weak domestic demand, macroeconomic disequilibria and political instability in several countries. These factors have translated into a marked reduction in the pace of economic activity in the region, with GDP growth estimated at around 1 percent in 2001, about half the growth rate achieved in 2000.[73] Through its depressing effects on wages, employment and, ultimately, effective demand for food, the reduction in economic activity constitutes a major setback from the perspective of food security.

Unlike in 2000 when the strong United States economy had a more robust positive impact on the northern part of the region (particularly Mexico) than on the south, poor performances were more evenly distributed throughout the region in 2001. Of major consequence for the whole region were the depressed performances of its three largest economies. In Mexico, GDP was expected to record zero growth after the very high rate (6.9 percent) achieved in 2000. After showing promising signs of recovery in 2000 and early 2001, Brazil's economy was hard hit by a serious electricity crisis and the deteriorating economic environment. Entering its fourth year of recession, Argentina's economy was severely affected by the virtual disappearance of external financing and difficulties in reducing the fiscal deficit and servicing public debt. These events cloud with uncertainty Argentina's prospects for an early recovery, and raise concern over their financial and trade implications within the Southern Common Market (MERCOSUR) and the rest of the region. Peru and Uruguay also faced very difficult situations, expected to translate into growth rates below 1 percent in 2001, while Chile and Venezuela, in spite of some slowdown, were expected to maintain growth rates of around 3 percent.

The slackening in economic growth has been transmitted across countries through a sharp reduction in trade. With weaker demand and lower prices for its export products, the region experienced a marked slowdown of its export earnings. With imports also slackening, although at a slower pace than exports, the region's trade deficit was expected to widen in 2001. As a result, its current account deficit was expected to increase from $47 billion in 2000 to $58 billion in 2001 – the latter figure representing 3 percent of the region's GDP. At the projected levels of current and capital accounts, the net transfers of resources to the region in 2001 would be almost nil. Indeed, for the third year running, gross capital inflows will have to be allocated entirely to debt amortization and factor services.

Recent agricultural performance

Below-average agricultural output growth in 2000.

With the exception of 1994–95 and 1999, which were unusually favourable years for agriculture, the performance of the region's agriculture sector in recent years has tended to lag behind that of its economy as a whole. This held true also for 2000. Agricultural production growth in 2000, at 2.1 percent, was markedly below that of overall economic activity and only slightly exceeded population growth. Low growth in crop production (0.6 percent) was partly compensated for by continued strong output growth (4.4 percent) in the livestock sector. The low crop growth was recorded in all three major producing countries: Argentina (with the exception of cereals), Brazil (with a reduced cereal crop) and Mexico. Among the subregions, only the Caribbean recorded an above-average output performance, with an increase in crop and livestock production of 3.1 percent. In Central America and South America, output growth was close to the regional average at 1.7 percent and 2.2 percent, respectively.

Some improvement in overall agricultural output performance is expected in 2001.

Some improvement is expected for the year 2001. Agricultural output is estimated to grow at 2.7 percent, although this is still

Table 17

ANNUAL REAL GDP GROWTH RATES IN LATIN AMERICA AND THE CARIBBEAN

	1997	1998	1999	2000	2001[1]	2002[1]
			(Percentage)			
Argentina	8.1	3.8	-3.4	-0.5	-2.7	-1.1
Brazil	3.3	0.2	0.5	4.4	1.8	2.0
Chile	7.4	3.9	-1.1	5.4	3.3	3.0
Colombia	3.4	0.6	-4.1	2.8	1.4	2.4
Mexico	6.8	5.0	3.7	6.9	0	1.2
Peru	6.7	-0.5	0.9	3.1	0.2	3.7
Venezuela	6.4	0.2	-6.1	3.2	2.7	1.8
Latin America and the Caribbean	**5.3**	**2.3**	**0.1**	**4.1**	**1.0**	**1.7**

[1] Projections.

Source: IMF. 2001. *World Economic Outlook*, December. Washington, DC.

Figure 24

LATIN AMERICA AND THE CARIBBEAN: SELECTED INDICATORS

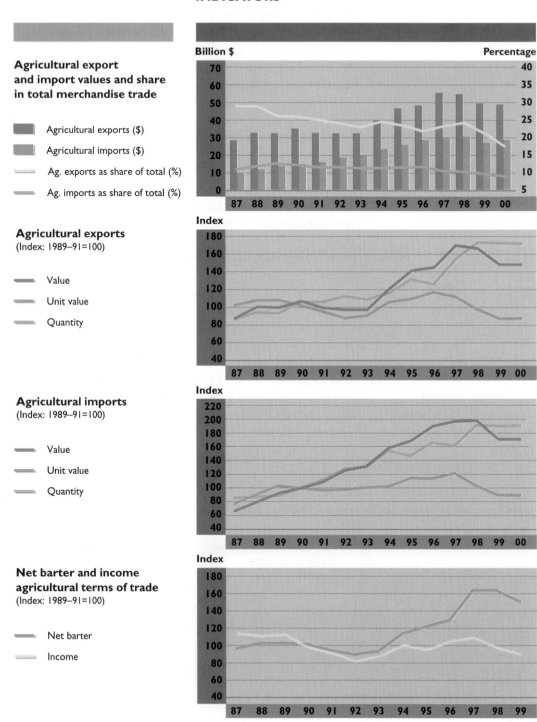

**Agricultural export
and import values and share
in total merchandise trade**

- Agricultural exports ($)
- Agricultural imports ($)
- Ag. exports as share of total (%)
- Ag. imports as share of total (%)

Agricultural exports
(Index: 1989–91=100)

- Value
- Unit value
- Quantity

Agricultural imports
(Index: 1989–91=100)

- Value
- Unit value
- Quantity

**Net barter and income
agricultural terms of trade**
(Index: 1989–91=100)

- Net barter
- Income

LATIN AMERICA AND THE CARIBBEAN: SELECTED INDICATORS

Real GDP
(Percentage change from preceding year)

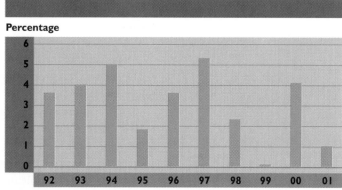

Dietary energy supplies
(kcal per capita per day)

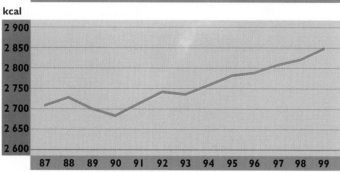

Agricultural production
(Index: 1989–91=100)

Total agricultural production

Per capita food production

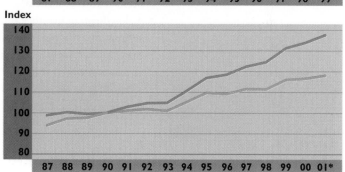

* *Preliminary*

Source: FAO and IMF

below trend (the average yearly growth for 1991–2001 was
around 2.9 percent). Weather and market conditions affected
countries and products in very different ways in 2001. In
particular:

- The 2.7 percent increase in overall output is the combined
  effect of above-average crop production growth (4.6 percent,
  with cereals expanding by 7.8 percent) and lower growth
  (1.8 percent) of the livestock sector.
- The robust crop production was largely a result of good
  harvests in the region's two major producers: Argentina
  (4.4 percent growth) and Brazil (6.8 percent).
- Most other countries in the region recorded below-trend crop
  output in 2001, with Chile and Paraguay as notable
  exceptions. Indeed, Central America averaged less than
  2 percent growth, while the Caribbean and several Andean
  countries experienced zero or even negative growth.
- Cereal production increased by an estimated 7.8 percent, the
  best regional performance in the past ten years. However, this
  was largely accounted for by the outstanding cereal harvest of
  Brazil, which recovered from the setback recorded during the
  previous year. Chile, Paraguay and Peru also contributed, to a
  lesser extent, to the strong increase in cereal production.
- On the other hand, 2001 was a poor cereal harvest year for
  the region's other major producers: Argentina, Colombia,
  Mexico and Venezuela.
- A slowdown in livestock output growth was recorded in all
  subregions, compared with the relatively high rates of the
  previous two years. Brazil, Colombia, Mexico and Venezuela
  all saw a decline, while output in Argentina and Uruguay saw
  a standstill or marginal decline under the effect of outbreaks
  of foot-and-mouth disease.

Table 18

NET PRODUCTION GROWTH RATES IN LATIN AMERICA AND THE CARIBBEAN

Year	Agriculture	Crops	Cereals	Livestock
		(Percentage)		
1992–96	2.9	2.5	4.5	3.6
1997	3.3	3.7	3.3	1.9
1998	1.7	2.6	-2.4	1.1
1999	5.4	4.5	4.8	6.3
2000	2.1	0.6	2.6	4.4
2001[1]	2.7	4.6	7.8	1.8

[1] Preliminary.
Source: FAO.

CHANGING PATTERNS IN AGRICULTURAL TRADE

The importance of agricultural trade for the Latin America and Caribbean region hardly needs emphasizing. The region is, in per capita terms, by far the most agricultural trade-oriented of all developing country regions. Its agricultural exports (at around $100 per capita/year) are five times greater than those of sub-Saharan Africa or Asia and the Pacific, and over three times larger than those of the Near East. The value of per capita agricultural imports in Latin America and the Caribbean also largely exceeds the average of all developing country regions except the Near East. Despite rapid industrialization, agricultural trade and related economic activities still constitute key sources of growth, employment and foreign exchange for the region.

The region's agricultural trading patterns have undergone major changes over recent decades.

However, the region's agricultural trade patterns and characteristics have undergone significant changes over recent decades, which have been a period of major transformations in the overall economic, political and institutional scene. The region's agriculture, especially its more modern and trade-oriented sectors, has shown considerable capacity to grasp the new opportunities arising from greater liberalization and integration of world markets. Nevertheless, the sector has faced difficulties in improving productivity and competitiveness, diversifying its product base and maintaining a strong presence in world trade. These difficulties have been linked to internal constraints and also to intensifying international competition, unstable and often depressed markets and persistent institutional barriers to agricultural trade.

This section presents statistical evidence underlying those issues. It provides, in particular, indicators of the economic importance of agricultural trade for Latin America and the Caribbean – both currently and in earlier periods – and explores the main characteristics, trends and pace of change of agricultural trade in the region.

Growing importance of agricultural trade relative to production

Agricultural exports have increased faster than production over the 1990s.

Recent decades have seen an expansion in the volume of agricultural trade at rates that have significantly exceeded those of agricultural production. This tendency, which underlines the growing interdependence and integration of the region's agriculture with world markets, has been particularly marked since the mid-1990s, a period of trade liberalization and revival of international trading arrangements (Figure 25). Indeed, while the volume of production rose by around 56 percent from 1980 to the late 1990s, that of exports almost doubled during the same period.

The growing importance of trade relative to output can also be observed with regard to imports. The case of cereals, the main group of imported commodities, is especially significant. Figure 26 shows a sizeable increase in per capita cereal supply – from about 220 kg to 290 kg yearly – between the early 1960s and 1999.

The expansion in cereal supply, which has contributed strongly to the considerable nutritional gains of the region over the past decades, has been achieved largely through an increasing recourse to imports. Indeed, while per capita production of cereals has declined from the levels achieved in the mid-1980s,

Figure 25

LATIN AMERICA AND THE CARIBBEAN: VOLUME OF AGRICULTURAL PRODUCTION AND TRADE

Agricultural exports

Agricultural production

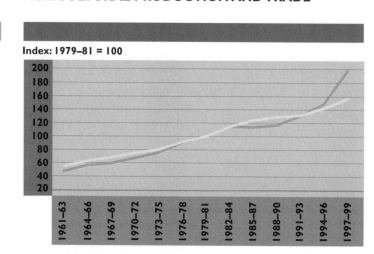

Index: 1979–81 = 100

Source: FAO

Figure 26

LATIN AMERICA AND THE CARIBBEAN: CEREAL PRODUCTION AND TRADE

Per capita cereal production

Per capita net cereal imports (including food aid)

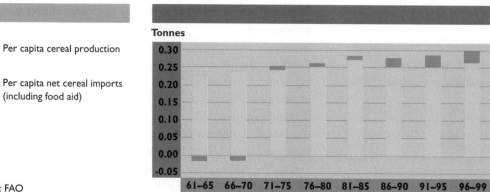

Tonnes

Source: FAO

imports have risen to represent about 12 percent of the total cereal supply in 1996–99.

Declining role of agriculture in total merchandise trade

Figure 27 summarizes the general trends of imports and exports of agricultural, fishery and forestry products and the shares of these exports and imports in relation to total merchandise trade.

In general, agricultural trade showed considerable dynamism during the 1970s, reflecting steep price increases for traditional commodity exports in the early and latter parts of the decade. This was followed by a virtual standstill during the 1980s, a period of deeply depressed markets in the region with dramatic price declines particularly during 1982–83, and a subsequent resumption of growth in the 1990s, especially strong during the "commodity boom" years of 1997–98.

But the share of agriculture in total exports has declined.

Despite its vigorous expansion during most of the period, however, agricultural trade has steadily lost its share in total trade, as the process of industrialization advanced and other traded products – especially manufactures – gained relative importance. While agricultural exports accounted for 43 percent of total exports during the early 1970s, they now account for just over 20 percent. The reduction in the share of agriculture in total imports has been much less marked, reflecting the growing recourse to external markets for meeting domestic food needs. Indeed, the agricultural import share has fluctuated around 12–13 percent during the past three decades and currently stands at around 10 percent.[74]

Figure 27

LATIN AMERICA AND THE CARIBBEAN: TRADE IN AGRICULTURAL, FISHERY AND FORESTRY PRODUCTS

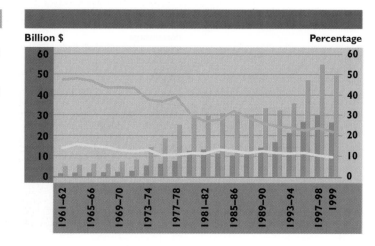

Agricultural imports (billion $)

Agricultural exports (billion $)

Agricultural imports as percentage of all imports

Agricultural exports as percentage of all exports

Source: FAO

The region has maintained a stable share of world agricultural exports.

Stable regional share in world agricultural trade

In a context of growing competition from traditional and emerging agricultural markets worldwide, the region has maintained a relatively stable position in world commodity trade. The region's share of total world agricultural exports has moved around the 15–17 percent level during the past three decades, with a slight declining trend until the late 1980s but subsequently increasing to represent almost 20 percent in recent years (Figure 28). These trends contrast favourably with the situation in most developing countries in other regions, in particular in Africa and the Near East, which have lost market share during the same period.[75]

A widely different pattern emerges with regard to Latin America and the Caribbean's position in world agricultural imports. The region's share in the total has shown a pronounced upward trend since the 1980s, when foreign exchange shortages had imposed severe restrictions on imports, including food imports. The region currently accounts for about 8 percent of the world's population and almost 10 percent of total world agricultural imports, up from 6 percent in the late 1980s (Figure 29).

The product composition of agricultural exports has become more diversified.

Diversified product composition of agricultural trade

Latin American and Caribbean countries have traditionally derived the bulk of their agricultural export earnings from a limited range of food and raw material products. In recent decades, however, there has been a sharp deterioration in the international market conditions of several key commodities exported by the region (see The price factor on page 117). This situation has prompted

Figure 28

LATIN AMERICA AND THE CARIBBEAN: REGIONAL SHARE IN WORLD AGRICULTURAL EXPORTS

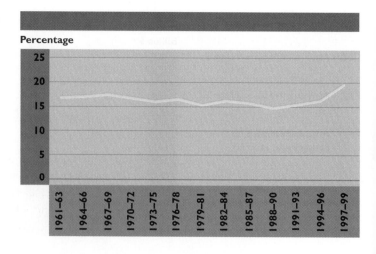

Percentage

Source: FAO

Figure 29

LATIN AMERICA AND THE CARIBBEAN: REGIONAL SHARE IN WORLD AGRICULTURAL IMPORTS

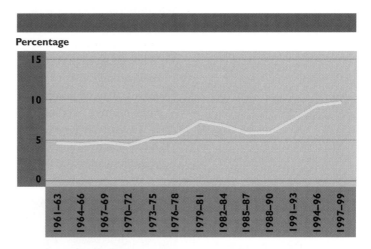

Percentage

Source: FAO

Table 19

LATIN AMERICA AND THE CARIBBEAN: SHARE IN TOTAL AGRICULTURAL EXPORTS OF MAIN AGRICULTURAL EXPORT PRODUCTS (BASE PERIOD 1970–72)

Export product	1970–72	1980–82	1990–92	1997–99
		(Percentage)		
Coffee, green	24.0	19.8	12.2	13.8
Sugar (centrifugal, raw)	17.5	19.4	11.3	5.3
Cotton lint	6.2	3.0	2.3	0.8
Bananas	5.2	3.7	7.4	5.5
Beef and veal	4.7	1.1	0.6	0.3
Maize	4.2	2.7	1.5	2.5
Beef and veal, boneless	3.6	2.3	2.5	2.3
Beef preparations	2.1	1.7	1.6	1.0
Cattle	2.0	0.8	1.2	0.6
Cocoa beans	1.6	1.3	0.7	0.3
Tobacco leaves	1.4	2.0	2.9	2.5
Wheat	1.3	2.5	2.1	2.5
Tomatoes	1.3	0.7	0.9	1.1
Soybean cake	1.2	6.2	7.9	7.6
Sugar, refined	1.2	2.5	1.4	2.0
Total	**77.5**	**69.6**	**56.6**	**48.0**

Source: FAO.

renewed efforts in many countries towards export diversification, through both a widening of the commodity product base and an increase in the value added of exports. Efforts to move away from overspecialization have achieved varying degrees of success in the different countries, but have contributed overall to considerable changes in the relative importance of the various export products. These changes are summarized in Table 19, which shows the 15 main agricultural products exported by the region, ranked by their importance in 1970–72, and the evolution of their respective shares in total agricultural exports.

Noteworthy features are:

- While these 15 products accounted for almost 80 percent of total agricultural exports in the early 1970s, they now account for less than 50 percent of the total. This is explained by the large number of other products that have gained importance in the list of major exported commodities.[76]

- Adverse movements in international markets for the region's traditional tropical product exports resulted in a

Women in a cooperative sorting coffee grains
In Latin America and the Caribbean the importance of some traditional export products such as coffee has declined steadily in recent years. Nevertheless, coffee is still the most important agricultural export commodity of the region.

FAO/10089/J. VAN ACKER

sharp decline in the relative importance of these products. Coffee remains the region's main exported commodity, but now accounts for less than 15 percent of all agricultural exports compared with one-quarter of the total in the early 1970s. Cotton, cocoa and, even more pronouncedly, raw sugar, also saw declines in their respective shares.

• The counterpart to the declining share of traditional tropical products was the emergence of oilseeds and related products as major export commodities and gains achieved by fruits, cereals and vegetables.

• Soybeans and soybean cakes, of inconsequential importance in the early 1970s, in recent years accounted for no less than 17 percent of the region's agricultural exports. Such expansion in market share was narrowly based, however, as it primarily stemmed from the spectacular development of the soybean industry in the two countries Argentina and Brazil (see Box 7).

The changes in composition and increasing diversification of agricultural exports are further highlighted in Table 20, which shows the relative share of the 15 most important agricultural exports in 1997–99. These products account for only about 60 percent of total agricultural exports, rather than almost 80 percent of the total accounted for by the 15 most important agricultural exports in 1970–72 .

Table 20

LATIN AMERICA AND THE CARIBBEAN: SHARE IN TOTAL AGRICULTURAL EXPORTS OF MAIN AGRICULTURAL EXPORT PRODUCTS IN 1997–99

Export product	(Percentage)
Coffee, green	13.8
Soybean cake	7.6
Soybeans	5.6
Bananas	5.5
Sugar (centrifugal, raw)	5.3
Soybean oil	3.9
Crude organic materials (29)	3.0
Tobacco leaves	2.5
Maize	2.5
Wheat	2.5
Orange juice, concentrated	2.3
Beef and veal, boneless	2.3
Sugar, refined	2.0
Oil of sunflower seed	1.9
Food, prepared	1.4
Total	**62.0**

Source: FAO.

Box 7

SOYBEANS IN ARGENTINA AND BRAZIL

One remarkable feature of the recent agricultural development in Latin America is the emergence of Argentina and Brazil as two of the world's largest producers and exporters of soybeans. In the early 1960s, soybean production in Brazil represented only 1 percent of global production, with virtually no production taking place in Argentina. At the turn of the decade, their combined share in global production still did not exceed 4 percent, the bulk of it still accounted for by Brazil. The 1970s saw the beginning of a phenomenal expansion in soybean production in Brazil, followed by Argentina with some years' lag. Their continued expansion over the 1980s and 1990s has led them to become the second and third largest producers, accounting for one-third of total world production in recent years.

The share of Argentina and Brazil in the global export market of soybeans and soybean products has also shot up quickly. Their combined share now represents around 40 percent of total world exports.

Many factors have contributed to this remarkable growth. In Brazil, the development of "tropical" soybean varieties by the national agricultural research and extension network EMBRAPA (Empresa Brasileira de Pesquisa Agropecuaria) enabled soybean production to expand from the temperate southwest of the country to areas in the centre west. Policy assistance by the government and recent macroeconomic stability also contributed to the rapid expansion.

The rapid expansion of soybean production in Argentina was induced by the high international prices in the early 1970s. Favourable agroclimatic conditions and improved cropping systems also contributed. Soybean yields rose quickly, especially in the 1970s, while planted areas expanded, reflecting a shift from coarse grains and pasture as well as new planting. Double cropping with wheat made soybean production more profitable. Policy reform in the 1990s, including the introduction of an export tax rebate and currency stability, further encouraged soybean production.

If market prices remain favourable, soybean production in Brazil and Argentina may continue to grow for the time being because both countries have still many potential areas to plant. However, some constraints are emerging as production expands. One such constraint is the increasing cost of transportation. Producers also face increasingly high marketing costs as production areas move into areas further inland. The continuation of large-scale mechanized farming is causing soil erosion in some areas, and increased cropping intensity is undermining natural soil fertility. Researchers and farmers are searching for more sustainable technologies and farming systems, including non-tillage cultivation and improved crop rotation.

ARGENTINA AND BRAZIL: SHARE IN GLOBAL PRODUCTION OF SOYBEANS

	1969–71	1979–81	1989–91	1999–2001
		(Percentage)		
Argentina	0.1	4.2	8.8	13.4
Brazil	3.5	15.7	18.4	20.4
Both countries	3.6	19.9	27.2	33.8

Source: FAO.

ARGENTINA AND BRAZIL: SHARE IN VALUE OF GLOBAL EXPORTS OF SOYBEANS AND DERIVED PRODUCTS[1]

	1969–71	1979–81	1989–91	1997–99
		(Percentage)		
Argentina	0.0	5.7	15.0	16.8
Brazil	3.8	17.5	21.2	22.3
Both countries	3.8	23.2	36.2	39.1

[1] Soybeans, soybean cake, soybean oil.
Source: FAO.

Geographic diversification of markets

The developed market economies remain the major outlet for the region's agricultural exports.

Most of the region's agricultural trade has traditionally been oriented towards industrialized country markets, which account for around 60 percent of agricultural shipments from, and over half of agricultural imports to, the region (Table 21).[77]

In recent decades, however, the geographic distribution of trade has changed significantly. While the European Union (EU) and the United States have maintained their position as the main outlets for exports from Latin America and the Caribbean, the relative position of the developing countries has risen. On the other hand, following the process of economic transformation in the formerly centrally planned economies in the 1990s, Eastern European countries lost their status as major trading partners.

Similar patterns can be observed on the side of imports, with a more marked reduction in the relative share of developed countries, to the advantage of developing countries, as suppliers of agricultural products to the region (Table 22).

Increasing importance of intraregional agricultural trade and of exports to Asia and the Pacific.

The process of market diversification towards developing country markets has reflected to a certain extent the emergence of Asia and the Pacific as increasingly significant markets for the region. However, the driving force in this process was the considerable *increase in intraregional agricultural trade* that took place, especially during the 1990s, as a result of intensifying efforts towards regional integration. The share of intraregional trade in total agricultural trade rose between 1990 and 1997, from 12 to 18 percent in the case of exports and from 28 to 38 percent in the case of imports.

Table 21

REGIONAL DESTINATION OF AGRICULTURAL EXPORTS FROM LATIN AMERICA AND THE CARIBBEAN

Destination	1980	1990	1995	1997
		(Percentage)		
Developed countries	60	66	64	63
European Union	30	34	32	32
United States and Canada	24	25	24	24
Developing countries	20	27	33	33
Developing America	10	12	17	18
Developing Africa	3	4	3	3
Near East	3	5	4	4
Asia and the Pacific	4	6	9	9
Eastern European countries	18	7	3	3

Source: UNCTAD. 2000. *Handbook of Statistics 2000.* Geneva.

The role of MERCOSUR was particularly important, given the size of the countries concerned and the degree of complementarity in several items of their product base. Tables 23 and 24 show that for Argentina, Brazil, Paraguay and Uruguay, the period between the mid-1980s and late 1990s was one of major geographic shifts in agricultural trade, in favour of other countries in the group. Argentina, for example, saw its share of agricultural exports destined for MERCOSUR partners rise from only 10–15 percent of the total in the 1980s to almost one-quarter in recent years. Similarly, the share of agricultural exports from Brazil to other MERCOSUR countries rose from negligible levels to almost 10 percent. The tendency towards intra-area trade concentration can also be observed in the case of agricultural imports, as shown in Table 24. Most remarkable was the increase in Brazil's share of imports from the area, from around 27 to 45 percent. In the cases of Paraguay and Uruguay, where agricultural trade was already heavily directed towards MERCOSUR country markets, this orientation was accentuated further during the period.

Agricultural trade balances and their economic significance

With agricultural exports exceeding agricultural imports by a considerable margin, the region has maintained a strong agricultural surplus position, even in periods of depressed markets for its main commodity exports (see Figure 27).

Table 22

REGIONAL ORIGIN OF AGRICULTURAL IMPORTS TO LATIN AMERICA AND THE CARIBBEAN

Origin	1980	1990	1995	1997
		(Percentage)		
Developed countries	70	61	57	56
European Union	14	17	16	12
United States and Canada	52	40	39	41
Developing countries	26	34	41	42
Developing America	22	28	37	38
Developing Africa	1	1	1	1
Near East	0	0	0	0
Asia and the Pacific	4	6	9	9
Eastern European countries	5	5	1	1

Source: UNCTAD. 2000. Handbook of Statistics 2000. Geneva.

Indeed, periods of depressed exports have closely coincided with contractions in agricultural imports, reflecting the region's strong reliance on export earnings from agriculture to finance imports, including of food.

Positive agricultural trade balances are largely accounted for by Argentina and Brazil, but most subregions have an agricultural surplus.

The region's overall agricultural trade balance has largely reflected that of its major net exporters, Argentina and Brazil, where large surpluses have tended to widen further during the past decade. Argentina and Brazil together account for about half of the region's total agricultural exports, but less than one-quarter of its total imports. Nevertheless, surplus situations are typically found in most years throughout the region, notable exceptions being the Caribbean subregion, which has been a net agricultural importer since the early 1990s, and Mexico (see Figure 30).

The significance of the agricultural trade balances should be assessed with regard to, on the one hand, the economic

Table 23

MERCOSUR: DESTINATION OF AGRICULTURAL EXPORTS

Exporting country	Destination				
	Argentina	Brazil	Paraguay	Uruguay	Total MERCOSUR
			(Percentage)		
Argentina					13.1
1986		12.1	0.2	0.8	11.8
1990		11.0	0.3	0.5	21.3
1994		18.1	1.9	1.3	23.1
1998		19.9	1.6	1.6	
Brazil					
1986	0.0		0.0	0.0	2.8
1990	0.5		0.4	1.0	1.9
1994	3.6		2.2	0.9	6.6
1998	4.8		3.1	1.6	9.5
Paraguay					
1986	13.5	42.3		2.3	58.2
1990	5.6	33.3		1.0	39.9
1994	4.1	47.4		0.8	52.3
1998	12.8	35.8		2.0	50.6
Uruguay					
1986	2.5	37.1	0.3		39.9
1990	2.0	30.3	0.2		32.5
1994	4.6	29.1	1.0		34.6
1998	8.2	44.9	6.3		59.4

Source: FAO.

importance of agricultural exports and, on the other hand, the
financial cost involved in agricultural imports. Table 25 presents
a number of indicators illustrating these crucial aspects of
agricultural trade. For the region as a whole, agricultural exports
account for about 23 percent of total merchandise exports, down
from 29 percent in the early 1980s, while agricultural imports
have represented around 10–12 percent of total imports during
the past three decades. Behind these averages, however, very
different situations are found at the subregional and individual
country levels.

Agricultural trade is an
important component of
total trade.

Although the region has considerably broadened its export
base, particularly through the expansion of the volume of
manufactured products, the share of *agricultural exports* in total
merchandise exports has remained high – about 47 percent in
recent years for the region as a whole, down from 70 percent in
the early 1980s. Except for a few economies primarily based on

Table 24

MERCOSUR: ORIGIN OF AGRICULTURAL IMPORTS

Importing country	Origin				
	Argentina	Brazil	Paraguay	Uruguay	Total MERCOSUR
	(Percentage of total)				
Argentina					31.8
1986		21.7	6.7	3.4	34.9
1990		23.6	8.0	3.4	37.0
1994		31.8	1.4	3.9	34.8
1998		27.3	3.2	4.3	
Brazil					
1986	15.7		4.1	7.6	27.4
1990	29.0		9.1	10.1	48.2
1994	32.4		5.7	8.2	46.3
1998	33.4		3.7	8.1	45.3
Paraguay					
1986	12.9	20.2		2.3	35.4
1990	13.2	19.9		1.7	34.8
1994	31.0	14.5		3.5	49.1
1998	19.5	49.3		7.7	76.5
Uruguay					
1986	16.6	25.1	6.3		47.9
1990	19.2	27.6	3.6		50.5
1994	28.8	29.6	1.1		59.6
1998	36.3	24.1	0.4		60.7

Source: FAO.

Figure 30

LATIN AMERICA AND THE CARIBBEAN: AGRICULTURAL TRADE BALANCES

▬▬ Exports

▬▬ Imports

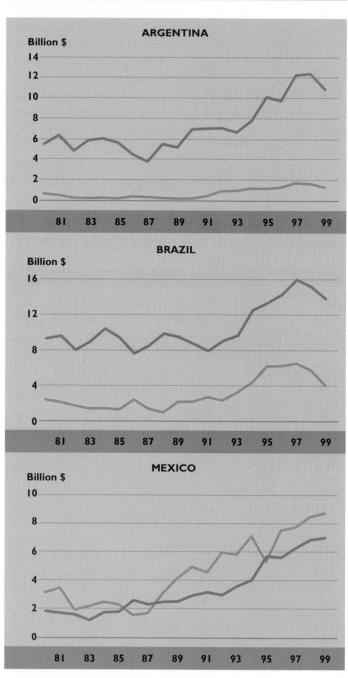

LATIN AMERICA AND THE CARIBBEAN: AGRICULTURAL TRADE BALANCES

 Exports

 Imports

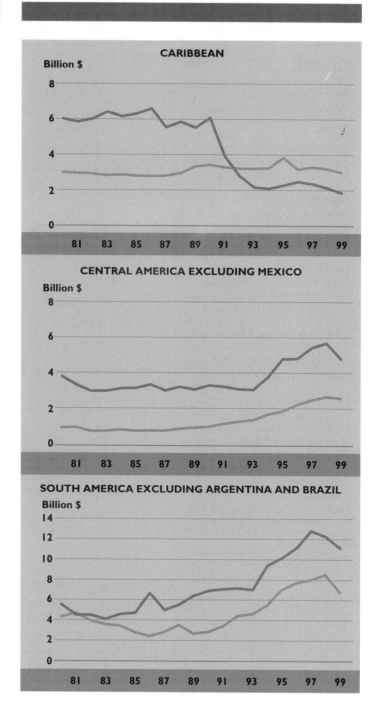

CARIBBEAN

Billion $

CENTRAL AMERICA EXCLUDING MEXICO

Billion $

SOUTH AMERICA EXCLUDING ARGENTINA AND BRAZIL

Billion $

Source: FAO

Table 25

LATIN AMERICA AND THE CARIBBEAN: AGRICULTURAL EXPORTS AND IMPORTS AS A RATIO OF TOTAL MERCHANDISE TRADE

	1979–81	1981–83	1989–91	1997–99
		(Percentage)		
Argentina				
Agricultural exports/total exports	69.9	69.6	56.7	46.7
Agricultural imports/total imports	6.6	5.6	5.4	5.4
Agricultural imports/total exports	7.0	4.4	2.7	6.2
Brazil				
Agricultural exports/total exports	44.3	40.8	26.9	29.6
Agricultural imports/total imports	10.2	8.8	11.1	9.1
Agricultural imports/total exports	12.0	8.3	7.5	10.9
Mexico				
Agricultural exports/total exports	12.8	6.9	11.3	10.0
Agricultural imports/total imports	14.0	15.0	14.1	10.1
Agricultural imports/total exports	18.4	11.7	17.9	12.4
Caribbean				
Agricultural exports/total exports	23.6	28.4	37.9	17.8
Agricultural imports/total imports	9.7	10.8	15.3	13.0
Agricultural imports/total exports	11.3	13.6	24.7	26.8
Central America, excluding Mexico				
Agricultural exports/total exports	71.9	69.6	64.4	49.1
Agricultural imports/total imports	12.1	11.8	12.3	13.0
Agricultural imports/total exports	17.3	17.9	20.4	23.9
South America, excluding Argentina and Brazil				
Agricultural exports/total exports	14.8	13.9	16.8	19.7
Agricultural imports/total imports	14.2	14.8	9.8	11.5
Agricultural imports/total exports	12.1	13.0	7.4	12.7
Latin America and the Caribbean				
Agricultural exports/total exports	29.1	27.2	25.9	23.3
Agricultural imports/total imports	11.5	11.9	12.2	10.2
Agricultural imports/total exports	12.6	11.5	11.4	12.7

Source: FAO.

oil and minerals, remittances or tourism, agricultural exports remain a major, if not the main, source of foreign exchange. This is true even for the more industrialized economies: agricultural exports represent around half of total exports in Argentina, 30 percent in Brazil, 32 percent in Colombia and 17 percent in Chile. The ratio exceeds 60 percent in several countries in Central America (Belize, Costa Rica, Guatemala, Nicaragua) and in Paraguay.

Many of these economies combine the seemingly paradoxical situation of being both agriculture-based and strongly dependent on *agricultural imports*. This is generally explained by the region's different structure of exports (chiefly non-food primary products, as seen above) and imports (primarily cereals). This form of agricultural specialization, which often accorded lower priority to producing food for domestic consumption, was expected to maximize the comparative advantages and competitiveness of the region and therefore contribute positively to current accounts. However, these expectations have not materialized in many periods and circumstances. Agricultural exports have been losing significance in national accounts, while the opposite has occurred for agricultural imports. Agricultural – basically food – imports have become increasingly important components of national diets, but the increases in food import bills have not always been matched by commensurate increases in foreign exchange.

The price factor
Because of their immediate effect on export earnings and import bills, fluctuations in commodity prices have often been the determining factor in cycles of prosperity and depression in many economies in the region. For the region as a whole, the general tendency of agricultural export unit values (in current dollar terms) has been that of stagnation or decline since the early 1980s, punctuated by temporary upsurges such as those in the "commodity boom" periods of 1979–81 and 1995–97 (Figure 31).

Figure 31
LATIN AMERICA AND THE CARIBBEAN: QUANTITY, VALUE AND UNIT VALUE OF AGRICULTURAL EXPORTS

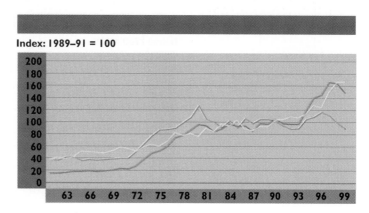

Quantity

Value

Unit value

Index: 1989–91 = 100

Source: FAO

The region has compensated for declining prices of their agricultural exports by increasing export volumes.

Despite such generally unfavourable price trends, the region has nevertheless been able to increase its export earnings from agriculture, more noticeably during the past decade, through a strong expansion in the volume of shipments. While the agricultural export unit value fell by about 10 percent between 1989–91 and 1999, the value of these exports increased by 50 percent during the same period.

These trends can also be observed at the individual commodity level. The comparatively steady growth in the volumes of exports, even during price crisis periods, confirms the premise that international market prices were determinant in agricultural export performances.

As noted earlier, the past two decades saw generally unfavourable price trends for the major tropical export products; relatively better price trends for cereals (bearing in mind that, with the notable exception of Argentina and Uruguay, most countries in the region are net cereal importers); and varying degrees of success in compensating for unfavourable price trends through gains in export volumes.

The economic importance of agricultural price movements is better assessed in relation to the prices of products imported by the region. Figure 32 shows two indices: *barter* terms of trade of agricultural exports (the ratio of the region's agricultural export unit value to manufactured good prices); and *income* terms of trade (the ratio of agricultural export value to manufactured good prices, or the *purchasing capacity* of agricultural exports).

The general picture is one of stable barter terms of trade during the 1960s and early 1970s; a marked improvement

Figure 32

LATIN AMERICA AND THE CARIBBEAN: AGRICULTURAL TERMS OF TRADE

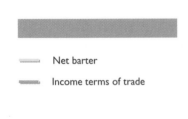

——— Net barter

▬▬▬ Income terms of trade

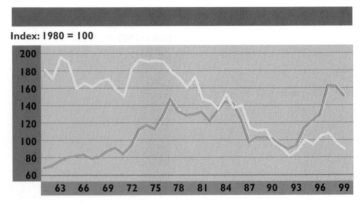

Index: 1980 = 100

Source: FAO

*Packaging for export in
Venezuela*

Various aspects of preparing
and packing plantains for
export: weighing boxes of the
fruits.

during the food crisis periods of the mid-1970s; a long and deep
deterioration from the mid-1970s through 1993, with some
temporary rebounds, such as during the 1984 food crisis; and
recovery in recent years. A more encouraging picture emerges
regarding income terms of trade: although these followed a
similar downward trend during the period 1985–92, they showed
considerable improvement in other periods. Once again, this
demonstrates the region's capacity to counter adverse price
trends through expanded volumes of agricultural exports.
Taking 1989–91 and 1999 as reference periods, agricultural
prices were estimated to fall 6 percent below those of
manufactured products; however, the *volume* of these exports
rose almost 70 percent during this period. The resulting increase
in export earnings from agriculture would have allowed the
purchase of 56 percent more manufactured products.[78]

Conclusions

The various aspects of agricultural trade examined in this section
have taken place against a policy environment characterized,
especially since the mid-1980s, by increasing liberalization of
trade and foreign exchanges. The new policy orientation has
involved reduced public intervention and increased efforts to
improve international competitiveness through a greater role of

The policy background to changes in agricultural trading patterns has been one of economic liberalization.

the private sector. Many countries replaced preferential or fixed exchange rates by managed crawling pegs or floating exchange rates. Average tariffs, and the degree of dispersion around them, were greatly reduced. Administrative and non-tariff barriers to trade were dismantled.

This process was carried out despite the slow progress in the liberalization of agricultural trade and support policies on the part of many of the region's trading partners. Industrialized countries have maintained high levels of protection, particularly in agriculture.[79] In addition to traditional tariff barriers, various non-tariff barriers to trade, such as sanitary and phytosanitary regulations, are increasingly important obstacles to the region's agricultural exports. High agricultural subsidies in the industrialized countries are also perceived as serving to erode the region's competitiveness in world markets.[80]

It was therefore in spite of significant constraints that the Latin America and Caribbean region has managed to expand the value and purchasing capacity of agricultural exports from the mid-1980s to the late 1990s. The revival can be credited to the region's new policy emphasis on free markets and its strenuous efforts to improve the countries' linkages with the world economies after the disappointing experience of previous inward-looking strategies. Much of the revival can also be attributed to the general strengthening of import demand from the region's main trading partners, fuelled in particular by an unusually long period of strong economic growth in the United States. Vice versa, the deteriorating trade performances of the region in recent years reflect to a major extent the economic slowdown in the industrialized countries, illustrating once again the dependence of the region's agricultural trade on external events beyond its control.

Regional trading arrangements have played an important role but are facing major challenges.

The renewed momentum of the region's agricultural trade between the mid-1980s and late 1990s also reflected the emergence or revitalization of regional trading agreements, following the example set by the European Community and the North American Free Trade Agreement (NAFTA) in the early 1990s. The phenomenon was rendered possible by the greater convergence of economic policies and political regimes within the countries of the region. Such convergence also produced, along with formal trading and cooperation agreements, a de facto integration that fostered intraregional trade and investment. The beneficial effects of this process also extended to agricultural trade, as seen in the case of MERCOSUR.

The region may have to face a number of major challenges in the years to come. It has been observed above that agricultural imports have tended to increase faster than agricultural exports, and the food import bill has become a major burden for many countries. This raises some fundamental issues: how to maintain a free-market, export-oriented agriculture without unduly penalizing domestic food production; how to assist the process of adjustment to import competition and improve domestic productivity and competitiveness without creating permanent mechanisms of protection. Whatever the courses countries choose, any trade-related policy should take into consideration the dangers of polarization or inequity. Sectors that are less able to take advantage of the broadened markets should be enabled to make the necessary adjustment through slower, but clearly established, mechanisms.

There are still challenges ahead for regional agriculture and governments.

Despite the progress achieved, the way towards fuller integration remains problematic. Past experience has shown (more recently in the case of MERCOSUR) the difficulties that may arise, in periods of economic stress, in reconciling regional objectives and national interests. The challenge for future years will be to maintain the momentum of integration and extend its benefits in a trade-creating and non-discriminatory manner across and within countries. Social equity is also a major consideration in this context. As suggested by the Economic Commission for Latin America and the Caribbean (ECLAC), social integration within countries should be sought as a complement to regional integration, through policies that reduce marginalization and ensure a more participatory pattern of international competitiveness.[81]

Finally, it has been seen that the product composition of trade is changing rapidly over time, with processed, differentiated and niche products growing in importance. This phenomenon, which is especially pronounced in the Latin America and Caribbean region, implies that the relevance of natural endowments in determining the export comparative advantage is progressively declining. It will be increasingly important, therefore, to direct policy action towards technology, management and marketing skills applied to a diversified range of products with greater value added. The public sector also has a significant role to play in creating a macroeconomic and regulatory environment that favours agro-industrial development while also streamlining credit markets and investing in marketing infrastructures, information and applied research.[82]

IV. Near East and North Africa

REGIONAL OVERVIEW
General economic performance

The Near East and North Africa region saw real GDP increase by 5.9 percent in 2000, largely a result of higher oil prices.

The Near East and North Africa region recorded real GDP growth of 5.9 percent in 2000, a strong recovery from the 1.1 percent seen in 1999 and well above the 1993–99 average of 3.3 percent.[83] The improved economic performance was largely based on the substantial increase in oil prices, the main economic factor for many countries in the region. Projections indicate real GDP growth of 1.8 percent in 2001. The deterioration in the overall economic conditions in the region in 2001 is largely a result of the sharp slowdown in world economic growth with its concomitant adverse effect on demand for oil and hence oil prices.

The events of 11 September have further undermined oil prices as well as prices of most non-fuel commodities. Oil-exporting countries are expected to be affected the most. However, the impact will be cushioned in a number of countries, in particular in the Near East, by the relatively conservative economic policies followed when oil prices were high. Increasing regional security concerns have contributed to a downturn in tourism, which is of particular importance for Egypt and Jordan.

In the Islamic Republic of Iran, GDP growth fell back slightly from 5.8 percent in 2000 to 5 percent in 2001. Improved agricultural production following a long-term drought, the strong performance of the construction and manufacturing sectors and an upturn in domestic demand are all expected to support economic growth in 2002.

Saudi Arabia experienced robust economic growth of 4.5 percent in 2000, but this is expected to slow to only 2.3 percent in 2001. A further slowdown, to just over 1.5 percent, is expected for 2002. The country is applying expenditure restraints to mitigate the effects of the oil price fluctuations and to reduce the high domestic debt.

The slowdown in world economic growth and the events of 11 September have led to weakened regional growth, projected at 1.8 percent for 2001.

Algeria, another oil-producing country, saw real GDP expand by 2.4 percent in 2000, and for 2001 growth of 3.6 percent is anticipated. An oil stabilization fund built up during the period of high oil prices will help cushion the downturn and growth is expected to be relatively well sustained at around 3.5 percent in 2002.

GDP growth in Morocco reached only 0.8 percent in 2000. A major factor behind this low figure was the negative effects of adverse climatic conditions on agricultural performance. Growth in 2001 is estimated to have reached 6.1 percent and for 2002 the projections are 4.4 percent growth in real GDP.

In Egypt, real GDP growth has slowed from 5.1 percent in 2000 to a projected 3.3 percent in 2001. A 25 percent depreciation of the currency since mid-2000 and the EU–Egypt Free Trade Agreement of mid-2001 are expected to stimulate the traded goods sector.

For the Eastern Mediterranean countries of Jordan, Lebanon and the Syrian Arab Republic, economic growth is projected to be somewhat lower than in the Near East and North Africa region as a whole, partly on account of the difficult security situation.

The Turkish economy rebounded from its 4.7 percent contraction in 1999. Growth in 2000 was 7.2 percent in real terms. For 2001, however, real GDP is again expected to shrink by 6.1 percent. Private consumption[84] and fixed investment expenditure collapsed owing to the uncertain policy outlook in the aftermath of the devaluation. These trends have been exacerbated by the knock-on effects of the attacks on the global economy. The economy is expected to pick up in 2002, with growth reaching a projected 4 percent.

Agricultural performance

Drought severely affected agricultural production in the region, with output stagnating in 2000 after contracting the previous year. Many countries continued to experience drought conditions in 2001.

The dominant factor affecting agriculture in the region for the year 2000 was drought. Agricultural production stagnated after recording a 4.2 percent contraction in 1999. Cereal output fell for the second consecutive year. Many countries continued to experience drought conditions also in 2001, for the third consecutive year in many cases, and agricultural production is estimated to have shrunk by nearly 2 percent. The outcome would be worse, but for the buffering effect of irrigation in the region.

In North Africa, agricultural production rose by only 0.7 percent in 2000 after seeing output rise by 7.1 and 2 percent in 1998 and 1999, respectively. Crop production fell by 0.7 percent, with cereal output down by 9.7 percent – the second consecutive drop. However, livestock output rose by 2.4 percent. Projections for 2001 suggest a modest rise in agricultural output of 0.7 percent. While crop production is projected to see a rise of 0.8 percent, cereal production is expected to rise sharply by 11.4 percent.

Agricultural output in Morocco fell by 3.7 percent in 2000 after a decline of 10.5 percent in the previous year. Drought

Figure 33

NEAR EAST AND NORTH AFRICA: SELECTED INDICATORS

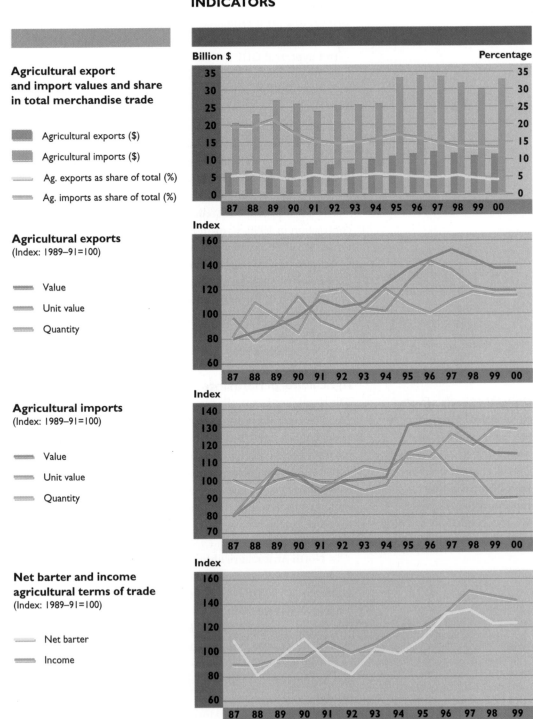

Agricultural export and import values and share in total merchandise trade

Agricultural exports ($)

Agricultural imports ($)

Ag. exports as share of total (%)

Ag. imports as share of total (%)

Agricultural exports
(Index: 1989–91=100)

Value

Unit value

Quantity

Agricultural imports
(Index: 1989–91=100)

Value

Unit value

Quantity

Net barter and income agricultural terms of trade
(Index: 1989–91=100)

Net barter

Income

NEAR EAST AND NORTH AFRICA: SELECTED INDICATORS

Real GDP*
(Percentage change from
preceding year)

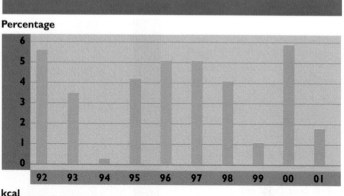

Dietary energy supplies
(kcal per capita per day)

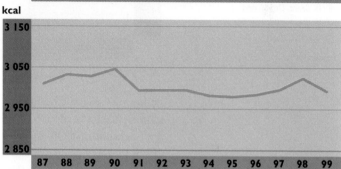

Agricultural production
(Index: 1989–91=100)

▬ Total agricultural production

▬ Per capita food production

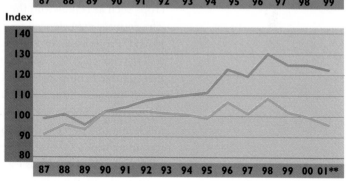

* *Excludes Algeria, Morocco
and Tunisia (according to
IMF classification)*
** *Preliminary*

Source: FAO and IMF

Figure 34
PETROLEUM PRICE INDEX*

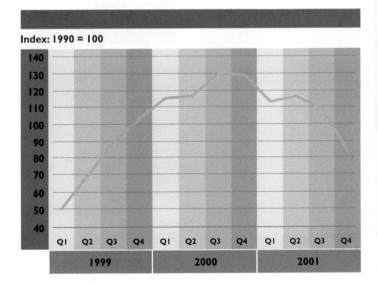

Index: 1990 = 100

* Spot crude-weighted average
  of UK Brent, Dubai, and
  West Texas Intermediate

Source: IMF

conditions severely hampered cereal production, which experienced a further 51.8 percent decline after dropping by 46.7 percent in 1999. Agricultural production stagnated in the 1990s largely because of the dominance of drought-sensitive crops such as cereals and the increased incidence of drought. The country experienced six droughts in the 1990–2000 period. Projections for 2001 show an increase in output of close to 5 percent in 2001, with aggregate cereal output having more than doubled compared with the level achieved in 2000.

In 2000, agricultural production in Algeria fell by 4.7 percent. Cereal production contracted by 61 percent following a 36 percent drop in 1999. For 2001, agricultural output growth of almost 9 percent is expected. The 2001 aggregate cereal output is estimated at 2.6 million tonnes compared with 0.9 million tonnes harvested in 2000 and with the past five-year average of 2.3 million tonnes.

Also in Tunisia, the agriculture sector was adversely affected by relatively severe drought conditions in 2000, and overall agricultural output declined by 4.9 percent. Cereal production fell by 42 percent, while livestock production increased by a modest 1.7 percent. In 2001, a further decline in agricultural output of about 8.7 percent is projected. With regard to cereals, however, official estimates put production in 2001 at 1.35 million tonnes, or 24 percent above the 2000 level. By contrast, olive production, which accounts for one-third of agricultural land, was at the lowest level for over 20 years. The harvest in 2001–02 was more than 50 percent below that of the previous year.

Agricultural production in Egypt grew by 4.4 percent in 2000 after expanding by 6.5 percent in 1999. Cereal production rose by 3.7 percent after expanding by 10.3 percent in 1999. In Egypt, nearly 100 percent of food production depends on the Nile and groundwater; hence it is more insulated from the effect of drought. However, for 2001 a contraction of 1.1 percent in agricultural output is expected. Cereal output is projected to fall by 6 percent.

The countries of the Gulf Cooperation Council (GCC)[85] saw agricultural production decline by 1 percent in 2000. Crop

Table 26
ANNUAL REAL GDP GROWTH RATES IN THE NEAR EAST AND NORTH AFRICA

Country/region	1996	1997	1998	1999	2000	2001	2002[1]
				(Percentage)			
Algeria	3.8	1.1	5.1	3.2	2.4	3.6	3.4
Egypt	5.0	5.3	5.7	6.0	5.1	3.3	3.3
Islamic Republic of Iran	5.9	2.7	3.7	3.1	5.8	5.0	4.8
Morocco	12.2	-2.2	6.8	-0.7	0.8	6.1	4.4
Saudi Arabia	1.4	2.0	1.7	-0.8	4.5	2.3	1.6
Turkey	6.9	7.6	3.1	-4.7	7.2	-6.1	4.1
Near East and North Africa[2]	**5.1**	**5.1**	**4.1**	**1.1**	**5.9**	**1.8**	**3.9**

[1] Projections.
[2] Including Bahrain, Cyprus, Egypt, Iraq, the Islamic Republic of Iran, Jordan, Kuwait, Lebanon, the Libyan Arab Jamahiriya, Malta, Oman, Qatar, Saudi Arabia, the Syrian Arab Republic, Turkey and Yemen.
Source: IMF. 2001. *World Economic Outlook*, December. Washington, DC.

Table 27
NET PRODUCTION GROWTH RATES IN THE NEAR EAST AND NORTH AFRICA

Year	Agriculture	Cereals	Crops	Food	Livestock	Non-food
			(Percentage)			
1992–96	3.3	3.3	3.7	3.4	2.9	3.1
1997	-2.7	-12.1	-6.4	-3.3	6.0	8.2
1998	9.0	16.8	11.0	9.8	3.3	-2.1
1999	-4.2	-17.7	-6.4	-4.3	1.7	-1.8
2000	0.0	-6.1	-0.2	-0.1	0.0	1.8
2001[1]	-1.9	2.8	-2.6	-1.9	-0.4	-1.7

[1] Preliminary.
Source: FAOSTAT.

production fell by 1.7 percent, with cereal output in particular contracting by 10 percent. Livestock output rose modestly by 0.8 percent. For 2001, projections show agricultural output rising by about 1.3 percent, with crop output stagnating but livestock production rising by 1.9 percent.

In the Near East in Asia subregion (excluding the GCC countries), agricultural production fell by 0.3 percent in 2000 after contracting by 7 percent in 1999. Crop production stagnated and livestock output fell by 1.3 percent. Projections for 2001 show output contracting by a further 3.2 percent, with crop and livestock production falling by 4.4 and 1.3 percent, respectively.

Cracked earth because of drought

The Near East and North Africa region is characterized by low and variable rainfall. Drought is a recurrent phenomenon in large parts of the region.

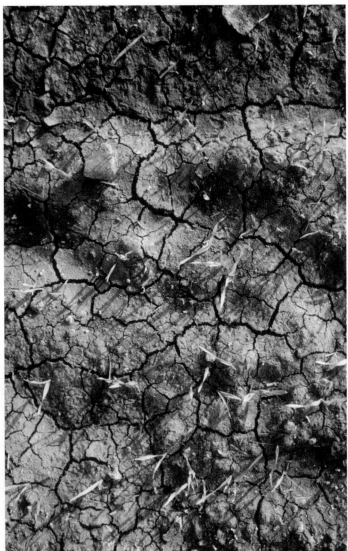

Agricultural production in Turkey contracted by 0.8 percent in 2000 after falling by 5.2 percent in 1999. However, cereal production increased by almost 8 percent after declining by 23 percent in 1999. Another relatively poor year is expected in 2001, with a further decline in agricultural output of 1.1 percent and cereal production expected to contract by 9 percent.

In Jordan, drought in 1998, 1999 and 2000 has severely affected the country's agricultural output. Although agricultural output recovered a little in 2000 with respect to 1999, a further decline of about 6 percent is expected in 2001.

As a consequence of continued drought conditions, Iran has seen agricultural output decline by a further 0.3 percent in 2000 after a decline of 6.3 percent in the previous year. Drought has continued to affect agriculture in 2001, with output anticipated to fall by about 8.5 percent. Cereal output is estimated to have declined even further, to 11.9 million tonnes, the lowest level in more than a decade. Three years of extreme drought have adversely affected about 90 percent of the rural, urban and nomadic population. It is estimated that 200 000 nomadic livestock owners have lost their only source of livelihood. In addition to a nationwide drought, heavy torrential rains during August 2001 devastated rice, cotton and wheat production areas and damaged thousands of hectares of farmland in the northern provinces of Iran.

CLIMATE VARIABILITY, ARIDITY AND VULNERABILITY TO DROUGHT

Very productive land is also very vulnerable to drought, and careful soil management is needed to avoid possibly irreversible damage.

The Near East and North Africa region is a vast zone of generally diverse climatic conditions, characterized by very low and highly variable annual rainfall and a high degree of aridity. In the past, the rivers have laid down deep, alluvial fertile soils and have supported several of the earliest irrigation societies and civilizations. However, very productive land is also extremely vulnerable to drought if mismanaged, leading to irreversible damage, such as desertification. This process differs from drought but represents the ultimate consequence of it if no adequate measures are taken in time. The general problem of water scarcity in the region and the critical role of proper water resource management and irrigation development were discussed in the 2001 edition of *The State of Food and Agriculture*.[86] This section discusses more specifically the impact of drought and the importance of drought preparedness.

Drought should be seen as a risk-management process with emphasis on monitoring and managing emerging stress conditions and other hazards associated with climate variability.

Drought – a structurally recurrent phenomenon in the region

The causes of drought in the region are very complex. Contrasting geographic locations and topographic variations (seaside, mountains, hills, flat lands, desert), with their oceanic or continental influences, exposure to western and eastern wind systems and exposure to the Azores' atmospheric pressure systems, are among the physical determinants that explain the spatial scale and intensity of droughts in the region. On the other hand, demographic pressures have led to widespread ecosystem degradation over recent decades and have exacerbated the region's vulnerability to drought through

Box 8

AFGHANISTAN

Two decades of conflict have reduced Afghanistan to one of the world's most impoverished nations. The economy is in a very poor state. There is no macroeconomic framework; transportation and communication facilities are very poor; no banks are operating in the country and the manufacturing and export sectors have become marginal operations.

Agriculture is the mainstay of the country's economy but after two decades of war and civil strife much of the agricultural infrastructure is damaged and in urgent need of rehabilitation. The area harvested for cereals is much smaller today than it was in 1978. Moreover, the country has experienced severe drought in parts of the country in 1999, 2000 and 2001, making the current food

security situation extremely precarious. The FAO/World Food Programme (WFP) Crop and Food Supply Assessment Mission of May 2001 found mounting evidence of emerging widespread famine conditions.[1] At the beginning of 2002, WFP was assisting about six million people in Afghanistan.[2]

For 2001, the estimated cereal output of 2 million tonnes implied a cereal import requirement of about 2.2 million tonnes, close to the very high level of the previous year. The outlook for the 2002 wheat crop (to be harvested in May 2002) is poor, with cereal production expected to decline further, aggravating an already grave food supply situation.

The livestock sector has also been severely affected by three years of consecutive drought and the ongoing increased cultivation of marginal and fragile arid lands, soil erosion, runoff and desertification.

Historical evidence corroborated by tree-ring studies in North Africa clearly indicates that drought is a structurally recurrent phenomenon in this part of the Mediterranean region. In Tunisia, drought episodes have been traced back to the year 707 and in the period 1907–97 alone 23 dry years were observed. In Morocco, the number of drought episodes over 1 000 years as revealed by tree-ring evaluation varied from century to century around an average of 22 dry years per century.[87]

Of the 22 drought years in the twentieth century, ten occurred

conflict. A lack of grazing land, the disruption of traditional grazing routes and a shortage of veterinary services are having catastrophic consequences, especially for Afghanistan's nomadic population, the *Kuchi*.

The years of war and civil strife have led to a neglect of the irrigation infrastructure and it is estimated that about one-half of the irrigated area has fallen into disuse. Traditional irrigation in Afghanistan consists of surface and groundwater systems using simple diversion and extracting techniques that supply water for irrigation and domestic use to households at the community level. This type of irrigation is the main source of water for much of the nation's cereal cultivation. Twenty-three years ago, the total irrigated area was about 2.7 million ha, of which about

2.3 million ha would have been classified as being covered by traditional irrigation systems. It is estimated that about 50 percent of the 2.3 million ha require rehabilitation and this action may be the shortest route to reducing food insecurity nationwide. Among other factors, repairing much of the structure would be relatively simple; the impact on food production would be immediate; and rehabilitation could serve as a significant source of employment internally and for the returning refugees. It is likely that this relatively low-cost investment with a short gestation period would be an effective channel by which food aid could be used to renew productive assets.

Increased domestic production of cereals will depend not only on rehabilitation of the irrigation system, but also on improving

Drought is a recurrent phenomenon in the Near East and North Africa region. Some analysts believe that the frequency and severity of drought have increased, although the evidence for this is not yet conclusive.

during the last two decades and included the three successive dry years of 1999, 2000 and 2001.

Drought is also a recurring event in the Near East. Jordan, for example, is predominantly arid and has experienced chronic water shortages and suffered from severe shortages since the 1960s. The recent droughts in Afghanistan, Iran, Jordan, Pakistan, the Syrian Arab Republic and the West Bank and Gaza Strip were the worst ever recorded in decades. The most recent Intergovernmental Panel on Climate Change (IPCC) reports confirm some global warming in the region and forecast more over the next century, but past changes in rainfall patterns and future predictions are not well established.[88]

AFGHANISTAN: TOTAL AREA HARVESTED FOR CEREALS

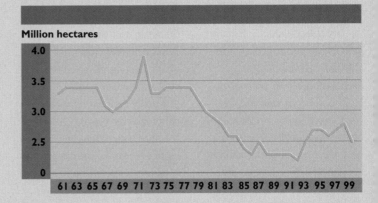

Million hectares

Source: FAOSTAT

the supply of vital inputs, increasing the availability of draught power and the strengthening of extension services.

Agriculture must be the key sector in any strategy to improve food security and livelihoods in both the near and longer term. Increased cereal production is essential for improved food security. Livestock is an important

source of food and draught power, and the livestock and horticulture sectors both have substantial export potential. Improved water harvesting and conservation and, very importantly, the rehabilitation of the traditional irrigation systems are the cornerstones on which to base a programme to improve food security and to build sustainable livelihoods.

[1] FAO. 2001. *Afghanistan: special alert.* GIEWS Report No. 318, September. Rome (available at www.fao.org/WAICENT/faoinfo/economic/giews/english/alertes/2001/SRAFGH31.htm).
[2] WFP news release, 5 February 2002.

Table 28

NUMBER OF DROUGHTS IN MOROCCO FROM THE FOURTEENTH TO THE TWENTIETH CENTURY

Century	Number of droughts
Fourteenth	31
Fifteenth	25
Sixteenth	12
Seventeenth	22
Eighteenth	16
Nineteenth	19
Twentieth	22

Source: J. Morton and C. Sear. 2001. *Challenges for drought management in West Asia and North Africa.* Paper prepared for the Ministerial Meeting on Opportunities for Sustainable Investment in Rainfed Areas of West Asia and North Africa, Rabat, Morocco, 25–26 June 2001.

Water shortage is already the main constraint in most countries of the region, and IPCC model simulations indicate that the water scarcity may worsen substantially as a result of future changes in climatic patterns.[89] Climate change, drought and desertification are interrelated but the concepts cannot be used interchangeably to address the complex issues of drought and water management in this region.

Water and land resource issues

Typically, heavy reliance on surface and groundwater prevails in all countries of the region, with 60–90 percent of water being used for agriculture. All over the region, water demand is steadily increasing while water supply is steadily decreasing. This is happening in the context of conflicting pressures from the domestic, agriculture, industrial and tourism sectors. The question of how to balance the water equation remains a big challenge for decision-makers.

The topic of renewable freshwater resources and water management in the region was previously addressed in *The State of Food and Agriculture 2001.*[90] Available data confirm that at least ten countries in the region were already experiencing severe water shortages in 1995.[91] Jordan, Kuwait, the Libyan Arab Jamahiriya, Qatar, Saudi Arabia and the United Arab Emirates have less than 200 m^3/person/year to meet their domestic requirements. The projections show that Algeria and Tunisia will join this group by 2025, while Egypt, Morocco and the Syrian Arab Republic are expected to experience severe water shortages by 2050. By 2025 only Iraq and Turkey are expected to be relatively better off.[92]

Impact of recent droughts on crop and livestock production

Following the recovery in 1998, three years of drought in many countries of the region have led to a sharp drop in agricultural output (see previous section). Crop production, particularly cereal production, has been severely affected.

The drought has also had a detrimental impact on livestock populations and productivity in the region. Livestock accounts for between 30 and 50 percent of total agricultural GDP and is a significant factor in sustaining the livelihoods of many rural dwellers. Large livestock losses therefore have a direct and severe impact on household food security, especially of the rural populations who live in remote and inaccessible areas and who are most vulnerable to drought. Over the last three years, drought is estimated to have affected at least 40 percent of the region's livestock populations. Heavy losses due to animal mortality, production losses and distress sales of animals have been widely reported in most countries. The effect will probably continue to be felt beyond 2002 as the situation has been aggravated by the cumulative effect of consecutive droughts.

The severe droughts have had a devastating effect on range vegetation, as well as on the availability of feed from grain and crop residues. Consequently, resource-poor farmers are often faced with purchasing feed at the expense of household consumption. The drastic fall in feed availability has already led to widespread distress sales of livestock, saturating the markets and leading to a sharp drop in prices. Average prices of live sheep tumbled by more than 50 percent between 1999 and 2000. Similar drops have been observed in almost all countries of the region, reflecting expectations of continued drought and a steep fall in disposable income.

Impact on population livelihood, household income and rural poverty

In addition to the collapse of agricultural activities, rural and urban water supplies during 1999–2001 were significantly affected. Water rationing was the general rule in most large cities around the region. Further, recurrent droughts have resulted in serious economic and social problems. For example, the drought experienced in Algeria, Morocco and Tunisia during the period 1999–2001 caused a dramatic disparity in their agricultural trade balance, disrupted local rural economies, increased migration to urban areas and exacerbated rural poverty. Similar situations prevailed in Iran, Jordan, the Syrian Arab Republic and Pakistan during this drought period.

Three years of drought have severely affected at least 40 percent of the region's livestock populations.

Three years of drought have worsened rural poverty and increased rural–urban migration.

Figure 35

CHANGE IN AGGREGATE CEREAL PRODUCTION FOR DROUGHT-AFFECTED COUNTRIES[1] IN THE NEAR EAST AND NORTH AFRICA, 1989–2001

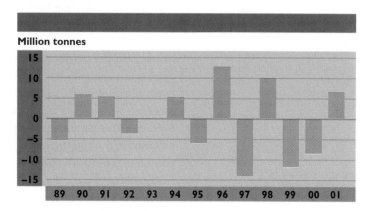

[1] Afghanistan, Algeria, Islamic Republic of Iran, Iraq, Jordan, Morocco, Syrian Arab Republic, Tunisia, Yemen

Source: FAOSTAT

Available information indicates that the incidence of poverty in the region increased significantly towards the end of the decade. In particular, the proportion living on below $2 per day increased from 25 percent to 30 percent of the population, a development attributable to increases in Egypt, Morocco and Yemen.[93]

The most vulnerable and seriously affected social groups were dryland farmers (including cereal producers), olive and fruit growers and sheep herders. Farmers' and herders' communities suffered severe loss of income through the loss of harvests, partial loss of flocks, low animal production yields and weak market prices. As a consequence of three successive dry years, many herders and farmers in the region found it necessary to purchase supplementary animal feed, water and treatments and other agricultural inputs, leading to increasing indebtedness.

The impact of drought on disposable household income is difficult to assess because of the limited availability of accurate data. Information gained from field surveys of large and small farms in a semi-arid cereal and livestock-producing area of Morocco is summarized in Table 29. The surveys were conducted in the same farming communities over two consecutive years: the first period was exceptionally dry (1992–93) and the second was considered to be a good wet year (1993–94). The results indicate that regardless of farm size, household income varied substantially: from a secure high level during the wet year to an insecure low level during the dry year. Drought had a severe impact on many households' incomes through complete crop failure and limited livestock earnings. Off-farm activities were among the most common coping mechanisms adopted by households, as would be the case in most parts of the region. The data on total expenditure on the other hand show that in a dry year households tend to allocate a higher proportion of expenditure to meeting farm operational production costs at the expense of their own members' consumption needs.

Impact on the environment

The region's irrigation systems are under considerable environmental strain, with almost all countries experiencing problems with salinity and waterlogging. A further cause for concern is the overexploitation of groundwater, particularly, but not only, in the countries of the GCC. In view of the fact that water is practically cost-free in most of the countries, the sustainability of irrigation systems is a major concern.

Degradation of natural resources is especially serious in the low rainfall areas that represent over 70 percent of the total rangelands in the region. For the nomadic population, their incomes depend directly on the rangelands' quality and quantity. In normal years, animals were kept on the rangeland for eight months and then fed for the remaining four. With prevailing drought conditions, which mean that there is a lack of forage and drinking water in large parts of the rangelands, livestock are fed for most of the year. Large numbers of farmers and herders have

Table 29

IMPACT OF DROUGHT ON ANNUAL HOUSEHOLD INCOME AND EXPENDITURE IN A SEMI-ARID AREA OF MOROCCO

	Farm size			
	Small (< 5 ha)		Large (20–50 ha)	
	Wet year	Dry year	Wet year	Dry year
	($)			
Household income	2 186	933	8 984	1 777
On-farm income	1 633	115	6 824	-111
Crops	420	-105	3 134	-510
Livestock	1 213	220	1 850	399
Off-farm income	553	818	2 060	1 888
Household expenditure	2 240	1 960	5 980	5 910
Crops and livestock	300	830	2 860	3 830
Family consumption	1 940	1 130	3 120	2 080

Source: IAV Hassan II field surveys during 1992–93 dry year and 1993–94 wet year; IFAD. 1999. Final Evaluation Report, Integrated Rural Development Project of Abda-Ahmar (Safi region, Morocco). Rome, IFAD and Rabat, Ministry of Agriculture.

migrated from their villages to search for water and livestock feed. This phenomenon requires immediate attention to prevent major population displacements and further environmental degradation.

Water scarcity is placing substantial strains on the environment, causing damage to the region's biological diversity.

The long period of drought has caused significant damage to the environment and to the region's biological diversity, including both animal and plant species. Wildlife has been severely affected as a result of the shortage of drinking water, lack of feed, dried wetlands and degradation of wildlife habitats. For instance, in the Hamoun wetlands of Iran, which are of international importance, aquatic life has disappeared. Herbivores are among the first animal species to be affected by a lack of feed. Dryness of wetlands and natural lakes has also occurred in Morocco, as well as other countries of the region, causing similar and probably irreversible environmental damage. In Jordan, the continued drought during 1999 and 2000 caused visible damage to the natural and artificial forests that make up 20 and 30 percent of the total area, respectively.

Government measures for drought prevention and relief of affected groups

Young farmer ploughing in an arid zone of Morocco
Drought can severely affect farm household incomes.

Current drought management and mitigation interventions in the region consist mostly of short-term drought relief operations.

FAO/18029/I. BALDERI

Although drought recurs relatively frequently in the region, drought management is mostly focused on short-term relief operations, implemented at considerable cost.

In 2000/01 Morocco earmarked around $650 million for drought relief and mitigation activities, representing about one-third of its entire annual investment budget.

The types of policy governments in the region have implemented in response to the recent prolonged droughts are exemplified by the practical experiences from North Africa (Morocco), the Near East (Jordan) and West Asia (Iran) outlined below. For these three countries (as for most countries in the region), when a nationwide drought occurs the policy applied consists of establishing a national drought programme to be monitored by an intergovernmental committee (National Drought Task Force). Headed by the Ministry of Agriculture, this political decision-making body proposes a package of emergency measures to be implemented across the country. Regional and provincial drought committees also exist to monitor implementation of the centrally planned measures. To implement the proposed activities, funds are made available to ease the adverse impacts of the drought and to assist affected rural populations in solving the problems associated with (i) drinking water, (ii) livestock protection, (iii) creation of job opportunities and (iv) agricultural tax relaxation or debt relief.

For the 2000 national drought relief programme in Morocco, the government earmarked around $650 million for drought relief and mitigation activities for the period April 2000 to July 2001. This important core fund accounted for one-third of the country's entire annual investment budget. The fund was disbursed to the various components as follows: 9.4 percent for drinking water, 19.4 percent for livestock feeding and sanitation, 60.5 percent to create jobs in rural areas, 4.5 percent to stabilize the market prices of cereal grains, 3.8 percent to limit forest degradation, 1.8 percent to cover agricultural credit forgiveness and the remaining 0.5 percent for communication and public awareness.[94] With regard to the level of investment, the period of implementation and the preliminary results, the programme has been credited with relative success, although an effective evaluation of its real impact has yet to be carried out.[95]

In Jordan, government financial assistance for the 1999 drought relief programme was about $58 million and a similar amount was allocated in 2000. The estimated total production loss for 2000 was $160 million.[96] The national drought mitigation programme focused on providing water and feed to sheep herders, supporting subsidized barley and feedstuff, flexibility in feed imports and the export of live animals and the introduction of mechanisms for delayed reimbursement and/or forgiveness of agricultural credits for the most affected communities. The government also distributed water and food aid to the nomadic population living in the driest area of the country, the steppe of Al-Baddia (Bedouins) and in similarly affected areas of other regions.

In Iran, drought-related crop and livestock production losses in 2001 are estimated at $2.6 billion.

The Government of Iran allocated about $138 million and $500 million in 2000 and 2001, respectively, to mitigate the effects of the ongoing drought. Half of the 2001 budget was allocated to the Agricultural Bank in order to provide loans to drought-mitigation projects focusing on, for example, on-farm soil and water conservation, water supply, maintenance of damaged traditional irrigation canals and watershed management. The other half was allocated to preparedness activities and to increase the capital of the Agricultural Product Insurance Funds. The approved budget for 2002 represents about 20 percent of the estimated losses inflicted in 2001 to crop and livestock production, which total around $2.6 billion.[97]

From reactive crisis management to proactive risk management in agriculture

Agriculture in the region is extremely sensitive to the large year-to-year climatic fluctuations. Although this climatic variability raises complex risk-management issues, many countries do not have a sustainable management policy to cope with these natural hazards. Irrigation and proper water-resource management has a vital role to play (as discussed in *The State of Food and Agriculture 2001*).

Countries with long-term drought-management policies are better able to deal with drought compared with countries that manage only the ensuing crisis.

In addition, experience elsewhere has shown that countries with long-term drought-management policies, like Australia, South Africa and some states of the United States, are generally better prepared to deal with drought than those that simply manage the ensuing crisis. Current new initiatives in the region directed towards such a strategy include the establishment in Morocco of the National Drought Observatory, located within the Ministry of Agriculture and working in close institutional collaboration with policy-makers and academics to develop a national drought policy plan. The aim of this initiative is to develop an institutional infrastructure that includes a drought early warning system and a delivery system for information to users and drought managers. A direct output will be to strengthen institutional capacity in drought early warning, monitoring and impact assessment.

A critical element of drought planning and mitigation in the region is the early detection of emerging drought and the timely and effective delivery of information to decision-makers. This requires continuous monitoring of climate and water-supply conditions within individual countries and also across countries within the region. It is within this context that initiatives have recently been taken to promote regional drought-preparedness networking efforts.

The concept of a global drought-preparedness network is an initiative that, with support from FAO and the World Meteorological Organization, could provide the opportunity for nations and regions to share experiences and lessons learned (successes and failures) through a virtual network of regional networks, using the World Wide Web as the information delivery system. An important element in such a global network would be FAO's Global Information and Early Warning System, which reports on regional food shortages and on emergency events, such as droughts, that may dramatically affect the food production system around the world.

V. Central and Eastern Europe and the Commonwealth of Independent States

REGIONAL OVERVIEW

Macroeconomic trends and agricultural performance

Economies of the transition countries recorded a respectable growth for the third consecutive year in 2001, although slightly lower than in 2000.

Economies of the countries in transition of Central and Eastern Europe and the Commonwealth of Independent States[98] (CIS) marked a respectable growth for the third consecutive year in 2001.[99] Real GDP in these countries grew at a rate of 4.9 percent in 2001, although this figure was less than that of the previous year (6.3 percent). As in the preceding two years, the strongest performance was recorded in the CIS, with an estimated growth of 6.1 percent (5.8 percent in the Russian Federation and 6.8 percent in the remaining countries of the CIS), while growth in the Central and Eastern European countries was an estimated 3.0 percent. The slightly weaker performance is largely a consequence of lower growth rates in the region's chief gas and oil producers – Azerbaijan, Kazakhstan, the Russian Federation and Turkmenistan – as well as the slowdown in economic growth in Poland, the largest economy in Central and Eastern Europe. Nevertheless, the fastest-growing economies of the region in 2001 were primarily oil and gas producers such as Azerbaijan and Turkmenistan.

Agricultural output showed a substantial growth in 2001 for the first time after ten years of decline and stagnation.

Net agricultural production (crop and livestock) in the transition economies grew more than GDP in 2001, at 5.9 percent.[100] The poor harvest in 2000 in most of the region, particularly in Central and Eastern Europe, was a factor in this improvement. Agricultural output in the countries of the former Soviet Union marked a positive growth in 2001 for the third consecutive year, while in Eastern Europe output growth in 2001 followed three preceding years of declining production. Net agricultural production grew fastest in Turkmenistan (38 percent), Azerbaijan (25 percent), Hungary (17 percent), Romania (16 percent) and Georgia (13 percent).

Seen from a longer-term perspective, the most recent trends in the growth rates of GDP and net agricultural production are quite promising. Over the past eight years (1993–2001) the

Figure 36

CENTRAL AND EASTERN EUROPE AND CIS: SELECTED INDICATORS

Agricultural export and import values and share in total merchandise trade

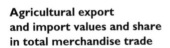

Agricultural exports ($)

Agricultural imports ($)

Ag. exports as share of total (%)

Ag. imports as share of total (%)

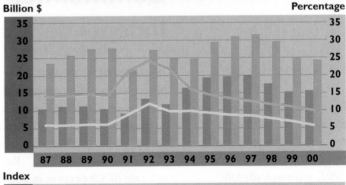

Agricultural production
(Index: 1989–91=100)

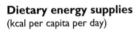

Total agricultural production

Per capita food production

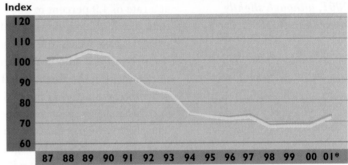

Real GDP
(Percentage change from preceding year)

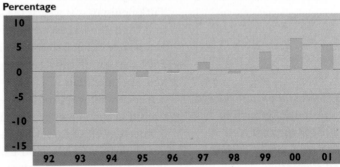

Dietary energy supplies
(kcal per capita per day)

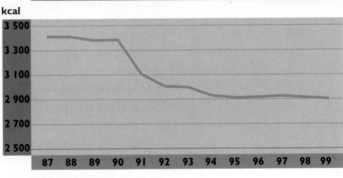

* Preliminary

Source: FAO and IMF

GDP and net agricultural production of transition economies have shrunk by an average of 0.4 and 1.9 percent, respectively, each year. After several years of "transitional recession", significant GDP growth resumed for most transition countries by 1999. However, agricultural production did not follow this turnaround until 2001. The substantive output growth in 2001 points to the first year of expansion for the region since the beginning of the economic reform process. Although the growth was to some extent a reflection of recovery from the poor crops of the previous year, it might be seen as a sign that the agriculture sector in the region could also be emerging from the adjustment recession.

Table 30

ANNUAL REAL GDP GROWTH RATES IN THE TRANSITION COUNTRIES OF CENTRAL AND EASTERN EUROPE AND THE CIS

	1997	1998	1999	2000	2001[1]	2002[1]
			(Percentage)			
Central and Eastern Europe	2.6	2.3	2.0	3.8	3.0	3.2
CIS[2]	1.1	-2.8	4.6	7.8	6.1	3.9
Russian Federation	0.9	-4.9	5.4	8.3	5.8	3.6
Excluding the Russian Federation	1.5	1.6	2.8	6.8	6.8	4.6
Countries in transition	1.6	-0.8	3.6	6.3	4.9	3.6

[1] Projections.
[2] Including Mongolia.
Source: IMF. 2001. *World Economic Outlook*, December. Washington, DC.

Table 31

NET AGRICULTURAL PRODUCTION GROWTH RATES FOR CENTRAL AND EASTERN EUROPE AND THE CIS

Year	Agriculture	Crops	Cereals	Livestock
		(Percentage)		
1992–96	-5.1	-3.3	-6.0	-7.2
1997	1.4	7.9	32.5	-5.1
1998	-6.7	-14.1	-27.2	-0.1
1999	0.5	2.4	6.9	-2.5
2000	-0.1	2.6	-3.5	-1.0
2001[1]	5.9	13.4	34.2	1.1

[1] Preliminary.
Source: FAOSTAT.

Figure 37

NET AGRICULTURAL PRODUCTION INDICES FOR CENTRAL AND EASTERN EUROPE AND THE CIS

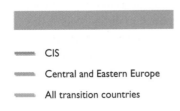

CIS

Central and Eastern Europe

All transition countries

Source: FAO

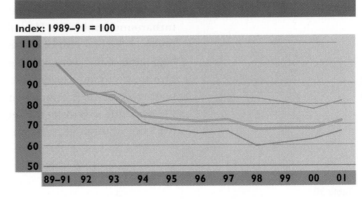

Index: 1989–91 = 100

LAND AND FARMS IN CENTRAL AND EASTERN EUROPE AND THE CIS IN THE PERIOD OF CENTRAL PLANNING

The general trends outlined above do not capture the significant institutional changes that have taken place over the past ten years in the countries of Central and Eastern Europe and the CIS; nor do they reflect the substantial country-level differences in performance. In the following paragraphs, a review is made of developments in one of the most fundamental institutional changes in agriculture in the region: land reform.

Before 1989–90, the countries of Eastern Europe and the former Soviet Union had similar organizational and institutional structures in agriculture. The "Soviet model" of state planning, supply and procurement on collective and state farms predominated in these countries. Land was owned primarily by the state, and farming was organized into two main sectors.

Predominant was the state and collective sector, characterized by large farms employing wage labour. These farms received inputs from state supply organizations and delivered output to state procurement organizations. Prices for commodities marketed by state and collective farms were state controlled, as were the prices of processed food products sold in state stores.

The second was the private sector, consisting of small (0.1–0.2 ha) plots farmed by collective and state farm employees who grew fruits, vegetables and potatoes, and raised livestock for meat and milk in their non-working hours. The private sector had very little land and produced mostly for self-consumption. Inputs were distributed by or taken from collective and state farms. Farm workers were allowed to market their surplus production in urban markets, where prices were usually higher than in state stores. However, restrictions on the size of private plot land holdings limited both the type and quantity of commodities that could be produced.

This dualistic Soviet model of agriculture was originally imposed in the 1930s in the former Soviet Union and the 1950s in Eastern Europe as a means of "squeezing agriculture" to ensure a source of food at constant prices for industrial cities. Starting in the 1960s, however, the Stalinist period policies[101] were largely abandoned for two reasons: stagnant productivity growth in the sector,[102] and the need to supply "prestigious" livestock products. The latter requirement was met by the development of an industrialized livestock sector with large state investments and increased production incentives.

While the nature of the Soviet model of agriculture was changing in the former Soviet Union and the more orthodox countries of Eastern Europe, other countries went so far as to virtually abandon the model. In postwar Poland and Yugoslavia, efforts at collectivization were relatively limited from the beginning and land was farmed predominantly by small, private farmers. Hungary and Yugoslavia rejected the Soviet model of agriculture in the 1960s: agricultural and food prices were partially liberalized; planning was abandoned and farm "cooperatives", rather than collective and state farms, were encouraged.

Pretransition agriculture was unable to achieve expected productivity increases because of the lack of incentives and pervasive state control.

However, even these quite palpable and fundamental reforms did not change what can be seen as the key features of socialist agriculture after the Second World War. First, all farming – even in Poland and Yugoslavia, where private property arrangements existed – operated within an environment of controlled prices for inputs and commodities and pervasive state controls over marketing and input availability. Continued perverse incentives and state control were the chief reasons why the reformed socialist agriculture of Eastern Europe did not deliver the large increases in productivity expected. Second, even the farming cooperatives of Hungary and Yugoslavia operated in an environment of soft budgetary constraints in which bankruptcy was virtually unknown.

LAND AND FARM REFORM IN CENTRAL AND EASTERN EUROPEAN AND CIS COUNTRIES

Building a market agriculture in the post-socialist economies consists of replacing these key features of socialist agriculture with the environment and institutions of a market economy. This task involves much more than just "getting the prices right". The old bureaucratic organizations need to be replaced by new

Secure, clear and transferable land-tenure rights are fundamental for market economy agriculture.

So is an efficient farm ownership and management structure.

But it has been recognized that privatization alone is not enough ... and the creation of family farms has become an important policy goal.

institutions that respond flexibly to market signals and are allowed to fail if they are not competitive. This involves a fundamental change in the relationship between the state and producers, in terms of the role the state can play in the economy and the tasks and responsibility of producers.

Three main aspects of land and farm reform have been particularly significant in the construction of a market agriculture. The first is the establishment of *secure, clear and transferable land-tenure rights*. Secure land tenure may include the right to utilize land as one sees fit without state interference, the right to reap returns on investments in land without confiscatory taxation, and the right to buy and sell land. Reliable court enforcement of contracts and land ownership registration can ensure secure tenure rights, which form a basis for transparent and efficient land and capital markets. Secure land-tenure rights are also a sign that the relationship between the state and producers has been fundamentally altered.

The second way in which land and farm reform can contribute to building a market agriculture is by *ensuring an efficient ownership and management structure for farms*. An efficient ownership structure minimizes transaction costs and clearly assigns ownership rights to the land, assets and income of the farm. An efficient management structure supports production at minimum cost.

All countries in Central and Eastern Europe and most CIS countries have come to recognize that the cooperative, collective and state farms of the socialist period had inefficient ownership structures and failed to encourage production at minimum cost. With the exception of a few CIS countries, this realization led to the privatization of farms. In Central and Eastern Europe, however, and in the Caucasus region and Moldova in the CIS it has also been recognized that privatization per se does not lead to the creation of farms with a clear (and therefore efficient) ownership structure. "Private" farms formed on the basis of the old state and collective farms have all too often continued to operate in similar ways to those of their predecessors. They have continued receiving state handouts, usually via agricultural bank credits (which are seldom repaid), and operating with excessive numbers of employees. In short, the privatization of farms by itself does not solve the problem of "soft budgets".

This recognition combined with a desire to return their agriculture to one of privately owned family farms encouraged most Central and Eastern European and a few CIS countries to dismantle the large, socialist-size farms by restoring land to previous owners or distributing land to farm employees. The creation of a family farm agriculture has thus been an important aim of agricultural reform in these countries.

The family farm, however, is not the only ownership–management structure found in farms in the transition economies. In both Central and Eastern European and CIS countries, farm ownership may be structured as a joint stock company, a limited liability company, a partnership or a family-run (single-owner) farm. As noted below, many CIS countries have had limited success in making these structures work efficiently.

The creation of a class of mid-sized commercial farms can also contribute to building a market agriculture.

The third way in which land reform can contribute to the building of a market agriculture is by *creating a class of mid-sized commercial farms*. Such farms are large enough to participate actively in markets, while being profitable and flexible enough to survive in a competitive international market environment. They are larger than "micro" subsistence farms, but considerably smaller than socialist-era large farms.

Just as with the previous two tasks, the creation of a class of mid-sized, commercial farms is not achieved by privatization alone. Subsistence farms do not utilize markets, while large privatized farms with soft budgets tend to distort them. Proactive policies promoting land consolidation, land leasing and land markets are therefore required, as well as the dissolution of large privatized farms with soft budget constraints.

The establishment of clear and secure rights of land tenure

The transition countries have followed different strategies for farm privatization.

There was wide agreement, even in the CIS countries, that land reform should include farm privatization and an increase in the area under individual land tenure. There were several reasons for this. The lack of incentives of collective and state farms was an obvious problem. Second, in Central and Eastern Europe, decollectivization was seen as a way to reintegrate agriculture into mainstream Western market development. Third, the process of land reform in China (the best-known land reform of the socialist world at the time), which involved the expansion of private plots and long-term leases of land, spurred the growth of agricultural production and the economy as a whole. Finally, the higher productivity of private plots compared to Soviet-type collective and state farms seemed to offer convincing proof of the superiority of private farms.[103] There was a widespread preference for privatization in Central and Eastern European and CIS countries (Table 32). Only Belarus, Kazakhstan, Tajikistan and Uzbekistan do not yet permit private ownership of land.

A small private farm in Hungary
The land (approximately 5 ha) and the tractor are the farmer's property. In Central and Eastern Europe most agricultural land is today cultivated by individual farmers.

The *principle* of privatization must be distinguished from the *strategy* of how it is achieved. Various strategies of privatization have been adopted.[104] The Central and Eastern European countries, with the exception of Albania, chose restitution to former owners or a combination of restitution and distribution. In the CIS, countries that chose a strategy at all opted for distribution among farm members.

Two mechanisms have been employed in the distribution of land among farm members. In the Central and Eastern European countries, and in the Caucasus region and Moldova in the CIS, land and property were divided into physical plots (land parcels) and distributed among members as private property. In the remaining CIS countries, land and property were divided into shares representing claims to a notional portion of the total land and assets of the farm.

Some countries have been more successful than others in creating clear and secure land-tenure rights.

The privatization of farms and farmland has thus not necessarily implied the establishment of clear and secure rights of land tenure. In many countries where farmland has been allocated via shares rather than physical plots, privatization has failed to establish such rights. In Table 32, columns 3 and 4 illustrate these differences. Ukrainian and Russian land-share owners experience difficulties in converting their paper shares into physical plots, and it is doubtful that they would be able to trade such shares.[105]

Table 32

CHARACTERISTICS OF LAND RELATIONS IN THE TRANSITION COUNTRIES OF CENTRAL AND EASTERN EUROPE AND THE CIS

	(1) Potential private ownership	(2) Privatization strategy	(3) Allocation strategy	(4) Transferability
Central and Eastern Europe				
Albania	All land	Distribution	Plots	Buy/sell, leasing
Bulgaria	All land	Restitution	Plots	Buy/sell, leasing
Czech Republic	All land	Restitution	Plots	Buy/sell, leasing
Estonia	All land	Restitution	Plots	Buy/sell, leasing
Hungary	All land	Restitution + distribution	Plots	Buy/sell, leasing
Latvia	All land	Restitution	Plots	Buy/sell, leasing
Lithuania	All land	Restitution	Plots	Buy/sell, leasing
Poland	All land	Sale of state owned land	None	Buy/sell, leasing
Romania	All land	Restitution + distribution	Plots	Buy/sell, leasing
Slovakia	All land	Restitution	Plots	Buy/sell, leasing
CIS				
Armenia	All land	Distribution	Plots	Buy/sell, leasing
Azerbaijan	All land	Distribution	Plots	Buy/sell, leasing
Belarus	HH[2] plots only	None	None	Use rights non-transferable; buy/sell of HH plots dubious
Georgia	All land	Distribution	Plots	Buy/sell, leasing
Kazakhstan	HH plots only	None	Shares	Use rights transferable; buy/sell of HH plots dubious
Kyrgyzstan[1]	None	None	Shares	Use rights transferable
Moldova, Republic of	All land	Distribution	Plots	Buy/sell, leasing
Russian Federation	All land	Distribution	Shares	Leasing, buy/sell dubious
Tajikistan	None	None	Shares	Use rights transferable
Turkmenistan	All land	None	Intrafarm lease	Use rights non-transferable
Ukraine	All land	Distribution	Shares	Leasing, buy/sell dubious
Uzbekistan	None	None	Intrafarm lease	Use rights non-transferable

[1] Kyrgyzstan allowed private ownership of land following the June 1998 referendum, but the corresponding legislation is still not fully in place.
[2] HH = household.

Source: C. Csaki, Z. Lerman and S. Sotnikov. 2000. *Farm sector restructuring in Belarus: progress and constraints.* World Bank Technical Paper No. 475. Europe and Central Asia Environmentally and Socially Sustainable Development Series. Washington, DC, World Bank.

The creation of farms with an efficient ownership and management structure

Central and Eastern European countries and some CIS countries have dismantled large farms; other CIS countries have preserved them, albeit privatized.

Recognizing that privatization alone does not ensure an efficient ownership and management structure, Central and Eastern European countries and several CIS countries dismantled the large farms by restoring the land to previous owners or distributing it among farm employees. In the remaining CIS countries there has been little agreement on the appropriate governance structure of farms. These countries have preserved the large farms, albeit usually with private ownership. In many cases, collective farms were privatized by insiders, with the ownership of assets falling to the management and employees. But the *distribution* of assets (including land) was never clearly defined. This lack of clearly defined ownership has often allowed the de facto governance structure to continue. This can be summed up as:

- persistence of large landholdings with excess labour;
- permanent job rights;
- limited interest in the profits of the farm;
- residual claim on income by the state through discretionary taxation and debt collection;
- continued poor financial performance.

The primary objection to the dissolution of large farms has been the belief that large farms are more efficient than smaller farms because they enjoy economies of scale. In reality, however, neither size nor economies of scale are the issues at stake: far more important are the efficient ownership and management of farms, which require clearly assigned ownership rights to land, assets and income.

By dividing the farm into notional ownership shares the "privatized" successors of collective farms do not clearly assign these rights. To do so in an equitable manner the buildings, machinery and land assets would need to be divided up into physical plots and pieces, as is done in the dissolution of such farms. Instead, such insider share privatization simply represents another form of collective property with all its ensuing problems.

In a number of CIS countries there have been attempts to resolve this dilemma. For example, in Kazakhstan, the Russian Federation and Ukraine large companies have been allowed to lease or buy the notional shares in the farms. This has often resulted in improved management, new investment and increased profitability. Such farms may appear to square the circle of reforming socialist-era farms. They are often larger than even the largest corporate farms in the United States and are run in a business-like manner. However, it is difficult to tell whether such farms will remain viable in the longer run.

By contrast, farm individualization into private family-run farms has generated a large portion of land in individual family farms in most Central and Eastern European countries (Table 33). By 1997, Albania, Latvia and Slovenia had farming sectors with a share of land in individual farming comparable with those in developed market economies, and the same was true of Armenia and Lithuania by 2000.

The formation of a class of mid-sized commercial farms
The experience of other developed countries seems to support a certain (rather wide) range of farm sizes appropriate for

Table 33

SHARE OF AGRICULTURAL LAND IN INDIVIDUAL TENURE IN CENTRAL AND EASTERN EUROPE AND THE CIS

Country	Agricultural land in individual tenure		
	1990	1997	2000
		(Percentage)	
Central and Eastern Europe			
Albania	4	100	...
Bulgaria	13	52	...
Czech Republic	5	38	26
Estonia	6	63	79
Hungary	6	54	41
Latvia	5	95	94 [1]
Lithuania	9	67	94
Poland	77	82	...
Romania	12	67	85
Slovakia	5	11	13
Slovenia	92	96	...
CIS			
Armenia	4	33	100 [1]
Azerbaijan	3	9	...
Belarus	7	12	12
Georgia	7	24	66
Kazakhstan	0.2	20	29
Kyrgyzstan	1	23	...
Moldova, Republic of	9	27	50
Russian Federation	2	11	12 [1]
Tajikistan	2	7	...
Turkmenistan	0.2	0	...
Ukraine	7	17	18 [1]
Uzbekistan	2	4	...

[1] = 1999.

Sources: 2000: National Statistical Offices; 1990 and 1997: C. Csaki, Z. Lerman and S. Sotnikov. 2000. *Farm sector restructuring in Belarus: progress and constraints.* World Bank Technical Paper No. 475. Europe and Central Asia Environmentally and Socially Sustainable Development Series. Washington, DC, World Bank.

The creation of mid-sized farms has proceeded differently across the transition countries.

modern, competitive commercial farming. "Micro" farms below 0.5 ha produce primarily for themselves, and thus are not part of commercial agriculture. Large socialist-type farms have not been sustainable in Western countries. Between these two extremes lie what may be called "middle-class" farms, neither "micro farms" nor socialist-type behemoths.

Once again, privatization in the Central and Eastern European and CIS countries did not immediately result in the formation of a substantial middle class of competitive, commercial family farms. On the contrary, in the Central and Eastern European countries, the Caucasus region and Moldova, restitution and land distribution initially resulted in a large number of small farms, often consisting of numerous scattered land parcels. These farms are usually too small to be significant commercial production units, though they do produce for the market. In the remaining CIS countries, where socialist-size farms have been privatized, the ownership (and sometimes management) structure is collective, rather than individual and family based.

In countries where secure tenure rights have been established – including the right to buy, sell and lease freely – there is reason to believe that the still sizeable inequalities in land distribution may be temporary. As successful farmers lease or buy more land and as the assets of unsuccessful corporate farms are sold, the distribution of farms will gradually become more equal through the transfer of land and farm assets. Farm surveys support part of this evolutionary hypothesis in that they show that much of the land held in Central and Eastern Europe is currently leased, and that operational units are larger than ownership units. Agricultural policy can assist in this transition by facilitating the operation of land markets and allowing competition to alter the structure of farming, including allowing uncompetitive individual and corporate farms to fail. Public assistance for the consolidation of small plots to build a more competitive farm structure can also help.

There is greater concern regarding the distribution of land in countries where secure land-tenure rights have not been established and where farm restructuring has involved share distribution. Without secure land-tenure rights, including the right of transfer, an evolutionary consolidation of small land plots into mid-sized farms is unlikely. Indeed, without the distribution of land shares in the form of physical plots, it is unlikely that corporate farms will break up. A long-term consequence of unequal land distribution is therefore likely to be the low growth of agricultural incomes in these countries.[106]

Conclusions

Central and Eastern European countries, the Caucasus region and Moldova seem to have made more progress towards providing a viable base for a market economy agriculture than the remaining CIS countries. The allocation strategies chosen by the latter countries have not succeeded in ensuring secure, clear and transferable land-tenure rights and an efficient farm ownership and management structure. Although all countries in the region now have augmented rights of individual tenure

Table 34

SHARE OF AGRICULTURAL LAND AND AVERAGE SIZE OF INDIVIDUAL FARMS IN THE UNITED STATES, THE EU AND SELECTED CENTRAL AND EASTERN EUROPEAN AND CIS COUNTRIES

Country	Year	Individual farms		Corporate farms	
		Share of agricultural land	Average size	Share of agricultural land	Average size
		(Percentage)	(ha)	(Percentage)	(ha)
United States	1998	92	173	8	676
European Union[1]	...	97	...	3	...
Central and Eastern Europe					
Albania	1998	100	1	–	
Bulgaria	1996	52	1	48	681
Czech Republic	2000	26	19	74	989
Estonia	2000	79	3	21	471
Hungary	2000	41	3	59	457
Latvia	1996	95	14	5	314
Lithuania	1997	78	4	22	372
Poland	1996	84	6	16	468
Romania	2000	85	...	15	...
Slovakia	2000	13	1	87	1 361
Slovenia	1997	94	5	6	333
CIS					
Armenia	1999	100	1	–	
Belarus	2000	12	1	88	3 130
Georgia	2000	66	1	34	100
Kazakhstan	2000	29	15	71	11 248
Kyrgyzstan	1996	9	6	91	6 423
Moldova, Republic of	2000	50	1	50	917
Russian Federation	1999	12	1	88	5 593
Ukraine	1999	18	1	82	1 850

[1] EU(10).

Note: Share of agricultural land in individual farms may differ somewhat from the figures in Table 33 owing to different sources.

Source: National Statistical Offices. European Commission. 2001. *The agricultural situation in the European Union: 1999 report.* Brussels, European Commission.

Women on a private farm preparing sacks of onions for sale at the general market of Budapest

The creation of a class of mid-sized commercial farms is an important way in which land reform can contribute to the building of a market agriculture.

Privatization alone does not create an efficient agricultural market economy; it also requires active government policies.

and more family farms, more robust reform is still required in many countries, especially CIS countries.

The task of building a competitive and sustainable market agriculture in the post-socialist economies consists of creating the policy environment and institutions of a market economy and fostering new commercial farms that respond flexibly to market signals and produce and market competitively. Privatization alone has not accomplished this task. Rather, experience has shown that the establishment of clear rights of land tenure, efficient ownership and management structures and the creation of a class of mid-sized commercial farms are the result of more comprehensive policies. These include measures to transfer land and other production assets to individuals, measures to facilitate a well-functioning market for land sales and leasing, and a policy environment that allows farms to adjust in response to market conditions and does not prop up the old, uncompetitive structures.

VI. Developed market economies

OVERVIEW
General economic performance

Economic growth in the developed market economies slowed in 2001.

Average real GDP in the developed market economies rose by 3.8 percent in 2000.[107] However, economic activity was already beginning to slow down owing to the rise in energy prices, a reassessment of corporate profitability and a tightening of monetary policy in late 1999 and 2000 in the United States and in the EU. In particular, developments in the information technology (IT) sector – the declining investment and output and consequent fall in IT-related trade – contributed significantly to the slowdown. The aftermath of the events of 11 September exacerbated the downturn, and real GDP growth in the developed market economies was projected at 1.1 percent for 2001.

Economic activity remained strong in the United States, where real GDP grew by 4.1 percent in 2000, the third year in a row that output expanded at more than 4 percent. However, in mid-2000 economic growth began to slow and following the 11 September terrorist attacks economic activity weakened further, causing real GDP growth to fall to about 1.3 percent in 2001.

In Japan, real GDP expanded by 1.5 percent after rising by only 0.8 percent in 1999 and contracting by 1 percent in 1998. Relatively strong investment and export growth helped generate the positive outcome for 2000. Weakened external demand and a fall in private and public investment underlie the contraction in economic growth of 0.5 percent projected for 2001.

Australia and New Zealand saw real GDP expand by 3.3 and 3.8 percent, respectively, in 2000. Output growth was projected to slow in 2001 but was expected to exceed 2 percent growth in both countries.

The EU area saw real GDP rise by 3.4 percent in 2000, an improvement over the 2.7 percent recorded in 1999. Weakened domestic demand, the downturn in the equity markets and the slowdown in external demand led to a reduction in economic growth in the second half of 2000, with the downturn being most marked in Germany. For 2001, output growth is estimated at 1.8 percent.

Agricultural performance

The year 2000 was marked by relatively slow agricultural production growth in the developed market economies, with

Figure 38

DEVELOPED MARKET ECONOMIES: SELECTED INDICATORS

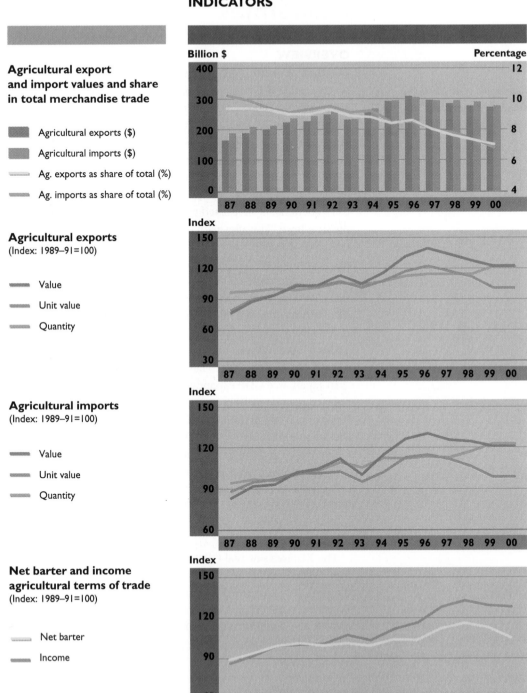

Agricultural export and import values and share in total merchandise trade

- Agricultural exports ($)
- Agricultural imports ($)
- Ag. exports as share of total (%)
- Ag. imports as share of total (%)

Agricultural exports
(Index: 1989–91=100)

- Value
- Unit value
- Quantity

Agricultural imports
(Index: 1989–91=100)

- Value
- Unit value
- Quantity

Net barter and income agricultural terms of trade
(Index: 1989–91=100)

- Net barter
- Income

DEVELOPED MARKET ECONOMIES: SELECTED INDICATORS

Real GDP
(Percentage change from preceding year)

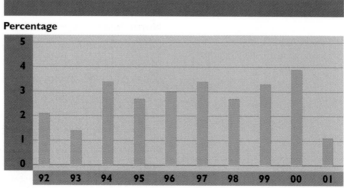

Percentage

Dietary energy supplies
(kcal per capita per day)

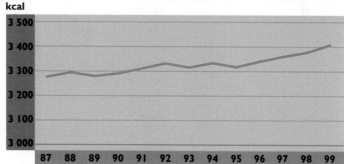

kcal

Agricultural production
(Index 1989–91=100)

▬▬ Total agricultural production

▬▬ Per capita food production

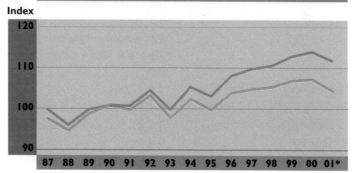

Index

* Preliminary

Source: FAO and IMF

The year 2000 was a year of relatively slow agricultural output growth.

output expanding by only 0.9 percent after growth of 2.1 percent the previous year. The slowdown was especially pronounced for livestock production, which rose by only 0.4 percent, whereas crop production increased by 1.4 percent.

Among the developed market economy subregions, only North America saw significant output growth in 2000, with total production increasing by an estimated 2 percent, marginally up from the 1.8 percent growth achieved in 1999. This reflects an expansion of 2.2 percent in the United States and only 0.5 percent in Canada (following a growth in output of more than 6 percent during the previous two years).

Agricultural production in the countries of the EU remained basically stagnant in 2000, recording a contraction of 0.2 percent. This was the net result of a 1.3 percent drop in livestock production and a 1.4 percent increase in crop production. Most of the large countries in the Union recorded negative growth rates, in most cases resulting from poor output performance in both the crop and livestock sectors. In France, Germany, Italy and the United Kingdom, agricultural output fell by between 0.5 and 3.0 percent. Relatively strong output growth of between 3 and 9 percent was seen in Finland, Greece and Spain.

Japan also saw a modest decline in agricultural production of around 0.5 percent in 2000, while the developed market economies of Oceania saw agricultural output increase by only 0.6 percent in 2000 after recording growth of 3.4 percent in 1999. The slowdown was entirely due to the lower output recorded in Australia. New Zealand saw output rise by 5.8 percent, recovering from the decline in output of 5.2 percent in 1999.

Agricultural production actually declined in 2001, according to preliminary estimates.

Preliminary estimates for 2001 point to a contraction of close to 2 percent in total agricultural production in the developed market economies. This contraction is largely attributable to a reduction in output of about 2.5 percent in the EU, with a significant decline in cereal production. Wheat output in the EU declined by more than 12 percent following a reduction in the area cultivated and adverse weather conditions. Barley and oat production is also expected to have fallen quite sharply. Poor weather conditions adversely affected grain production, in particular the wheat crop in France, the Netherlands, Spain and the United Kingdom. In Spain, harsh drought conditions had a substantial negative impact on the unirrigated wheat crop.

In North America, agricultural production appears to have declined significantly in 2001. A reduction in cereal production, in particular, is expected, partly as a result of drought conditions

Table 35

NET PRODUCTION GROWTH RATES IN DEVELOPED MARKET ECONOMIES

Year	Agriculture	Crops	Cereals	Food	Livestock
			(Percentage)		
Developed market economies					
1992–96	1.5	2.6	4.0	1.6	0.9
1997	1.6	2.1	-2.1	1.5	0.9
1998	0.7	-0.1	2.9	1.2	1.9
1999	2.1	2.0	-2.7	2.0	1.7
2000	0.9	1.4	3.9	1.0	0.4
2001[1]	-1.9	-3.8	-8.0	-2.2	-0.4
EC					
1992–96	0.3	1.3	1.6	0.3	0.0
1997	0.3	1.2	-0.7	0.2	-0.1
1998	0.2	-0.8	3.4	0.2	1.7
1999	2.4	3.5	-4.6	2.3	0.6
2000	-0.2	1.4	6.9	-0.1	-1.3
2001[1]	-2.6	-4.1	-7.2	-2.6	-1.1
North America					
1992–96	3.0	3.8	5.8	3.1	2.4
1997	3.1	3.6	-1.8	3.2	1.3
1998	1.3	0.6	3.9	2.3	2.5
1999	1.8	0.2	-2.8	1.4	3.3
2000	2.0	1.5	1.4	2.2	2.0
2001[1]	-1.7	-3.2	-7.1	-2.3	-0.2
Oceania[2]					
1992–96	2.9	11.0	20.5	4.9	0.6
1997	2.1	-2.9	-10.7	1.2	4.6
1998	3.3	7.6	5.2	4.3	1.8
1999	3.4	9.5	8.7	4.2	0.5
2000	0.6	0.5	4.9	0.1	1.8
2001[1]	1.3	-6.7	-16.3	1.0	2.6
Japan					
1992–96	-0.4	-0.2	3.9	-0.3	-0.7
1997	0.2	1.4	-2.6	0.1	-0.7
1998	-4.4	-8.1	-10.4	-4.3	-0.7
1999	1.4	2.7	2.8	1.4	-0.1
2000	-0.5	-0.6	4.0	-0.5	-0.6
2001[1]	-1.2	-1.2	-4.3	-1.2	-0.9

[1] Preliminary.
[2] Australia and New Zealand.
Source: FAO.

in the wheat plains and partly because 2000 was a bumper year for coarse grains. Canada also saw a reduction in wheat production of about 23 percent – a result of drought in some parts of the country and excess moisture in others. Coarse grain production is estimated to be down by 8 percent over 2000.

A further decline in production of around 1 percent is estimated for Japan in 2001. Although rice yields were very high in 2001, the area cultivated was reduced by about 70 000 ha and rice output is estimated to have fallen by almost 5 percent.

Among the developed market economy subregions, only the countries of Oceania are estimated to have seen a modest increase in agricultural output of between 1 and 2 percent in 2001. This increase is largely due to growth in livestock production.

Agricultural policy changes[108]

No major agricultural policy reforms were introduced in 2001.

No major agriculture sector-wide reform programmes were introduced or announced in the developed market economies in 2001. In some countries, a degree of progress was made in implementing previously announced reforms, while important new developments, such as the United States Farm Bill and the mid-term review of the EU Agenda 2000 programme, are expected in 2002. Policy discussion in many countries focused on such areas as sustainable development, food safety, the environment, rural development, the multifunctional role of agriculture, market concentration and competition policy, but actual policy changes in these areas were few. Institutional changes in some countries reflected the increasing priority given to food safety and rural development issues.

The levels of support and degrees of market protection fell for some commodities but no new programmes to lower or phase out agricultural producer support prices were announced. A number of countries increased support prices for certain commodities. Some countries introduced or extended support measures to lower input costs, while Australia, Canada and the United States introduced or extended support measures to farmers facing a reduction in farm income.

Table 36
OECD INDICATORS OF SUPPORT TO AGRICULTURE[1]

Indicator	1986–88	1999–2001	1999	2000	2001[2]
PSE					
Billion $	239	248	273	242	231
Percentage PSE	38	33	35	32	31
TSE					
Billion $	302	330	357	321	311
Percentage TSE	2.3	1.3	1.4	1.3	1.3

[1] All OECD countries.
[2] Estimates.
Source: OECD. 2002. *Agricultural policies in OECD countries: monitoring and evaluation.* Paris.

Support to agriculture declined somewhat in 2000 and 2001, but remains high with wide differences among countries and commodities.

Support to agriculture and the degree of protection to the sector provided through various policy instruments remained high in the developed market economies, but varied widely among countries and commodities. In 2000, the overall support to agriculture for all the Organisation for Economic Co-operation and Development (OECD) countries, measured by OECD's total support estimate (TSE) (see Box 9), amounted to $321 billion, or about 1.3 percent of GDP. This figure marks a drop compared with that of the previous year and, in terms of percentage TSE, is well below the 1986–88 average of 2.3 percent of GDP. In 2001, the total TSE in the OECD area declined to $311 billion.

Support provided directly to agricultural producers in all OECD countries, as measured by OECD's producer support estimate (PSE) (see Box 9), decreased from $271 billion in 1999 to $242 billion in 2000. In 2001, PSE is estimated to have

Box 9

OECD INDICATORS OF SUPPORT

OECD uses a number of indicators to measure support to agriculture. Two key indicators are the producer support estimate (PSE) and the total support estimate (TSE), defined here.

Producer support estimate
This is an indicator of the annual monetary value of gross transfers from consumers (resulting from policies that keep domestic prices above world market levels) and from taxpayers (resulting from budgetary financed policies) to agricultural *producers*. The **percentage PSE** expresses producer support as a percentage of gross farm receipts.

Total support estimate
This is an indicator of the annual monetary value of all gross transfers from taxpayers and consumers arising from policy measures that support the *agriculture sector*. It includes transfers to producers (PSE) and general services provided to agriculture. The **percentage TSE** expresses overall support as a percentage of GDP.

declined further, to $231 billion. The fall in support over the last two years was mainly due to a narrowing of the gap between prices received by farmers and world prices. The PSE expressed as a percentage of gross farm receipts fell from an average of 38 percent in the 1986–88 period to 32 percent in 2000 and is estimated to have fallen by a further 1 percent in 2001, although the figures vary substantially among countries and commodities.

New policies setting environmental targets, reducing pollution or encouraging more sustainable agricultural production were introduced in a number of countries. Australia and the EU, for example, presented goals for biodiversity conservation. Other countries, including Belgium, France and Denmark, introduced measures to reduce pollution from livestock production, while measures to reduce pesticide

Wheat crop in a natural reserve in the Tiber Valley in Italy
The crop is grown without chemical fertilizers and artificial nutrients. A number of countries are introducing incentives for organic farming and more environmentally friendly production methods.

FAO/13383/A. LOMBARDI

Many countries are encouraging more environmentally friendly agricultural production.

levels were introduced in France, Denmark and the Netherlands. New or enhanced incentives in favour of organic farming were introduced in 2001 in Austria, France, Norway and Switzerland. These countries also increased payments to farmers to encourage them to adopt more environmentally friendly production methods. Australia and the United States saw the introduction or extension of important natural resource conservation programmes.

In 2001, as in the previous year, several policy measures were introduced following natural disasters or concern about animal, plant or human health. The EU continued to provide support to beef farmers hurt by weak demand following the bovine spongiform encephelopathy (BSE) crisis, and several Member States announced additional measures to help farmers affected by the BSE crisis and the foot-and-mouth disease outbreak.

Food safety is another priority area for many countries.

Many countries have continued to strengthen their institutional structures and regulatory frameworks in order to improve food safety. The establishment of the European Food Authority in the EU was a significant development in this regard. New agencies and systems are also being developed in a number of other countries. Biotechnology and its relationship with food safety and the environment continued to be central concerns for many consumers and governments. A number of international meetings were held in 2001 and several countries introduced mandatory labelling requirements for genetically modified foods, while others were proposing to do so.

An important development in the area of trade policies in 2001 was the removal by the EU and New Zealand of tariffs on imports from the 48 least developed countries, although in the case of the EU the removal will be delayed for a few years for rice, sugar and bananas. Norway and Poland have announced similar tariff removal programmes, to be implemented in 2002.

NOTES

1   Unless specified otherwise, the macroeconomic projections and estimates in this section are drawn from IMF. 2001. *World Economic Outlook*, December. Washington, DC.

2   IMF. 2001. *World Economic Outlook*, October. Washington, DC.

3   World Bank. *World Development Indicators 2001*. Washington, DC.

4   If South Africa is included, both investment and saving ratios diminish in the 1990s compared with the 1980s.

5   Op.cit., note 1.

6   FAO press release, May 2000.

7   FAO. 1994. *Women, agriculture and rural development, a synthesis report of the Africa region*. Rome.

8   FAO. 1998. *Rural women and food security: current situation and perspectives*. Rome.

9   K.A. Saito, H. Mekonnen and D. Spurling. 1994. *Raising productivity of women farmers in sub-Saharan Africa*. World Bank Discussion Paper 230. Washington, DC.

10 Op. cit., note 8.

11 Op. cit., note 9; and F. Orivel, 1995. Education primaire et croissance économique en Afrique sub-Saharienne: les conditions d'une relation efficace. *Revue d'Économie du Développement*, 1.

12 Specifically, per economically active person in agriculture.

13 C. Udry, J. Hoddinott, H. Alderman and L. Haddad.1995. Gender differentials in farm productivity: implications for household efficiency and agricultural policy. *Food Policy*, 20(5): 407–423; C. Udry. 1996. Gender, agricultural production, and the theory of the household. *Journal of Political Economy*, 104(5): 1010–1046; P. Moock. 1976. The efficiency of women as farm managers: Kenya. *American Journal of Agricultural Economics: Proceedings Issue*, 58(5): 831–835; and op. cit., note 9.

14 C. Udry, J. Hoddinott, H. Alderman and L. Haddad. 1995. Gender differentials in farm productivity: implications for household efficiency and agricultural policy. *Food Policy*, 20(5): 407–423; and C. Udry. 1996. Gender, agricultural production, and the theory of the household. *Journal of Political Economy*, 104(5): 1010–1046.

15 Op. cit., note 9.

16 P. Moock. 1976. The efficiency of women as farm managers: Kenya. *American Journal of Agricultural Economics: Proceedings Issue*, 58(5): 831–835.

17 Op. cit., note 9.

18 M. Rekha. 1995. *Women, land and sustainable development: barriers to women's access to land*. Washington, DC, International Centre for Research on Women Reports and Publications.

19 Op. cit., note 8.

20 A.R. Quisumbing. 1996. Male–female differences in agricultural productivity: methodological issues and empirical evidence. *World Development*, 24(10): 1579–1595.

21 FAO. 1989. *Report on the Global Consultation on Agricultural Extension*. Rome.

22 A review of the economics of tsetse control/eradication can be found in L.T. Budd. 1999. *DFID-funded tsetse and trypanosomosis research and development since 1980. Vol. 2 Economic Analysis*. Pre-publication draft. London, DFID; and International Livestock Centre for Africa/International Laboratory for Research on Animal Diseases. 1988. *Livestock production in tsetse affected areas of Africa*. Proceedings of a meeting held 23–27 November 1987, Nairobi, Kenya. Two volumes. For wide-ranging information also see the PAAT Web site (available at: www.fao.org/paat/html/home.htm).

23 Trypanosomiasis transmitted by the tsetse fly (*Glossina* sp.) only occurs in Africa but other members of the genus Trypanosoma cause diseases outside Africa. There are three main tsetse-transmitted species of trypanosomiasis and over 20 species of tsetse. About 2–10 percent of tsetse flies carry animal-infective trypanosomes while only about 0.1 percent carry human-infective trypanosomes.

24 J.C.M. Trail, K. Sones, J.M.C. Jibbo, J. Durkin, D.E. Light and M. Murray. 1985. *Productivity of Boran cattle maintained by chemoprophylaxis under trypanosomiasis risk*. ILCS Research Report No. 9. Addis Ababa, International Livestock Centre for Africa.

25 WHO. *The World Health Report 2000*. Geneva. The disease had practically disappeared between 1960 and 1965 but is today resurgent. For further information on sleeping sickness see the WHO fact sheet (available at www.who.int/health-topics/afrtryps.htm).

26 When trypanosomiasis prevalence exceeds 30 percent it is virtually impossible to practise mixed farming. See B.S. Hursey and J. Slingenbergh. 1995. The tsetse fly and its effects on agriculture in sub-Saharan Africa. *World Animal Review*, 84/85: 67–73.

27 B. Swallow. 1999. *Impacts of trypanosomiasis on African agriculture*. Nairobi, International Livestock Research Institute.

28 L.T. Budd. 1999. *DFID-funded tsetse and trypanosomosis research and development since 1980. Vol. 2: Economic Analysis*. Pre-publication draft. London, DFID.

29 M. Kamuanga, C. Antoine, A.-S. Brasselle, B.M. Swallow, G.D.M. d'Ieteren and B. Bauer. 1999. *Impacts of tsetse control on migration, livestock production, cropping practices and farmer-herder conflicts in the Mouhoun Valley of southern Burkina Faso*. Paper presented at the 25th meeting of the International Scientific Council for Trypanosomiasis Research and Control (ISCTRC), Mombasa, Kenya. Quoted in Budd, 1999 (op. cit., note 28).

30 M. Gilbert, C. Jenner, J. Pender, D. Rogers, J. Slingenbergh and W. Wint. 1999. *The development and use of the Programme Against African Trypanosomiasis Information System*. Paper prepared for the International

Scientific Council for Trypanosomiasis Research and Control (ISCTRC) Conference, 27 September to 1 October 1999. Mombasa, Kenya.

31 FAO. 1998. Cost of trypanosomiasis. *Agriculture 21*. Rome.

32 Q. Jihui and T. Tisue. 2000. Achievable breakthrough: viewpoint on the challenge of creating tsetse-free zones in sub-Saharan Africa. *IAEA Bulletin*, 42/1: 47–50.

33 F.E. Brandl. 1988. *Economics of trypanosomiasis control in cattle. Farming systems and resource economics in the tropics.* Vol. 1. Kiel, Wissenschaftsverlag Vauk.

34 Ibid.

35 Op. cit., note 28.

36 Macroeconomic estimates and projections in this section are from IMF. 2001. *World Economic Outlook*. December, Washington, DC.

37 C.A. Carter and A. Estrin. 2001. *China's trade integration and impacts on factor markets.* Mimeo, University of California, Davis, California, USA. January; and S. Li, F. Zhai and Z.Wang. 1999. *The global and domestic impact of China joining the World Trade Organization. A project report.* Beijing, Development Research Centre, The State Council, China.

38 K. Anderson and C.Y. Peng. 1998. Feeding and fueling China in the 21st Century. *World Development*, 26(8): 1413–1429.

39 W. Martin. 2002 (forthcoming). Implication of reform and WTO accession for China's agricultural policies. *Economies in Transition*.

40 National Bureau of Statistics of China.

41 A. Nyberg. and S. Rozelle. 1999. *Accelerating China's rural transformation.* World Bank, Washington, DC.

42 J. Huang and H. Bouis. 1996. *Structural changes in demand for food in Asia.* A 2002 Vision for Food, Agriculture, and Environment, Discussion Paper 11. Washington, DC, International Food Policy Research Institute; and J. Huang and S. Rozelle. 1998. Market development and food consumption in rural China. *China Economic Review*, 9(1998): 25–45.

43 J. Huang and C. Chen. 1999. *Effects of trade liberalization on agriculture in China: institutional and structural aspects.* United Nations ESCAP CGPRT Centre, Bogor, Indonesia.

44 National Bureau of Statistics of China.

45 J. Huang and H. Ma. 1998. The 20-year reform and the role of agriculture in China: capital flow from rural to urban and from agriculture to industry. *Reform*, 5: 56–63; op. cit., note 41.

46 N.R. Lardy. 1995. The role of foreign trade and investment in China's economic transition. *China Quarterly*, 144: 1065–1082.

47 National Bureau of Statistics of China.

48 A. de Brauw, J. Huang, S. Rozelle, L. Zhang and Y. Zhang. 2002 (forthcoming). The evolution of China's rural labour markets during the reform. *Journal of Comparative Economics*.

49 Ibid.

50 A. de Brauw, J. Huang and S. Rozelle. 2001. *Sequencing and the success*

of gradualism: empirical evidence from China's agricultural reform. Working Paper. Department of Agricultural and Resource Economics, University of California, Davis, California, USA.

51 N. Lardy. 2001. *Integrating China in the global economy.* Brookings Institution, Washington, DC.

52 J. Huang and S. Rozelle. 2001. *The nature and extent of current distortions to agricultural incentives in China.* Paper presented at the second project meeting on WTO Accession, Policy Reform and Poverty Reduction in China. World Bank Resident Mission, Beijing, 26–27 October 2001.

53 T. Sicular. 1988. Plan and market in China's agricultural commerce. *Journal of Political Economy* 96(2): 383–87.

54 Op. cit., note 52.

55 The Uruguay Round Agreement on Agriculture foresaw the gradual reduction, at different rates for developed and developing countries, but not the elimination, of export subsidies. Least developed countries are exempt from export subsidy reduction commitments.

56 W. Martin. 2002 (forthcoming). Implication of reform and WTO accession for China's agricultural policies. *Economies in Transition.*

57 Op. cit., note 43.

58 Op. cit., note 56.

59 Op. cit., note 50.

60 Op. cit., note 52; A. Park, H. Jin, S. Rozelle and J. Huang. (Forthcoming.) Market emergence and transition: transition costs, arbitrage, and autarky in China's grain market. *American Journal of Agricultural Economics.*

61 National Bureau of Statistics of China.

62 L. Brandt, J. Huang, G. Li and S. Rozelle. (Forthcoming.) Land rights in China: facts, fictions, and issues. *China's Economic Review.*

63 Ministry of Agriculture. 2001. *China Agricultural Development Report, 2001.* Beijing, China Agricultural Press.

64 L. Zhang, Y. Zhang, J. Huang and S. Rozelle. 2001. *The evolution of land rights in China in the 21st century.* Working paper. Centre for Chinese Agricultural Policy, Chinese Academy of Sciences, Beijing.

65 Op. cit., note 63.

66 M. Shen. *Financial reforms and China's rural economic performance.* Department. of Economics, Stanford University, Stanford, California, USA. (Ph.D. thesis)

67 J. Huang and H. Ma. 1998. The 20-year reform and the role of agriculture in China: capital flow from rural to urban and from agriculture to industry. *Reform,* 5: 56–63.

68 J. Stigliz and A. Weiss. 1981. Credit rationing in markets with imperfect information. *American Economic Review,* 71(3): 393–410. June.

69 Cheng shows that China's AMS in the entire period of the 1990s was negative. See G. Cheng. 2000. *Impacts of WTO Agreement on Agriculture on China's agricultural development.* Beijing, China Economic Press.

Ma claims that the subsidies provided by government to agriculture, from production to consumption and marketing, were less than 2.3 percent of agricultural output in 1999. It is worth noting that most of these subsidies went to maintain an expensive domestic grain and cotton quota procurement system and export subsidies for maize and cotton. The former is being phased out and the latter was removed on 1 January 2002. Even the limit on AMS measures might not be binding since it is unlikely that China can afford high budgetary spending on agricultural subsidies. See M. Ma. 2001. *Agricultural subsidies: the last stumbling block to China's entry to the WTO?* Working paper. Hong Kong SAR, Deutsche Bank.

70 Op. cit., note 52.

71 J. Huang and R. Hu. 2002. *Funding options for agriculture research in the People's Republic of China.* Project report. Agricultural and Social Sector Department, Asian Development Bank, Manila.

72 Ministry of Agriculture. *China Agricultural Development Report, 2000.* Beijing, China Agricultural Press.

73 Unless otherwise specified, macroeconomic estimates and projections in this section are drawn from IMF. 2001. *World Economic Outlook,* December. Washington, DC.

74 Latin American and Caribbean countries remain nevertheless significantly less dependent on food imports than most other developing countries; the agricultural/total imports share is currently around 25 percent in sub-Saharan Africa, 18 percent in the Near East and North Africa and 8 percent in Asia and the Pacific.

75 The share of developing countries as a whole in world agricultural exports has plunged from around 35 percent during the 1970s to 25 percent in recent years. Only Asia and the Pacific and Latin America and the Caribbean regions have been able to maintain or consolidate their position in world markets. The counterpart of the developing countries' reduction in market share has been a strong gain on the part of industrial countries, in particular the EU. Indeed, while in the early 1970s the EU(15) accounted for around 30 percent of world commodity exports, this share is now about 40–45 percent. Most of this increase reflects intensified trade among EU member countries. Excluding intratrade, however, EU(15) exports still represent 18 percent of the world total.

76 Although the focus of this review is on primary commodities, the diversification of the product base was more significant for products with greater value added (see FAO. 1997. *The State of Food and Agriculture 1997.* Rome, Special chapter). The chapter indicates that Latin America and the Caribbean's ratio of agro-industrial production to agricultural GDP was around 40 percent by the mid-1990s, compared with around 20 percent for the other developing country regions. A significant part of this production is for external markets.

The region accounted for around 12 percent of the world's exports, and around 4 percent of imports, of industrially processed food products in 1994. The region has seen spectacular examples of agro-industrial development and trade expansion. For instance, the production of juices from tropical products in Brazil rose more than twentyfold between the mid-1980s and the mid-1990s. Chile's "case study" success as an export-oriented agricultural industry was based not only on fresh fruit but also on the development of processed products such as wine and food preserves. Argentina's food-processing industry has a long-established tradition; the Bunge y Born cereal transformation multinational is one of the largest in the world.

77   The dependence on industrialized country markets, especially the United States, is even more marked for non-agricultural products. About 70 percent of all merchandise exports from Latin America and the Caribbean are destined for industrialized countries; nearly half of the region's total exports go to the United States.

78   A more thorough analysis of long-term trends in agricultural terms of trade will be found in a forthcoming publication prepared for FAO by Prof. George P. Zanias: *The evolution of primary commodity terms of trade and the implications for developing countries*. This study confirms the tendency for net barter agricultural terms of trade to deteriorate in all developing country regions since the early 1980s, but also confirms the gains in purchasing capacity achieved by agricultural exports, especially since the late 1980s – a feature attributed mainly to export diversification.

79   Average tariff protection in agriculture in the industrialized countries is about nine times higher than in manufacturing.

80   See, for example, OECD. 2001. *Agricultural policies in OECD countries. monitoring and evaluation*. Paris. The report states: "Despite some shift away from market price support and output payments, these continue to be the dominant forms of support in most countries, insulating farmers from world market signals and distorting global production and trade."

81   ECLAC. 1994. *Latin America and the Caribbean: Policies to improve linkages with the global economy*. Santiago, Chile.

82   These issues have been discussed in detail in various sections and special chapters of *The State of Food and Agriculture*. See in particular: 1995, Agricultural trade: entering a new era?; 1997, The agroprocessing industry and economic development; 2001, The future of the agricultural trading environment: issues in the current round of negotiations on agriculture.

83   Macroeconomic estimates and projections in this section are drawn from IMF. 2001. *World Economic Outlook*, October and/or December. Washington, DC.

84   Economist Intelligence Unit. Turkey: *Country Report 2001*. London.

85 Bahrain, Kuwait, Oman, Qatar, Saudi Arabia and the United Arab
    Emirates.

86 FAO. 2001. *The State of Food and Agriculture 2001*, pp. 166–171. Rome.

87 N. Chbouki. 1992. *Spatio-temporal characteristics of drought as inferred
    from tree-ring data in Morocco*. University of Arizona. (Ph.D. thesis); and
    C.W. Stockton. 1988. Current research progress toward
    understanding drought. In *Drought, water management and food
    production*, Proceedings, International conference, Agadir, Morocco,
    21–24 November 1985.

88 Intergovernmental Panel on Climate Change. 2001. *Special report on the
    regional impacts of climate change: an assessment of vulnerability*. Geneva.

89 Ibid.

90 Op. cit., note 86.

91 The thresholds indicative of periodic water shortage, chronic water
    shortage and absolute water shortage are 1 500 m^3, 1 000 m^3 and
    500 m^3 of renewable freshwater per person per year, respectively.

92 FAO. 1997. *Irrigation in the Near East Region in figures*. Water Report
    No. 9. Rome.

93 World Bank. 2001. *Global economic prospects and the developing
    countries*. Washington, DC. At the same time, the proportion of people
    living on less than US$1 per day declined slightly.

94 *Le Programme national de lutte contre les effets de la sécheresse*. 2000.
    Publication du Comité Inter-Gouvernements Permanent du
    Développement Rural; Secrétariat général du Comité, Ministère de
    l'agriculture, Rabat, Morocco, April 2000.

95 Ameziane. 2000. *Stratégies d'adaptation à la sécheresse*. Colloque
    national de l'agriculture et du développement rural, Rabat, 19–20 July
    2000. Ministère de l'agriculture, Rabat, Morocco.

96 FAO/TCOR. 2000. *Jordan: Drought impact assessment and project profile*.
    Rome.

97 UN interagency mission report on the extreme drought in Iran;
    FAO/TCOR report on drought impact assessment and proposal of
    project profiles, FAO, Rome, 2001.

98 Central and Eastern Europe includes: Albania, Bosnia and Herzegovina,
    Bulgaria, Croatia, the Czech Republic, Estonia, Hungary, Latvia,
    Lithuania, Macedonia, Poland, Romania, Slovakia, Slovenia and
    Yugoslavia. The CIS includes: Armenia, Azerbaijan, Belarus, Georgia,
    Kazakhstan, the Republic of Moldova, the Russian Federation,
    Tajikistan, Turkmenistan, Ukraine and Uzbekistan.

99 Macroeconomic estimates and projections in this section are drawn
    from IMF. 2001.*World Economic Outlook*, December. Washington, DC.

100 Preliminary figures. FAO.

101 These policies were characterized by strict production planning, low
    wages, little investment and (in the former Soviet Union) considerable
    controls on movement of the rural population.

102 L. Wong and V. Ruttan. 1990. A comparative analysis of agriculture productivity trends in centrally planned economies. *In* K. Gray, ed. *Soviet agriculture: comparative perspectives*, pp. 23–47. Ames, IA, USA, Iowa State University Press.

103 Z. Lerman. 1998. Does land reform matter? Some experiences from the former Soviet Union. *European Review of Agricultural Economics*, 25: 307–330.

104 J. Swinnen. 1997. The choice of privatization and decollectivization policies in central and eastern European agriculture: observations and political economy hypotheses. *In* J. Swinnen, ed. *Political economy of agrarian reform in central and eastern Europe*. Aldershot, UK, Ashgate.

105 Z. Lerman, K. Brooks and C. Csaki. 1994. *Land reform and farm restructuring in Ukraine*. World Bank Discussion Paper No. 270. Washington, DC; and M. Pugachev. 2000. *Organizational forms of the new agricultural enterprises in Ukraine*. Ukraine Agricultural Policy Project discussion paper. Kiev, Ukraine, Iowa State University, Institute for Policy Reform.

106 C. Csaki, Z. Lerman and S. Sotnikov. 2001. *Farm debt in the CIS: a multi-country study of the major causes and proposed solutions*. World Bank Discussion Paper No. 424. Washington, DC.

107 Macroeconomic estimates and projections are drawn from IMF. 2001. *World Economic Outlook*, December. Washington, DC.

108 This section draws on OECD. 2002. *Agricultural policies in OECD countries: monitoring and evaluation 2002*. Paris.

PART III

AGRICULTURE AND GLOBAL PUBLIC GOODS TEN YEARS AFTER THE EARTH SUMMIT

I. The role of agriculture and land in the provision of global public goods

INTRODUCTION

Ten years after the Earth Summit in Rio de Janeiro, the World Summit on Sustainable Development will review implementation of Agenda 21.

Ten years after the United Nations Conference on Environment and Development (UNCED) held in Rio de Janeiro in 1992 – also known as the Earth Summit or Rio-92 – South Africa will be hosting the "World Summit on Sustainable Development" in Johannesburg. At the Rio Summit, world leaders adopted Agenda 21, a blueprint for attaining sustainable development in the twenty-first century. At the Johannesburg Summit, to be held in August–September 2002, attention will focus on many of the key challenges and opportunities the global community faces in implementing the various chapters of Agenda 21.

FAO is the Task Manager for four chapters of Agenda 21, namely: Planning and management of land resources (Chapter 10), Combating deforestation (Chapter 11), Sustainable mountain development (Chapter 13), and Sustainable agricultural and rural development (Chapter 14). It is also a major partner in the implementation of several other chapters of Agenda 21, notably, Combating desertification and drought (Chapter 12), Biological diversity (Chapter 15), Oceans and seas (Chapter 17), Freshwater (Chapter 18) and Toxic chemicals (Chapter 19), and in the implementation of some of the multilateral environmental agreements (MEAs) that came out of Rio-92. These include the United Nations Framework Convention on Climate Change (UNFCCC), the Convention on Biological Diversity (CBD) and the Convention to Combat Desertification and Drought in those Countries Experiencing Serious Drought and/or Desertification, particularly in Africa (UNCCD).[1]

The concept of global public goods is gaining importance in discussions on sustainable development.

A concept that has gained importance in the discussions on sustainable development leading up to the Johannesburg Summit is that of global public goods (GPGs). This concept is increasingly viewed as a useful framework for addressing global environmental problems and increasing political will and financing for better coordinated global efforts. A large body of recently available literature has focused on various aspects of GPGs, such as health, knowledge, cultural heritage, financial stability, peace and security.[2] The importance of GPGs with regard to agriculture and natural resources, however, has received less attention in this debate.

ECONOMIC CONCEPT OF LOCAL AND GLOBAL PUBLIC GOODS

The concept of public goods is linked to the economic notions of externalities and market failure. An externality refers to a situation where, for example, a firm's actions have unintended or unwanted side-effects that benefit (positive externality) or harm (negative externality) another party that would otherwise not be associated with the firm's product.[3] In general, the benefit or cost imposed is not compensated for through market transactions. Market failure occurs when the positive contributions or negative consequences of an action are not adequately reflected in the market price of the related products. These are, thus, either over- or undersupplied.

Public goods are a special case of externalities and are goods for which consumption cannot be confined to a particular consumer or group of consumers.[4] Strictly speaking, pure public goods are goods having characteristics of non-excludability and non-rivalry in consumption.[5]

Pure public goods exhibit the characteristics of complete non-excludability and complete non-rivalry, while goods characterized by complete excludability and rivalry are termed *private goods*. Between these two extremes, a series of so-called quasi-public goods are characterized by different degrees of non-excludability and non-rivalry. For example, while actions to promote biodiversity and landscape conservation or to mitigate climate change are generally considered as pure public goods, national parks with free access could be considered as non-excludable, but rival in consumption. Likewise, national parks with regulation or entry fees, and those without congestion, could be considered as excludable, but non-rival.

Public goods are often location specific – for example, flood control, the off-site effects of soil erosion and watershed protection – and can be referred to as *local public goods*. However, some extend beyond the local or regional area, and their impact is transboundary in nature. Public goods whose impact is global in nature are referred to as *global public goods*. Examples could include biodiversity and global climate change mitigation. Kaul, Grunberg and Stern provide the following definition of a GPG:

> *A GPG is a public good with benefits that are strongly universal in terms of countries (covering more than one group of countries), people (accruing to several, preferably all, population groups) and generations (extending to both current and future generations, or at least meeting the needs of current generations without foreclosing development options for future generations).[6]*

Global public goods are goods with universal benefits but provided by a smaller group.

PUBLIC GOODS ASSOCIATED WITH THE LAND-CLUSTER CHAPTERS OF AGENDA 21

Table 37 illustrates some of the public goods associated with the land-cluster chapters of Agenda 21 (the list should not necessarily be considered as exhaustive). These include public goods that are of local and global nature and semi-public goods characterized by different degrees of rivalry and excludability. The public goods are also classified according to the local, regional or global nature of their impact.

Agriculture and land can provide or contribute to important global public goods: biodiversity, climate change mitigation and others.

Several land-use options, outlined in Chapter 10, are aimed at promoting the conservation of biodiversity through the maintenance of species diversity and restoration of degraded lands. Such measures also have the potential to make the largest contribution to incremental carbon sequestration in both soil and biomass and promote endangered species in the surrounding areas.

Chapter 11 – Combating deforestation – also addresses pure public goods such as biodiversity, the stability of the

Table 37

PUBLIC GOODS ASSOCIATED WITH THE LAND-CLUSTER CHAPTERS OF AGENDA 21 AND THE RANGE OF THEIR IMPACT

Chapter of Agenda 21	Associated public good	Range of spillover
10 – Planning and management of land resources	Ecosystem stability	Regional, global
	Biodiversity conservation	Local, regional, global
	Carbon sequestration	Global
11 – Combating deforestation	Forest biodiversity	Local, regional, global
	Ecosystem stability	Regional, global
	Wildlife	Local, regional, global
	Reduction of greenhouse gas emission from forest fires	Local, regional, global
	Carbon sequestration	Global
12 – Combating desertification and drought	Incremental carbon sequestration	Global
	Protection of waterbodies	Local, regional, global
	Biodiversity conservation in drylands	Local, regional, global
13 – Sustainable mountain development	Ecosystem stability	Regional, global
	Hydrological stability	Local, regional
	Carbon sequestration	Global
14 – Sustainable agriculture and rural development	Conservation of agrobiodiversity	Local, regional, global
	Carbon sequestration	Global
15 – Biological diversity	Conservation of agrobiodiversity	Local, regional, global
	Carbon sequestration	Global

hydrological cycle and global climate system, and the maintenance or restoration of ecosystem stability (the latter having the characteristics of a local or regional public good). Combating desertification (Chapter 12) and the rehabilitation of degraded and mountain ecosystems (Chapter 13) can contribute to wildlife protection, biodiversity and climate change mitigation through carbon sequestration.

Public goods related to sustainable agriculture and rural development (Chapter 14) include widely shared resources and benefits such as the conservation of agrobiodiversity, farmers' knowledge on agrobiodiversity, watershed and flood protection benefits, and climate change mitigation through carbon sequestration. Agricultural research and knowledge provided by Consultative Group on International Agricultural Research (CGIAR) centres are vital contributions to GPGs in so far as these innovations are shared by the global community. Agriculture can also contribute to the generation of negative externalities, such as nutrient depletion, increase in flood frequency downstream and loss of natural forests and wetlands. Conventional and highly commercialized farming systems are often blamed for destroying species diversity and natural regeneration processes.

Other cases of transboundary or global public goods could include food safety, transboundary plant and animal pests and diseases,[7] the protection of international water bodies and the destruction of obsolete pesticide stocks.

PROGRESS IN THE PROVISION OF GLOBAL PUBLIC GOODS SINCE RIO-92

Progress in the provision of land-related global public goods has been slow since Rio-92.

Agenda 21 mainly calls for policy action towards reducing negative externalities generated by economic activities, but the provision of GPGs is not directly addressed. Indicators for measuring progress are therefore difficult to formulate and assess directly. A brief overview of progress with regard to some of the GPGs covered by Agenda 21 is provided below.

Rehabilitation of degraded lands. This includes the complete rehabilitation of severely degraded lands, improvement of currently used marginal lands or drylands and improvement in land-management practices. Information on all these aspects is sparse and the total area brought under land rehabilitation is difficult to assess. Some 20 percent of the world's susceptible drylands are affected by human-induced soil degradation, placing at risk the livelihoods of more than 1 000 million people.[8] Overall, progress has been very slow; soil loss and desertification persist with particular intensity and impact for many lower-

FAO/20565/M. MARZOT

The rich forests of Homs in the Syrian Arab Republic require careful management and control The maintenance of forest ecosystems contributes to wildlife protection, biodiversity and climate change mitigation through carbon sequestration

income countries. These degraded lands, if rehabilitated, could provide opportunities to enhance carbon sequestration and improve the livelihoods of people who are at risk.

Creation of protected areas of global importance. Efforts towards the conservation of biodiversity have mainly taken the form of establishing protected areas and reserves. Recent estimates show an increase in natural heritage reserves of global importance – to 131 million ha in developed countries and 133 million ha in developing countries. However, these areas have been created through the transfer of natural forests and shrubs into reserves, rather than through restoration of degraded lands.

Area under natural forests and plantations. The recent Global Forest Resources Assessment (see Box 1 on page 36) pointed to a reduction in natural forest cover of 16.1 million ha per year between 1990 and 2000 (from 3 808 million ha to 3 682 million ha). Plantation cover increased slightly from 155 million ha to 187 million ha over the same period. This resulted in a net loss of 12.5 million ha in forest cover, but the net rate of deforestation appears to have slowed when compared with that of the pre-1990 period.

Shift towards sustainable agricultural practices. Since Rio-92 there has been an increased emphasis on organic farming in developed countries and a shift towards conservation agriculture and integrated pest management (IPM) practices. This shift includes changes in cropping patterns to legume crops, the use of composted or uncomposted organic manure and the selection of appropriate species and varieties for the biological control of pests. Conservation agriculture has been adopted on almost 60 million ha in a diverse group of countries (see Box 10). These developments have helped greatly to enhance soil nutrition and soil organic matter and increase soil carbon storage.

Physical progress/potential in the direct promotion of GPGs. A recent estimate of global carbon storage predicted that sustainable harvesting and management of forests worldwide

Box 10

CONSERVATION AGRICULTURE

Conservation agriculture[1] is a strategy that can prevent, and even reverse, the declining soil fertility that commonly results from mechanized tillage or ploughing. The term conservation agriculture encompasses several techniques, but in general this method of crop production calls for reduced tillage and leaving crop residues on the land to protect the soil from wind, encourage biological activity and create organic matter in the soil. Leaving soil residues on the surface creates a structure that admits water, so that it reaches the plants' roots – instead of running off the surface and taking the soil with it.

Conservation agriculture began in the United States in the late 1970s as a reaction to growing soil erosion and fertility problems and the spiralling fuel costs that followed the 1973 oil embargo and made tillage an expensive practice. Today, about 60 million ha of farmland worldwide are cultivated in this way. The United States remains a leader in conservation agriculture, although the most dynamic growth in this method has occurred in South America. In southern Brazil, Argentina and Paraguay, as much as half the arable land is now cultivated using conservation agriculture.

After a few years, the benefits can include:
• higher and more stable yields;
• significant savings in irrigation water;
• less loss of topsoil;

could help in storing an additional 184 Tg (1 Tg = 10^{12} g) of carbon per year in forests and wood products during the next 50 years, with a range of 108–251 Tg per year.[9] Likewise, typical agricultural soils contain 100–200 tonnes of carbon per hectare over a depth of 1 metre. For intensively cultivated soils, a change in land-use practices could result in increased organic matter and carbon sequestration. However, it is difficult to assess to what extent land and forest resources have contributed to global climate change mitigation since Rio-92.

Physical progress in the conservation of biodiversity. In terms of conserving biodiversity, there have been significant improvements in the understanding of the nature and extent of change in major ecosystems, many of which are rich in biodiversity. Similarly, significant progress has been made in

• cost and energy savings from not ploughing;
• less runoff, reducing flooding and chemical contamination of rivers;
• better local water supplies because of reduced runoff;
• less silting of watercourses.

The conversion to conservation agriculture requires the purchase of different sowing equipment or adaptation of existing equipment. Because this method requires the minimal use of chemical pesticides, farmers must learn to control pests and diseases through IPM, which emphasizes the use of pests' natural enemies. This takes time, and because the pests and diseases are no longer controlled by ploughing, farmers who adopt conservation agriculture initially need to use more herbicide, not less. After a few years, however, the higher returns should cancel out the extra costs. Eventually, IPM enables farmers to reduce herbicide use greatly, or abandon it altogether.

Conservation agriculture has another desirable effect. Plants consist largely of carbon, and when they decay or are burned, they release carbon dioxide – the most significant single "greenhouse gas" contributing to climate change. With better management, agricultural land can return this carbon to the soil as organic matter – a process known as carbon sequestration.

[1] More information on conservation agriculture can be found at www.fao.org/ag/AGS/AGSE/agse_e/Main.htm

raising awareness and in the creation of protected areas and *ex situ* collections of gene pools of importance to food and agriculture.

Funding for agricultural research for the benefit of the global community has been declining.

CGIAR research as GPGs. Developing countries largely depend on the research and knowledge provided by international and national research centres. Thus, agricultural research and dissemination of knowledge in developing countries, especially where it concerns areas that have poor resources, could be considered as public goods. Specifically, research undertaken and knowledge disseminated by the CGIAR centres are often considered as GPGs[10] and are shared among the global community. Nevertheless, over the past ten years, funding for the CGIAR system and technological research has continuously declined, with the result that the CGIAR centres are experiencing increasing financial stress. Inadequate funding could affect the ability of the centres to conduct research and disseminate the knowledge required for improved food production and the alleviation of hunger and poverty.[11]

Expansion of the knowledge base. The documentation and registration of farmers' knowledge about agrobiodiversity could be considered another example of a GPG. National reporting to the CBD suggests that about two-thirds of countries have conducted such case studies (e.g. on pollinators, soil biota, integrated landscape management and farming systems).[12]

There has been progress in understanding and preserving biodiversity.

International undertaking on protecting plant genetic resources. Recognition of the concept of Farmers' Rights in the recent agreement reached on protecting plant genetic resources is an important step forward that will help protect global agrobiodiversity in gene banks, farmers' fields and in the wild. The concept of Farmers' Rights is intended to form the basis of a formal system of recognition and reward to encourage and enhance the continued role of farmers and rural communities in the conservation and sustainable use of plant genetic resources.[13] The agreement ensures that global benefits resulting from the use of plant genetic resources are shared equitably and calls for mandatory payments when commercial benefits are derived from the use of these resources.[14]

FINANCING GLOBAL PUBLIC GOODS

Compensation of the providers is indispensable for adequate provision of global public goods.

Because the consumption of public goods is non-excludable, there is a temptation (assuming a *beneficial* public good) to benefit without paying, i.e. free-riding. Consequently, mechanisms for compensating the providers are necessary to ensure that socially desirable levels of the good will be provided. This is true also for GPGs, where the benefits accrue to the global community while the providers are inevitably a much smaller group.

Agenda 21 calls for measures that generate both public and private goods, although funding mechanisms for their implementation were not specifically designated for one or the other. However, the global progress review report on financing for sustainable development provided a disappointing picture of the past performance in meeting the Rio-92 financing objectives and mechanisms.[15] Despite the promise made by developed countries of increasing official development assistance (ODA) to 0.7 percent of their gross national product (GNP), ODA after

Official development assistance has declined since Rio-92, particularly for agriculture and rural areas.

An example of a conservation agriculture technique in a maize crop in Brazil
Here the crop develops in a mulch cover that protects the entire soil surface from erosion, improving water infiltration and controlling weed growth

FAO/30003/T. FRIEDRICH

Rio-92 declined sharply from 0.33 to 0.22 percent of donor GNP, followed by a slight increase to 0.24 percent in 1999. ODA to agriculture (broadly defined) suffered a decline in real terms of more than 40 percent between 1988 and 1999. Within agriculture there were sharp decreases in ODA to agricultural services, crop production and forestry, although the share for environmental protection, research and training and extension increased.

Foreign direct investment (FDI) is concentrated on a few countries. FDI flows to most least developed countries have been negligible, and the agriculture and natural resource sectors have not benefited. FDI is motivated by market opportunities, which means that in general this financing instrument cannot be expected to generate much in the way of public goods. Moreover, it is not usually guided by sustainability considerations.[16]

On the other hand, global financing mechanisms such as the Global Environment Facility (GEF) – see Box 11 – have been an important source of funding for many multilateral environmental agreements, and thus the provision of GPGs. The GEF has helped fund over 800 projects; between 1991 and 1999 more than $2 billion were allocated to projects on biodiversity, climate change, international waters, ozone depletion and land degradation, and even larger amounts were mobilized as cofinancing. The largest portion of funding went to biodiversity projects, closely followed by projects on climate change.

Other funding mechanisms for global public goods have emerged.

Finally, some new sources are emerging for financing GPGs. National funds are being created under CBD, UNCCD and UNFCCC. Another source of funding is provided by the capital flows with technology transfer to developing countries envisaged under the Clean Development Mechanism (CDM) (resulting from the as yet unratified Kyoto Protocol). However, as with conventional funding mechanisms (ODA and FDI flows), the flow of resources under these various mechanisms has been uneven, and many are yet to be developed or implemented fully.

THE NEED TO INCREASE INTERNATIONAL FINANCIAL COOPERATION FOR PROMOTING GLOBAL PUBLIC GOODS

It is necessary to increase official development assistance, particularly to agriculture and rural areas.

Increasing ODA to the target set at Rio-92 occupied an important place in the preparations for the UN Conference for Financing for Development. The Monterrey Consensus called for concrete efforts towards the target of 0.7 percent of GNP as ODA to developing countries.[17]

There is, however, a need to focus particular attention on agriculture and rural areas. Indeed, a successful strategy for alleviating poverty and hunger must begin by recognizing that they are mainly rural phenomena and that agriculture is central to the livelihoods of rural people. A reversal of the declining trend in overall resources for hunger reduction, agriculture and rural development is necessary. It is also important to recognize that attaining the environmental objectives outlined in the land-cluster chapters of Agenda 21 will require much greater effort directed towards the agriculture sector and rural areas.

One important means of increasing political will and financing commitments to agriculture and rural development would be the recognition of the important potential role of agriculture and rural areas in the provision of GPGs. Indeed, only limited funding is currently available for such GPGs.

Additional funding must be mobilized to compensate the providers of global public goods.

Ensuring the provision of GPGs linked to the land-cluster chapters of Agenda 21 requires more than increased financing for development in general and for the agriculture and rural sectors specifically. Financing mechanisms must be geared directly to the provision of such goods. It is important to retain the idea that GPGs are goods and services benefiting the global community but provided by a narrower group of people, and that compensation to the providers is in the interest of the global community. Indeed, financing mechanisms for GPGs must be perceived and designed as a payment for goods and services provided.

A further important issue is whether increased financing for global public goods can also contribute to global poverty alleviation. While this will depend on specific circumstances and on the design of the mechanisms compensating the providers, there is a strong case for identifying synergies between the provision of GPGs and poverty alleviation and designing compensation mechanisms accordingly.

Synergies should be sought between the compensation of global public goods and poverty alleviation.

One option would be to link additional ODA flows to the effective mobilization of domestic resources for the provision of GPGs. Additional funding would be required, however, and serious consideration should be given to the creation of new financing mechanisms that provide both GPGs and transfer resources between developed and developing countries. A particular challenge is to design mechanisms in such a way as to also ensure an important contribution to poverty alleviation. (A review of some of the existing or potential financing mechanisms is provided in Box 11.)

Box 11

NEW OPPORTUNITIES FOR FINANCING GLOBAL PUBLIC GOODS RELATED TO THE LAND-CLUSTER CHAPTERS OF AGENDA 21

Global Environmental Facility (GEF). The GEF, established in 1991 and restructured after Rio-92, is intended to ensure international cooperation and financing to address major threats to the global environment. It brings together 166 member governments, the scientific community and a number of private sector and non-governmental organizations (NGOs). The implementing agencies are the United Nations Development Programme (UNDP), the United Nations Environment Programme(UNEP) and the World Bank. It finances and mobilizes cofunding for projects in the following focal areas: 1) biodiversity, 2) climate change, 3) international waters and 4) ozone depletion. Projects to address land degradation are also eligible for funding in so far as they relate to the four focal areas. Specific proposals, including land degradation as a separate focal area, are to be submitted for final approval at the GEF Assembly in October 2002.[1]

Debt-for-nature swaps, especially in sub-Saharan Africa. Sustainable debt financing is an important option for mobilizing resources for public and private investment. Debt-for-nature swaps is a mechanism through which the international debt of developing countries is written off and diverted towards financing environmental projects that yield global environmental benefits. Studies have shown that the highest deforestation rate is found in those countries of Africa that are also highly indebted. This suggests that there is significant potential for checking deforestation and promoting global public goods (GPGs) in these countries (e.g. reforestation and land-management activities) through such mechanisms.

Climate Change Fund. Under UNFCCC, both developed and developing countries are obliged to reduce greenhouse gas (GHG) emissions in the atmosphere and increase the sink capacity through the management of biomass and soils. A Climate Change Fund has been proposed to help the least developed countries build their capacity and finance for implementing the provisions outlined under the

Convention. Although the structure of the proposed fund is not yet clear, some countries have already committed contributions to the establishment of the Fund.

Clean Development Mechanism (CDM). The CDM, designed under the as yet unratified Kyoto Protocol, allows countries to finance emission reduction projects in developing countries and receive carbon emission reduction credits for their investment. The CDM could prove to be one of the most innovative financing mechanisms for promoting land-related GPGs. (The CDM is discussed in more detail in the following section.)

National Environmental Funds. Environmental funds have been established in a few developing countries under two UN Conventions – the UNCCD and the CBD – and are increasing in numbers. They are usually managed by private organizations and are capitalized by grants from governments and donor agencies as well as from environmental taxes and charges. Such funds could find wider application.

Improved mobilization of domestic resources. Domestic resource mobilization for the promotion of GPGs should enhance the existing financing mechanisms and help open new opportunities in an effective way. The removal of perverse subsidies; full-cost pricing of natural resources and services; the establishment of property rights over land, water and forests; fiscal reform towards implementation of environmental taxes and drawing on the willingness to pay of the beneficiaries of local and global public goods could all help create an enabling environment for mobilizing domestic resources and attracting external resources.

[1] Global Environment Facility (GEF). 2001. *Note on the proposed designation of land degradation as a GEF focal area.* GEF Council, 5–7 December 2001.

CONCLUSIONS

There is a need for increased focus on the land-cluster-related GPGs in the overall debate on GPGs, alongside other aspects that have so far received more attention, such as health, knowledge, cultural heritage, financial stability and peace and security. The global nature of these land-related GPGs lends justification to enhanced financing for their provision and to the development of new financial mechanisms for this purpose. The increased focus on the provision of GPGs and the need for globally coordinated efforts towards poverty alleviation would call for instruments, policies and programmes to be devised that at the same time address the effective implementation of the land-cluster chapters of Agenda 21 and contribute to poverty alleviation.

The following section considers in more detail the envisaged new financial mechanism for the provision of GPGs: the Clean Development Mechanism (CDM) deriving from the Kyoto Protocol on global climate change.

II. Harvesting carbon sequestration through land-use change: a way out of rural poverty?

INTRODUCTION

The key principle from UNCED in 1992 was the need to address both development and environmental problems in conjunction.

The key principle underlying the agreements that came out of the United Nations Conference on Environment and Development (UNCED) meeting held in Rio de Janeiro in 1992 was the requirement to address both development and environmental concerns in dealing with the pressing problems of environmental degradation facing the world. The agreements reached in Rio de Janeiro led to the establishment of a new international environmental governance system in the form of several multilateral environmental agreements (MEAs), including the UN Framework Convention on Climate Change (UNFCCC), the Convention on Biological Diversity (CBD) and the UN Convention to Combat Desertification in those Countries Experiencing Serious Drought and/or Desertification, particularly in Africa (UNCCD). Under these and other MEAs, a range of mechanisms to promote the generation of environmental goods and services together with economic development has been proposed and in some cases implemented.

The following explores the potential impacts on poverty alleviation of one of the main mechanisms proposed under the UNFCCC: the introduction of markets for carbon emission credits. An important group of potential participants in such a market is that of land users, including farmers and forest dwellers, who may supply credits for emission reductions through changes in their land-use practices. The lessons learned from examining the potential impacts of this mechanism on poverty alleviation and food security among land-user groups are also applicable to understanding the potential impacts of mechanisms proposed under other MEAs that will involve land-use change.

CLIMATE CHANGE AND LAND USE: CAUSES AND IMPACTS
Background on the issue of climate change
There has been considerable controversy over the degree and potential impacts of climate change, with some optimists claiming that global warming is an unproven hypothesis

Climate change has been controversial but there is now increasing consensus that changes are human-induced.

exaggerated by the alarmists,[18] and others asserting that the rate is significant and increasing and the impacts are likely to be huge.[19] Most of the controversy over climate change stems from the difficulty of separating human-induced changes from those occurring naturally, since it is claimed that climate change is a historical trend supported by the evidence of past ice ages. However, the impacts of changes in climate have recently been observed with increasing frequency and severity. There is now consensus in the scientific community that the changes observed over the last few decades are almost certainly in large part the result of human activities and the ensuing emissions of GHGs into the atmosphere.[20] Of these gases, carbon dioxide is dominant, accounting for about 50 percent of the warming effect of all climate-impact gases,[21] but other gases such as methane and nitrous oxide also contribute considerably to trapping heat, thus increasing global warming.

The third Intergovernmental Panel on Climate Change (IPCC) assessment report asserts that there has been an increase in the global average temperature of 0.2 °C to ±0.6 °C during the twentieth century.[22] Furthermore, sea levels have risen by approximately 15–20 cm worldwide and precipitation has registered an average increase of about 1 percent. However, while areas located at high latitudes are experiencing significant increases in rainfall, precipitation has actually declined in many tropical areas. At the same time, atmospheric concentrations of GHGs have increased by about 30 percent over the last two centuries.

If nothing is done to reduce these emissions, an increase in global warming of 1.4–5.8 °C over 1990 levels is projected to occur by 2100, and on average the sea level is projected to rise by 9–88 cm. The magnitude of the projected changes, which take into consideration ozone and aerosol emissions based on estimates of population growth, energy sinks, land-use and technological changes, has significantly increased since the second IPCC assessment report dated 1996. At that time, increases in global warming were projected to be about 2 °C, with a range of uncertainty from 1 °C to 3.5 °C.[23] Without a reduction in GHG emissions global warming will continue.

A new report from the United States National Academy of Science states that greenhouse warming and other human alterations of the climate system may increase the possibility of large, abrupt, regional or global climatic events, the effects of which are very difficult to estimate but will certainly be irreversible.[24]

The agriculture[25] sector is of key importance in the issue of climate change – both as one of the sources of the problem and as a recipient of its impacts. Even taking into consideration the lowest projections of a temperature increase of 1.4 °C, serious consequences for the physical and socio-economic infrastructure, as well as for agriculture, are projected. These include:

- decreased water availability for populations in water-scarce regions (particularly the subtropics);
- damage to human settlements and human-built environments from increased heavy precipitation and sea-level rise, such as coastal flooding and other damage from storms and floods;
- hazards to life and health such as increased incidence of tropical diseases, migration of tropical diseases to more temperate climates, increase in water-borne diseases and increase in heat-stress mortality.

Agriculture and forestry both contribute to and are affected by climate change.

The bulk of the impacts of climate change are likely to be felt in the developing countries owing to their geographic location and their greater dependence on the agriculture sector, which is highly sensitive to climatic conditions.

Increasing concentrations of GHGs are primarily associated with the burning of fossil fuels and cement production, which are largely undertaken by industrialized countries. Indeed, these countries are estimated to be responsible for approximately 70 percent of all human-caused GHG emissions. However, emissions from agricultural sources are also significant, accounting for an estimated 12–40 percent of current human-caused emissions.[26] The IPCC estimates that agriculture and forestry practices emit about 50 percent of total methane, 70 percent of nitrous oxide and 20 percent of carbon dioxide.[27]

The role of carbon sequestration through land use in mitigating climate change

Most of the world's carbon is stored in soils and forests, but large amounts have been released into the atmosphere as a result of agricultural and forestry activity.

Scientists estimate that about 80 percent of global carbon stocks are stored in soils or forests and that a considerable amount of the carbon originally contained in soils and forests has been released as a result of agricultural and forestry activities and deforestation.[28] Through photosynthesis, agricultural and forestry practices sequester and fix carbon into soil, plants and trees, thus reducing atmospheric GHGs. Consequently, changes in land-use and land-management practices could lead to a substantial refixation or sequestration of carbon in the soil and in trees.[29]

Reducing deforestation, generating increased forest stocks through the expansion of forestry plantations, adopting agroforestry activities, reducing soil degradation and rehabilitating degraded forests are all examples of measures that can potentially sequester carbon and thus counteract the impact of emissions made elsewhere.[30]

This can be reversed through increasing forest stocks and shifting to agricultural practices that fix more carbon in soils.

Dixon *et al.* estimate that the global economic potential for sequestration through land-use change ranges from 0.5 to 2 GtC/year (gigatonnes of carbon per year) for the next 50 years.[31] According to Lal *et al.*, the adoption of conservation tillage and residue management could lead to an increase of 49 percent in agricultural carbon sequestration; similarly 25 percent can be achieved by changing cropping practices, 13 percent by land restoration efforts, 7 percent through land-use change and 6 percent by improved water management.[32]

A study conducted by Tipper *et al.* indicates that the establishment of tree plantations on areas previously used as pasture may increase carbon stored in vegetation by about 120 tonnes of carbon/ha, while with the adoption of agroforestry practices such as growing timber and fruit trees interspersed with annual crops (e.g. maize) or perennial crops (e.g. coffee) can contribute around 70 tonnes of carbon/ha.[33] Finally, where closed forests are threatened, protection can prevent emissions of up to 300 tonnes of carbon/ha and, where forests are degraded, careful management and restoration can increase carbon storage by around 120 tonnes of carbon/ha.

The Clean Development Mechanism and the potential for carbon payment programmes to stimulate land-use change

The Kyoto Protocol calls for both a reduction of GHG emissions and increased sequestration in forests and soils.

The Kyoto Protocol sets the target of reducing global emissions of GHGs to 5.2 percent below 1990 levels by 2008.[34] It recognizes that net emissions may be reduced either by decreasing the rate at which GHGs are emitted to the atmosphere or by increasing the rate at which they are removed from the atmosphere through sinks and considers the two means as complementary. Increasing carbon sequestration is thus recognized as a means by which countries can offset emissions, though a variety of mechanisms. The one of greatest interest in the context of poverty alleviation is the Clean Development Mechanism (CDM).

Through the CDM, developing countries can be compensated for reducing GHG emissions and increasing carbon sequestration.

The CDM is a system established under Article 12 of the Kyoto Protocol that allows investors from Annex B countries (industrialized countries with legally binding emission reduction commitments) whose GHG emissions surpass their commitment levels to obtain a carbon credit from developing countries, which, in return, cut their emissions or increase carbon sinks through actions such as conserving forests or investing in clean technologies.[35] Ostensibly, the CDM would result in investment on the part of industrialized countries in projects that promote sustainable development as well as carbon sequestration in developing countries.[36] Carbon emission abatement costs are substantially lower in developing countries than in industrialized ones, which is the basis for establishing the market. It is envisioned that payments for emissions offsets to developing countries could be used to finance sustainable development, although the rules under which this will take place are still unclear.

The establishment of the CDM has been controversial, as has allowing sequestration through land-use change as a means of offsetting carbon emissions in general. The main objections are as follows:

- It has been argued that such offsets will continue to allow the major GHG emitters to continue their emitting practices while slowing growth in developing countries.
- Climate change mitigation through carbon-sequestering land-use changes is much more complicated and uncertain than that obtainable through reduction in emissions.
- Sequestered carbon is volatile (e.g. it can be re-released into the atmosphere), whereas a reduction in emissions leads to a permanent decrease.

An example of agroforestry: millet cultivation under **Acacia albida** *in Mali*

Agroforestry activities contribute to carbon sequestration and at the same time may enhance agricultural income

FAO/15859/R. FAIDUTTI

- Sequestration activities are difficult to monitor.
- Sequestration activities are less certain in terms of the final carbon outcomes, as they are subject to natural factors as well as human interventions.

The CDM mechanisms for compensating land-based carbon sequestration are not yet clear, but reforestation and afforestation currently qualify for compensation.

Despite the problems with sequestration activities based on land-use change, there is still considerable interest in pursuing means of climate change mitigation, primarily because of the low costs involved and the potential it offers for improving the sustainability of land-use practices. In November 2001, the Marrakesh Accords were signed by 178 countries; these set the ground rules for CDM operation and confirmed the eligibility of reforestation and afforestation as legitimate activities, but excluded the conservation of standing forests (avoided deforestation) and farming-based soil carbon sequestration, at least for the first commitment period ending in 2012. The Accords also set a cap on the maximum limit of emission reduction credits that can be obtained from sequestration at approximately 175 million tonnes of carbon dioxide equivalent.[37]

Recent developments indicate that the ultimate demand for carbon emission credits under the CDM may be much smaller than was originally envisioned. The withdrawal of the United States from the Kyoto Protocol reduced potential demand by an estimated 40–55 percent. Another major issue that could reduce the demand for carbon emission reductions is the degree to which the Russian Federation will enter the market as a supplier and at which time. A full-scale and immediate entrance of the Russian Federation into the market could drive market prices down by one-third.[38] These developments indicate that prices for carbon emission reductions could drop as low as $3.60 per tonne of carbon.

Projects for carbon-sequestering land-use changes are already being implemented.

Considerable uncertainty remains over the final form the CDM will take and how sequestering based on land-use changes will be treated. The Marrakesh Accords established a CDM board, which is currently in the process of developing guidelines and best practices. Meanwhile, there is considerable interest in harnessing carbon credits to promote sustainable agricultural development. Over 30 projects to offset carbon through land-use change have been developed on a bilateral payment basis, although it is still unclear whether they will qualify for CDM-based credits.[39] These projects include a number that specifically target smallholders and limited-income producers. The Scolel Té Project in Chiapas, Mexico, is one such example. In this project, carbon credits generated by forestry activities undertaken by groups and communities of small farmers are brokered through a trust fund that also provides technical and financial assistance to the participants. The costs of sequestering carbon in this project are estimated at $12 per tonne of carbon.[40] Other prominent examples include the Profafor Project in Ecuador, and the TIST Project in the United Republic of Tanzania, both of which involve smallholder provision of forestry emission credits.

Several development agencies, NGOs and private firms, such as FAO, the International Fund for Agricultural Development (IFAD), the United Kingdom Department for International Development (DFID), the World Bank, Winrock International and Ecosecurities Ltd, are all working on developing relevant information or actually engaged in developing projects that meet both sustainable development and carbon sequestration goals. Interest is not limited to producing sequestration benefits for the CDM, but extends to possible future programmes that may generate payments for mitigating climate change impacts. The World Bank is currently proposing the establishment of a BioCarbon Fund, which will be designed to deliver cost-effective carbon emission reductions, together with cross-cutting benefits in terms of biodiversity and land management.[41]

POVERTY AND LAND USE

Can compensation for land-based carbon sequestration under the CDM at the same time contribute to poverty reduction?

The impact of possible carbon-sequestering land-use changes on poor land-users is uncertain. There has been little empirical research on the economics of poor land-users actually participating. The issues are of great importance given that the majority of the world's poor are rural dwellers, dependent on land-use activities for their survival. In order to understand how carbon payment programmes could affect these estimated 800 million rural poor, it is necessary to look at the types of land-use pattern associated with poor land-users and their implications for carbon emissions, and at the potential private and social costs and benefits associated with the adoption of practices that reduce emissions and generate sequestration.

The relationship between poverty and natural-resource management is one that has been widely researched and debated. The notion of poverty as a major cause of resource degradation in the form of deforestation and forest and land degradation was the basis of many of the agreements that came out of the UNCED summit in 1992. However, research and experience with such programmes over the past ten years have shown that there are no clear and unambiguous correlations or causal links between poverty and resource degradation.

For the purpose of the following discussion, land-use practices can be divided into those that have an impact on above-ground carbon sinks, particularly forests, and those that affect soil-based carbon sinks. Currently, in view of the latest developments with the CDM, forestry-based activities[42] have assumed greater prominence, although soil carbon sequestration is still considered important. The institutional framework and rules for the global management of climate change are still in considerable flux, and soil carbon sequestration may be eligible for credits under the CDM in future commitment periods.

Forestry and types of land use affecting above-ground carbon sinks

For forestry, the link between deforestation and poverty is not clear.

In a comprehensive review of the evidence on the relationship between macroeconomic growth and deforestation, Wunder concludes that the results are ambiguous: in some countries higher income levels are associated with higher rates of deforestation, while in others the opposite is true.[43] He concludes that the outcome is dependent on the relative strength of two opposing effects: the growth of capital endowments, which enables deforestation, versus a "price-incentive effect" in which deforestation becomes less attractive because of higher potential returns from other economic activities. The relative strength of these effects depends on the resource endowment of the country and the type of growth path followed.

Likewise, at a micro level, the evidence concerning the relationship between income levels and deforestation is complex, with no clear direction of causality. On the one hand, increasing income levels may result in an increased capacity of producers to engage in deforestation, because of easier access to capital. On the other hand, high levels of poverty result in low labour values and thus greater incentives to undertake labour-intensive clearing of forests. In many cases, poverty is more likely to be associated with forest degradation than with deforestation, because the partial or temporary clearing of forest lands is more feasible within the constraints of poor land-users. Frequently, poor land-users gain access to forest resources only in the wake of large-scale logging efforts that put roads and other basic infrastructure into place. Poor land-users may then move in and advance deforestation.

Land uses that affect soil-based carbon sinks

For the degradation of agricultural land also, the link to poverty is ambiguous.

Carbon emission is also generated by land-management practices that result in a depletion of soil resources through erosion, or changes in the chemical and biological composition of the soil. Critical determinants of the impact of a farming system on erosion are the extent to which land cover is maintained, particularly during periods of rainfall, and the characteristics of the soil and topography involved. A major cause of soil erosion is the cultivation of the soil in preparation for agricultural production, particularly through mechanical means. Other widely used practices that generate erosion include the growing of annual crops on sloping lands or inadequate length of fallow periods for crops grown under extensive farming systems.

Payments for carbon sequestration based on land use will not necessarily involve the poor unless specific efforts are made to identify and involve them.

Poverty is often associated with the adoption of farming systems on steep hillsides or with short fallow cycles, largely because of constraints on the access to land. However, the adoption of mechanical forms of tillage is negatively associated with poverty, as is tillage under forms of animal traction. Thus, the same ambiguous result is found in terms of the relationship between poverty and land-degrading practices: where capital is a requirement for the adoption of practices that result in degradation, poor land-users are not associated with it; when the farming system involves the depletion of natural capital assets in the form of soil resources, then the system is associated with poverty.

These findings have several implications for the potential impact of carbon sequestration payment programmes on poverty alleviation. Payments for carbon sequestration based on land use will not necessarily involve poor land-users; for example, there are many situations where the poor will be neither the most competitive nor the largest potential suppliers of carbon sequestration through land-use change. However, there are countries and situations where the reverse is true, but these need to be more clearly identified in order to design effective schemes that can generate both sequestration and development objectives. To do so, a better understanding of the factors that will drive the potential response of poor land-users and increase their potential competitiveness as suppliers will be necessary.

POOR LAND-USERS AS CARBON CREDIT SUPPLIERS

Can the poor be competitive suppliers of carbon sequestration services?

The potential for carbon markets to achieve poverty alleviation depends on the degree to which the poor will be willing and competitive suppliers of credits. Opportunity costs faced by land users are a key determinant of who the willing sellers will be and the prices they would supply at. The opportunity costs of adopting sequestration are simply the benefits that producers would have to give up in order to provide sequestration. However, identifying such costs is not simply a matter of comparing profits from different farming systems. Issues such as the degree of food security offered by a system, and the timing and amount of labour required, are also important components of the opportunity costs of producers, which in turn determine the prices at which they would be willing to supply carbon sequestration services. In addition, the potential profits from sequestration will depend on the rate and total quantity of sequestration services that the producers can supply – factors that are largely determined by agro-ecological circumstances. The following section discusses how poverty might have an impact on the opportunity costs and productivity of carbon sequestration supply, and thus the capacity of poor producers to participate in carbon markets.

How do the poor make their land-management decisions?

Fundamental to this discussion is a conceptual framework for land-management decisions of land users and their implications for the generation of private and public benefits. In this framework (schematically presented in Figure 39), the land-using household is taken as the key decision-making unit. Households operate under given socio-economic and environmental conditions, which shape their ultimate decisions on land use. These include macrolevel factors such as the degree of market integration, the presence of infrastructure, and agroclimatic conditions. These factors will affect the incentives and constraints land users face in making their decisions. In addition, households have a given endowment of resources, e.g. land, labour and capital, which they allocate to various activities in their efforts to maintain a livelihood. These livelihood-generating activities can be divided into those that are land-use based and non-land-use based. Land-use-based activities may be for the purposes of generating private production benefits, or for the generation of environmental services for payment. The way in which households allocate their resources to land-use activities results in both private and public outcomes: private benefits in the form of products for their own consumption or income from marketed products, and public benefits (or costs) in the form of environmental services or, more specifically, carbon sequestration (or emissions).

Under what conditions would the poor be willing participants in carbon sequestration schemes?

The impacts of land-use changes adopted for carbon sequestration purposes can be divided into two main categories: 1) land-use changes that result in a shift in the source of livelihood maintenance and 2) land-management changes that have an impact (either augmenting or depleting) on current sources of livelihood. The opportunity costs facing producers and thus their willingness to supply carbon credits are different in each case.

Figure 39
CONCEPTUAL FRAMEWORK FOR LAND-MANAGEMENT DECISIONS

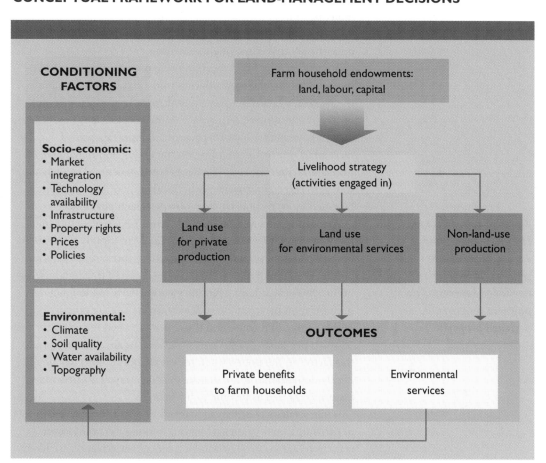

Carbon sequestration is sometimes accomplished through changes in livelihood sources, e.g. a shift from agriculture to forestry.

Land-use changes involving a shift in the source of livelihood

A common example of the first category is when sequestration is accomplished through a change in land use from agriculture to forestry. Referring back to Figure 39, this would result in a shift in activities from private production to environmental service production from land use. In addition, the shift could affect the amount of time or capital households invest in non-land-use activities. Of course, the degree to which this shift occurs can vary, with a mix of agricultural and environmental service provision being adopted (depending also on off-farm options).

It is important to recognize that livelihood activities generate more than just a stream of income or products; they also provide security by allowing households to cope with unexpected events, such as crop failure or sickness in the family. For many poor rural households, meeting subsistence food requirements from their own production provides a degree of protection from market-based consumption risk. This is a significant benefit to many producers who are located in areas of poor market integration, or where markets do not function well. Thus the opportunity cost of moving to environmental service payments as an important livelihood source among poor producers could be higher than that facing producers who are fully integrated into the market, who do not rely upon their own production as a source of consumption insurance. However, for poor households, carbon payments could also present an important way of increasing security, depending on the timing and the degree of uncertainty they involve. If payments are structured in such as way as to provide insurance benefits, then poor land-users may be much more responsive than others to such payments.

The poor can, in some circumstances, provide carbon sequestration services through changes in livelihood sources, if the payment programmes are designed properly.

Poor land-users also often adopt land-use activities that allow them to maintain a set of assets that they can rapidly liquidate in response to unexpected crises. A standing forest represents a potential source of income that can be accessed through logging in the case of a sudden need for income. Participation in a sequestration programme reduces or removes the potential use of this source of income and thus creates a need for other means of insurance to deal with crisis situations. Again, the impact of this factor on the poor's willingness to supply credits will be highly dependent on the degree to which payments provide insurance as well as income to households.

While security concerns may result in higher opportunity costs of providing environmental services among the poor, lower returns to agricultural production on converted lands are likely to have the opposite effect. The stream of income from capital-intensive commercial agriculture is likely to be higher than that obtained from low-input subsistence-oriented systems on converted forest lands. Thus the payment necessary to entice a land user to forego such income is likely to be lower for poor producers than those capable of engaging in more commercial systems. The implications are that low-income land-users could potentially be lower-cost providers of sequestration services, if programmes are structured so as to address their consumption insurance needs.

In other instances, carbon sequestration does not involve changes in livelihood but merely different practices, e.g. changes in agricultural or forestry practices.

Land-management changes affecting current livelihood sources

The opportunity costs facing a land user in the adoption of practices that have an impact on current livelihood sources are likely to include changes in agricultural practices that generate soil carbon sequestration and forest-management practices that reduce degradation. The key issues here are the degree to which

Compensation for carbon sequestration can help farmers overcome capital constraints to adopting more sustainable practices that will benefit them in the long run.

the change affects the private benefit outcomes to the household (e.g. the size of the arrow from activity to outcome in Figure 39) and the time frame over which these impacts are likely to occur. Carbon sequestration payment programmes may generate benefits by allowing land users to take measures that result in higher productivity that they were previously either unaware of or incapable of adopting. Alternatively, sequestration payments could compensate land users for decreases in productivity associated with the adoption of sequestering practices.

An example of the first instance could be adopting no-till or low-till practices. Over time, the adoption of such practices often leads to higher agricultural productivity and higher net returns to farmers. In this case, the farmers benefit from adopting sequestration practices in two ways: from the payments that are received for making the changes and from improvements in the environmental conditions they are operating under – the latter leading to increased land-use productivity. One important reason poor farmers do not adopt such measures is their inability to make investments that require costs in the short run in order to obtain benefits in the long run. Among low-income groups the cost of accessing capital through various forms of credit is generally higher than that facing higher-income groups, which prevents them from making investments they otherwise would like to undertake. Payments for carbon sequestration services offer an interesting way of reducing the cost of capital to low-income land-users. Here again, a key issue is the degree to which payments are structured to allow producers to overcome this investment constraint. Payments that do not provide sufficient capital at the initial phase of adoption of sequestering land-use practices are not likely to be attractive to poor producers.

The adoption of new land-management practices can often generate new labour requirements, either in terms of the overall labour input or in the timing of labour requirements. The opportunity cost of labour is another issue that will determine land users' response to carbon-sequestering land-use changes. Land users may be unwilling to shift to sequestering practices, even if they result in an overall increase in productivity, if they are unable to meet the labour requirement or if the returns to labour are lower than those they could obtain elsewhere. In terms of the implications for poor land-users, the effects could be contradictory. On the one hand, the opportunity costs of labour among the poor may be quite low, because there is limited potential for labour to be engaged in highly productive activities. This would indicate that poor land-users would be willing to supply labour to sequestration activities at a lower price. On the other hand, poor land-users are likely to be more constrained in their ability to augment the labour supply on-farm, owing to the higher probability of being located in areas of poorly functioning labour markets. Here, the critical determinants of poor land-user participation in sequestration supply will be the degree to which land-management practices result in increased labour burdens and the timing and level of sequestration payments.

In cases where sustainable practices involve reduced productivity, carbon sequestration payments must compensate farmers for income losses.

The alternative scenario, where the adoption of carbon-sequestering practices leads to a decrease in productivity, generates a set of opportunity costs to the land user similar to those described under land-use changes. Essentially, the carbon payment is substituting for another source of income (e.g. a shift from land-use production to environmental service production in Figure 39). The willingness of the producer to engage in such a change will depend not only upon payments meeting foregone production income, but also on the impact on consumption levels and food security. The opportunity cost of labour and capital will also be relevant. In this case, the degree to which the shift in land-management practice results in a permanent decrease in productive potential is likely to be important.

Under what conditions would the poor be competitive carbon sequestration providers?

Can the poor be efficient providers of carbon sequestration services?

While the opportunity costs to land users in supplying carbon sequestration services are a critical determinant of the price at which they respond to payments, it is also important to consider how efficiently they will be able to supply carbon in order to estimate their potential competitiveness in the market. Primary determinants of this factor are the rate and cost at which carbon can be supplied through various land-use and land-management changes across varying agro-ecological circumstances. These are determined by environmental conditions, as shown in Figure 39. There is considerable spatial heterogeneity in the biophysical capacity of land and trees to sequester carbon and the cost of the technologies required to accomplish this. The competitiveness of poor land-users in supplying carbon sequestration will be dependent on the biophysical conditions under which they operate.

The cost per tonne of carbon sequestered varies widely according to the activities, agro-ecological circumstances and technologies required. A simulation model of the marginal abatement costs of sequestration through land-use change constructed by McCarl *et al.* indicates that least-cost strategies involve mainly soil carbon sequestration and to some extent afforestation, fertilization and manure management.[44]

The costs of abatement also vary widely among categories of carbon-sequestering land-use changes. Estimates of sequestration costs in forestry from Latin America range from less than $1 per tonne up to $30 per tonne.[45] For forestry-based activities, those that involve planting rapidly growing species in uniform stands in favourable agroclimatic conditions generally have the greatest potential to generate sequestration benefits at a low cost in the short run. This fact has led to concerns about the potential for carbon payment programmes to stimulate large-scale forest plantation projects, which could crowd out smaller land users and result in negative impacts on other environmental services, particularly those relating to biodiversity.[46] However, this risk has been specifically addressed in the design of the CDM, which requires sustainable development objectives as well as climate change mitigation. Thus, the CDM rules are expected to emphasize the importance of identifying and promoting the adoption of land-use activities that generate cross-cutting benefits with other environmental services as well as sustainable economic benefits to the land users themselves.

The potential for, and costs of, carbon sequestration differ widely across soils and climatic conditions.

The ability of soils to sequester carbon through land-management changes varies widely depending on the type of soil, the degree to which it is degraded and climatic conditions. Antle and McCarl compared the different amounts of carbon that could be sequestered across varying sites and technologies in the United States and found considerable variation.[47] Estimates indicate that higher costs are incurred in achieving increases in soil carbon in highly degraded soils. Thus, areas of land that may have the greatest physical potential to supply soil carbon sequestration may also be those where it is most expensive.

To determine if and when the poor can be efficient carbon sequestration providers, more information is needed on geographic distribution of the poor across biophysical conditions.

There is insufficient reliable information on the geographic distribution of poverty across the biophysical characteristics affecting the cost of carbon sequestration supply. A review of studies on the geographic correlation between land degradation and poverty found that most studies at a macro scale of analysis did not find such a link, and that in several cases both the percentages and absolute numbers of the poor were higher in areas of high agro-ecological potential.[48] However, several microlevel studies did find significant correlations between land degradation and poverty. In terms of the geographic distribution of poverty with regard to forests, there is some indication of high concentrations of the poor in marginal forest areas, although the data were not of sufficient scale and scope to draw any general conclusions.

FAO/17203/G. BIZZARRI

Workers in a forest nursery in Pakistan
Planting trees on degraded lands may provide farmers with an additional source of income if it generates marketable carbon credits

These findings underline the need for better identification of the geographic distribution of the poor across biophysical conditions at a fairly detailed scale of analysis but with a broad – even global – coverage. It would then be necessary to identify, on the basis of these data, the means by which sequestration could be generated and the associated costs in areas that have good potential for achieving both carbon sequestration and poverty alleviation goals.

Carbon market design, transactions costs and poor land-users

There is still considerable work to be done in finalizing the rules under which sequestration programmes such as the CDM will operate. How these issues are settled is likely to have major implications for the potential of such programmes to reach the poor. The following section discusses some of the key issues regarding implementation, such as permanence, contract design and enforcement and transaction costs.

Permanence

The permanence of carbon sequestration as a means of mitigating climate change is of concern because carbon-sequestering land-use changes are reversible, and sequestered carbon can be emitted if management practices are subsequently changed. In addition, the carbon storage capacity of ecosystems is limited – they reach a point of saturation after which no further carbon can be stored. Estimates indicate that soil carbon sequestered through tillage changes generally reaches saturation after about 20 years, while forest-based sequestration has a longer saturation period. The reversibility and saturation potential of sequestration activities are likely to result in some sort of discount factor being applied to prices paid for such services, according to the length of time before saturation and the perceived risk of sequestration reversal.[49] In addition, these factors raise important issues about how payments should be structured to create incentives to maintain carbon stocks in saturated areas, or to refrain from reversing sequestration through changes in land-use practices. Presumably, once land users have reached a point of sequestration saturation they will cease to keep such areas under a sequestering land-use regime, unless doing so would provide sufficient private benefits to warrant the costs involved. Where this is not the case, either payments for storage would be required, or the price of the carbon offset would be considerably discounted. Likewise, sequestration efforts that are perceived to involve a high risk of reversal will probably be considered less valuable.

Sequestered carbon can be re-emitted through deforestation or the reversal of land-use practices. The permanence of sequestration is a cause for concern.

Concerns about permanence could result in reduced levels of payment for sequestration services provided by the poor, if the poor are perceived as being more likely to reverse sequestration practices. This may well be the case, owing to the higher need among the poor to insure against consumption risk and their more limited capacity to do so. As discussed above, the liquidation of natural capital assets is a typical means of managing unforeseen crises, and poor carbon sequestration providers may therefore be more likely to reverse sequestration practices in the absence of other insurance mechanisms. This could result in lower carbon payments to poor providers, or exclusion from the market as suppliers.

However, permanence issues may also work to the benefit of poor land-users if they are perceived to be permanent adopters in view of the overall productivity benefits they stand to gain. This would be the case where the practices adopted for sequestration would generate a long-term overall benefit to the land users but lack of capital had prevented their previous adoption; the land users' incentives to maintain these practices would here be generated from private benefits rather than ongoing payments. This situation is likely to arise more frequently among poor land-users. Referring back to Figure 39, in such cases there will be a strong positive feedback between environmental service outcomes and improvement in the producers' environmental conditions.

Another problem is the uncertainty of actual sequestration meeting expectations.

Uncertainty and contract design

A further risk arising in the market for carbon sequestration services stems from the uncertainty of actual sequestration levels meeting the projected potential. Land users may enter into a sequestration agreement based on the assumption that they will be able to generate a certain amount of carbon, but find that after some years they have not met expected levels even though they have followed the recommended practices. Furthermore, sequestration services will only merit compensation if they provide an additional benefit above an estimated baseline, which is subject to a degree of uncertainty.

The design of carbon contracts and subsequent monitoring procedure will determine the extent to which this risk will be shared between buyers and sellers. Land users could be paid on a per hectare basis for adopting practices that are known to generate carbon, regardless of the amount that is actually sequestered, in which case the seller would assume the risk of any shortfall. Alternatively, land users could be paid for actual carbon sequestered, in which case they would assume the risk. The efficiency of either scheme will be determined by the relative costs associated with monitoring land-use practices versus actual carbon tonnage and by the biophysical and economic conditions that influence sequestration supply.[50]

For poor land-users, contracts based on the per hectare adoption of land-use practices are clearly more beneficial. Poor land-users are unlikely to be capable of bearing the risk associated with carbon supply shortfalls. However, they are also more likely to present a higher degree of spatial heterogeneity in terms of carbon supply because of the smaller size of their areas, the greater variation in management levels applied to land-use practices and perhaps an even greater heterogeneity in the biophysical resources under their control. In addition, monitoring either land-use practices or carbon tonnage outcomes among poor producers is likely to be much more expensive because of the size of the area and tonnage involved. The following section considers the transaction costs involved in dealing with poor producers.

Transaction costs

The costs of implementing and monitoring carbon sequestration programmes are higher when they involve poor smallholders.

High transaction costs[51] associated with poor suppliers of sequestration services represent a major barrier to participation in carbon markets. These costs arise from the small scale under which poor land-users operate and the higher degree of uncertainty regarding their rights to land-based property. Frequently, poor land-users do not hold secure and clear title to their land assets, or they operate under systems of common property management that require a capacity for group coordination in order to institute changes. In addition, more than one type of property right may exist for a given land area, such as rights to trees, water and post-harvest residue collection. The poor may have access to only one type of property right affecting a given piece of land and often this is only on informal terms. These factors result in much higher costs in instituting carbon-sequestering land-use changes and a greater degree of uncertainty in the capacity to supply sequestration services.

The costs associated with identifying, negotiating, contracting and enforcing sequestration payments are obviously much higher when dealing with small and geographically scattered producers operating under heterogenous agro-ecological and institutional conditions. Reducing the transaction costs associated with payments for carbon sequestration (or any other type of environmental service) is a key issue that must be addressed in order to channel the benefits of such programmes to the poor.

Ensuring the participation of the poor will require coordination and capacity building.

Coordinating and consolidating sequestration supply among groups of poor landholders will be necessary for their effective participation in carbon markets. Carbon transactions may be conducted through local-level organizations that are already in place, such as local governments, farmers' associations or NGOs. Identifying areas and situations where large groups of low-income land-users are engaged in similar types of land-use activity – such as in areas of resettlement or agrarian reform or in communally held lands – could be an important means of consolidating the effective provision of sequestration services among the poor.

Addressing the problem of complex and unclear property rights will be more difficult, although it is clear that some sort of institutional development will be required. While such a process will necessarily involve government institutions, at least in order to formalize any reforms, the process of negotiating and coordinating solutions to the problem may be handled most effectively by NGOs, which could facilitate the development of coordination norms and agreements among stakeholders at the local level.

It also involves identifying situations with high crossover benefits between carbon sequestration and poverty alleviation.

Capacity building at a national level, in order to facilitate market transactions, and a system of honest and low-cost carbon market brokerages will be necessary if carbon markets are to offer benefits to the poor. The clearer identification of locations and situations where there is likely to be a high crossover benefit between carbon sequestration supply and poverty alleviation will also contribute significantly to making carbon payments accessible to the poor. International agencies and research institutes can play an important role here. Reliable information on where the least-cost sequestration potential through land-use change is obtainable, and the extent to which poor land-users are associated with such opportunities, will be critical for both investors and suppliers in attaining a carbon market that addresses both poverty alleviation and sustainable development goals. The development and dissemination of investment opportunity profiles that result in competitively priced carbon credits as well as poverty alleviation could greatly stimulate the capacity to achieve these goals.

CONCLUSIONS

Involving the poor requires special efforts, but can help contribute to the objectives of Agenda 21.

The analysis presented suggests that poor land-users are not likely to become beneficiaries of payments for carbon sequestration credits unless concerted efforts are made in terms of institution and capacity building and information provision. Even where such measures are being taken, payments for carbon-sequestering land-use changes do not represent a panacea for either the reduction of rural poverty or the mitigation of climate change. Nonetheless, carbon sequestration payments can play an important role in promoting sustainable development among the poor in line with the development goals of Agenda 21 and may represent an important new means of finance for such efforts.

Payments for environmental services can enable poor land-users to adopt sustainable agricultural practices, particularly in situations where a lack of investment capacity is the primary constraining factor. It is important to recognize that conflicts as well as synergies may become apparent between the dual goals of environmental and economic development; nevertheless, the complementarity between environmental and poverty alleviation goals can be greatly enhanced through policy and institutional reforms.

Equity and efficiency goals must both be addressed in designing mechanisms to promote environmental objectives.

Above all, it is necessary to consider that both equity and efficiency are fundamental criteria in designing mechanisms to stimulate the provision of environmental goods and services that benefit the global community. This was the basis for the agreements reached at Rio de Janeiro in 1992, although it has not been consistently applied since then. It is neither fair nor effective to demand the provision of environmental goods and services from the poor, unless such measures also offer the potential for improvements in their livelihoods. In order to ensure that this will be the case, much more information, institutional reform and capacity building will be required.

NOTES

1 For the purpose of this section, Agenda 21 Chapters 10–15 are termed the "land-cluster" chapters.

2 For example, see I. Kaul, I. Grunberg and M.A. Stern. 2000. *Global public goods*. Oxford, UK, Oxford University Press. The volume pays little attention to the global public goods related to agriculture and food security concerns, except for a brief description by Geoffrey Heal in a chapter on natural resources and GPGs.

3 Smoke emission from a factory is an example of a negative externality, while for an orchard keeper the pollination of his or her trees by bees belonging to a neighbouring beekeeper would be a positive externality.

4 Street lighting and the armed forces are two classic examples of public goods.

5 Paul Samuelson's seminal work, "The pure theory of public expenditures" (*Review of Economics and Statistics*, November 1954, pp. 387–89), provides a basis for defining public goods. Samuelson primarily identified two of the characteristics of public goods: non-excludability and non-rivalry. Non-excludability indicates that once a good is produced the benefits cannot be separated and those individuals who do not pay for it cannot be excluded from consumption. An example would be the recreational opportunities provided by the rural landscapes. Non-rivalry indicates that the consumption of a public good by one individual does not reduce the opportunity for consumption by another individual.

6 Op. cit., note 2.

7 See *The State of Food and Agriculture 2001* for a discussion of the economic aspects of transboundary plant pests and animal diseases.

8 United Nations Environment Programme. 2000. *Global Environment Outlook 2000* (available at www.grid.unep.ch/geo2000/english/index.htm).

9 National Center for Environmental Research. *1999 Progress Report: Estimating the cost of carbon sequestration in global forests* (available at http://es.epa.gov/ncerqa/progress/grants/98/deci/sohngen99.html).

10 Is international agricultural research a global public good? Speech by Robert Picciotto, Director-General, Operations Evaluation, World Bank, Washington, DC (available at www.worldbank.org/html/cgiar/publications/icw00/rpspeech.pdf).

11 V.W. Ruttan. 2000. The continuing challenge of food production. *Environment*, 42: 25–30.

12 UNEP/CBD/COP/5/INF/10 (available at www.biodiv.org/doc/meetings/cop/cop-05/information/cop-05-inf-10-en.pdf).

13 P. Esquinas-Alcázar. 1998. Farmers rights. *In* R.E. Evenson, D. Gollin and V. Santaniello, eds. *Agricultural values of plant genetic resources*. Wallingford, UK, CABI.

14 Agreement reached on protecting plant genetic resources. FAO Highlights, Rome (available at www.fao.org/News/2001/010703-e.htm).

15 United Nations Commission on Sustainable Development. 2000 (available at www.un.org/documents/ecosoc/cn17/2000/ecn172000-2.htm).

16 T. Panayotou. 2000. *Globalisation and environment.* Center for International Development (CID) Working Paper No. 53, July 2000. Cambridge, Massachusetts, Harvard University.

17 UN. 2002. Draft outcome of the International Conference on Financing for Development, Monterrey Consensus, UN General Assembly, 30 January 2002. A/AC.257/L.13.

18 W. Beckerman. 1995. *Small is stupid – blowing the whistle on the greens.* London, Duckworth; J.L. Simon. 1995. *The state of humanity.* Cambridge, MA, USA, Blackwell.

19 P.R. Ehrlich and A.H. Ehrlich. 1996. *Betrayal of science and reason – how anti-environmental rhetoric threatens our future.* Washington, DC, Island Press; N. Meyers and J. Simon 1994. *Scarcity or abundance? A debate on the environment.* New York, USA, W.W. Norton.

20 Committee on Abrupt Climate Change, Ocean Studies Board, Polar Research Board, Board on Atmospheric Sciences and Climate, National Research Council. 2001. *Abrupt climate change: inevitable surprises.* Washington, DC, National Academy Press; National Research Council (NRC). 2001. *Climate change science: an analysis of some key questions.* Washington, DC, National Academy Press; Intergovernmental Panel on Climate Change (IPCC). 2001. *The science of climate change 2001.* Report of Working Group I (available at www.usgcrp.gov/ipcc/default.html).

21 Deutsche Gesellschaft für Technische Zusammenarbeit (GTZ). 2001. *On track towards climate protection.* Eschborn, Germany.

22 The third Intergovernmental Panel on Climate Change (IPCC) assessment report. 2001. *Climate change 2001: impacts, adaptations, and vulnerability.* Report of Working Group II (available at www.usgcrp.gov/ipcc/default.html).

23 Op. cit., note 21.

24 Op. cit., note 20.

25 Agriculture is defined using the FAO definition and includes cropping, forestry and fisheries.

26 J.M. Antle and B. McCarl. 2001. The economics of carbon sequestration in agricultural soil. *In* T. Tietenberg and H. Folmer. *International yearbook of environmental and resource economics*, Vol. VI. Cheltenham, UK and Northampton, MA, USA, Edward Elgar Publishing.

27 Op. cit., note 22.

28 Ibid.

29 R. Lal, J.M. Kimble, R.F. Follett and C.V. Cole. 1998. *The potential of US cropland to sequester carbon and mitigate the greenhouse effect.* Chelsea, MI, USA, Ann Arbor Press.

30 R. Tipper. 1997. *Mitigation of greenhouse gas emissions by forestry: a review of technical, economic and policy concepts.* Working paper, Institute of

Ecology and Resource Management, University of Edinburgh, Scotland. A review of various land management practices that could increase soil carbon sequestration is contained in: FAO. 2001. *Soil carbon sequestration for improved land management practices.* World Soil Resources Report No. 96. Rome.

31 R.K. Dixon, J.K. Winjum, K.J. Andrasko, J.J. Lee and P.E. Schroeder. 1994. Integrated systems: assessment of promising agroforest and alternative land-use practices to enhance carbon conservation and sequestration. *Climatic Change,* 27: 71–9.

32 Op. cit., note 29.

33 R. Tipper, ed. 1998. *Assessment of the cost of large scale forestry for CO_2 sequestration: evidence from Chiaps, Mexico.* Report PH12. International Energy Authority Greenhouse Gas & R&D Programme (available at www.eccm.uk.com/climafor/publications.html).

34 M. Grubb, C. Vrolijk and D. Brack. 1999. *The Kyoto Protocol: A guide and assessment.* London, Earthscan.

35 L. Olsson and J. Ardö. 2001. Soil carbon sequestration in degraded semiarid agro-ecosystems – perils and potentials. *Ambio.* In press.

36 K. Brown and D.W. Pearce, eds. 1994. *The causes of deforestation.* London, UCL Press.

37 An amount equal to 1 percent of the base year's emissions (1990) of the Annex B countries, multiplied by five. T. Black-Arbelaez. 2002. *Applying CDM to biological restoration projects in developing nations: key issues for policy makers and project managers* (available at www.gefweb.org/ Documents/Forest_Roundtable/Applying_CDM_Rev1.pdf).

38 Op. cit., note 37.

39 R. Nasi, S. Wunder and J.J. Campos. 2002. *Forest ecosystem services: can they pay our way out of deforestation?* Discussion paper prepared for GEF for the Forestry Roundtable, New York, 11 March 2002 (available at www.gefweb.org/documents.pdf); and S. Bass, O. Dubois, J. Ford, P. Moura-Costa, M. Pinard, R. Tipper and C. Wilson. 1999. *Rural livelihoods and carbon management. An issue paper.* Report from the workshop on the implication of carbon offset policies for the rural poor and landless, Edinburgh, UK, 20–21 September 1999 (available at www.ecosecurities.com or www.ecce.uk.com).

40 For further information see the project Web site (available at www.eccm.uk.com/scolelte/index.html).

41 Personal communication, Louise Aukland Ecosecurities.

42 The definitions of afforestation and reforestation under the CDM have not yet been issued, and so may include activities such as reversing forest degradation or increasing areas under agroforestry.

43 S. Wunder. 2001. Poverty alleviation and tropical forests – what scope for synergies? *World Development,* 29(11): 1817–1833.

44 B.A. McCarl and B.C. Murray. 2001. *Harvesting the greenhouse: comparing biological sequestration with emissions offsets.* Unpublished paper,

Department of Agricultural Economics, Texas A&M University, College Station, TX, USA.

45 Op. cit., note 37.

46 Ibid.

47 Op. cit., note 26.

48 FAO. 2001. *Two essays on socio-economic aspects of soil degradation.* FAO Economic and Social Development Paper No. 149. Rome.

49 Op. cit., note 44.

50 Op. cit., note 26.

51 Transaction costs are defined as the costs of completing a contract, which includes the costs incurred by buyers and sellers finding each other, the costs associated with bargaining and the costs associated with monitoring and enforcing the contract.

ANNEX

TABLE

COUNTRIES AND TERRITORIES USED FOR STATISTICAL PURPOSES IN THIS PUBLICATION

Developed countries	Countries in transition	Developing countries			
		Sub-Saharan Africa	Asia and the Pacific/ Far East and Oceania	Latin America and the Caribbean	Near East and North Africa
Albania	Albania	Angola	American Samoa	Anguilla	Afghanistan
Andorra		Benin	Bangladesh	Antigua and Barbuda	Algeria
Armenia	Armenia	Botswana	Bhutan	Argentina	Bahrain
Australia		Burkina Faso	British Virgin Islands	Aruba	Cyprus
Austria		Burundi	Brunei Darussalam	Bahamas	Egypt
Azerbaijan	Azerbaijan	Cameroon	Cambodia	Barbados	Gaza Strip
Belarus	Belarus	Cape Verde	China China, Hong Kong SAR China, Macau SAR	Belize	Iran, Islamic Rep.
Belgium/ Luxembourg		Central African Rep.	Cocos Islands	Bermuda	Iraq
Bosnia and Herzegovina	Bosnia and Herzegovina	Chad	Cook Islands	Bolivia	Jordan
Bulgaria	Bulgaria	Comoros	East Timor	Brazil	Kuwait
Canada		Congo, Rep.	Fiji	Cayman Islands	Lebanon
Croatia	Croatia	Côte d'Ivoire	French Polynesia	Chile	Libyan Arab Jamahiriya
Czech Republic	Czech Republic	Democratic Republic of the Congo	Guam	Colombia	Morocco
Denmark		Djibouti	India	Costa Rica	Oman
Estonia	Estonia	Equatorial Guinea	Indonesia	Cuba	Qatar
Faeroe Islands		Eritrea	Kiribati	Dominica	Saudi Arabia
Finland		Ethiopia	Korea, Dem. People's Rep.	Dominican Republic	Syrian Arab Republic
France		Gabon	Korea, Rep.	Ecuador	Tunisia
Georgia	Georgia	Gambia	Lao People's Dem. Rep.	El Salvador	Turkey
Germany		Ghana	Malaysia	Falkland Islands (Malvinas)	United Arab Emirates
Gibraltar		Guinea	Maldives	French Guiana	West Bank
Greece		Guinea-Bissau	Marshall Islands	Grenada	Yemen
Greenland		Kenya	Micronesia, Fed. States	Guadeloupe	
Hungary	Hungary	Lesotho	Mongolia	Guatemala	
Iceland		Liberia	Myanmar	Guyana	
Ireland		Madagascar	Nauru	Haiti	
Israel		Malawi	Nepal	Honduras	
Italy		Mali	New Caledonia	Jamaica	

Developed countries	Countries in transition	Developing countries			
		Sub-Saharan Africa	Asia and the Pacific/ Far East and Oceania	Latin America and the Caribbean	Near East and North Africa
Japan		Mauritania	Niue	Martinique	
Kazakhstan	Kazakhstan	Mauritius	Norfolk Islands	Mexico	
Kyrgyzstan	Kyrgyzstan	Mozambique	Northern Mariana Islands	Montserrat	
Latvia	Latvia	Namibia	Pakistan	Netherlands Antilles	
Liechtenstein		Niger	Palau	Nicaragua	
Lithuania	Lithuania	Nigeria	Papua New Guinea	Panama	
Malta		Réunion	Philippines	Paraguay	
Monaco		Rwanda	Samoa	Peru	
Netherlands		Saint Helena	Singapore	Puerto Rico	
New Zealand		Sao Tome and Principe	Solomon Islands	Saint Kitts and Nevis	
Norway		Senegal	Sri Lanka	Saint Lucia	
Poland	Poland	Seychelles	Taiwan Province of China	Saint Vincent and the Grenadines	
Portugal		Sierra Leone	Thailand	Suriname	
Republic of Moldova	Republic of Moldova	Somalia	Tokelau	Trinidad and Tobago	
Romania	Romania	Sudan	Tonga	Turks and Caicos Islands	
Russian Federation	Russian Federation	Swaziland	Vanuatu	United States Virgin Islands	
San Marino		Togo	Viet Nam	Uruguay	
Slovakia	Slovakia	Uganda	Wallis and Futuna Islands	Venezuela	
Slovenia	Slovenia	United Republic of Tanzania	Tuvalu		
Saint Pierre and Miquelon		Zambia			
South Africa		Zimbabwe			
Spain					
Sweden					
Switzerland					
Tajikistan	Tajikistan				
The Former Yugoslav Republic of Macedonia	The Former Yugoslav Republic of Macedonia				
Turkmenistan	Turkmenistan				
Ukraine	Ukraine				
United Kingdom					
United States					
Uzbekistan	Uzbekistan				
Yugoslavia	Yugoslavia				

Special chapters of
The State of Food and Agriculture

In addition to the usual review of the recent world food and agricultural situation, each issue of this report since 1957 has included one or more special studies on problems of longer-term interest. Special chapters in earlier issues have covered the following subjects:

1957	Factors influencing the trend of food consumption
	Postwar changes in some institutional factors affecting agriculture
1958	Food and agricultural developments in Africa south of the Sahara
	The growth of forest industries and their impact on the world's forests
1959	Agricultural incomes and levels of living in countries at different stages of economic development
	Some general problems of agricultural development in less-developed countries in the light of postwar experience
1960	Programming for agricultural development
1961	Land reform and institutional change
	Agricultural extension, education and research in Africa, Asia and Latin America
1962	The role of forest industries in the attack on economic underdevelopment
	The livestock industry in less-developed countries
1963	Basic factors affecting the growth of productivity in agriculture
	Fertilizer use: spearhead of agricultural development
1964	Protein nutrition: needs and prospects
	Synthetics and their effects on agricultural trade
1966	Agriculture and industrialization
	Rice in the world food economy
1967	Incentives and disincentives for farmers in developing countries
	The management of fishery resources
1968	Raising agricultural productivity in developing countries through technological improvement
	Improved storage and its contribution to world food supplies
1969	Agricultural marketing improvement programmes: some lessons from recent experience
	Modernizing institutions to promote forestry development
1970	Agriculture at the threshold of the Second Development Decade
1971	Water pollution and its effects on living aquatic resources and fisheries
1972	Education and training for development
	Accelerating agricultural research in the developing countries
1973	Agricultural employment in developing countries
1974	Population, food supply and agricultural development
1975	The Second United Nations Development Decade: mid-term review and appraisal
1976	Energy and agriculture
1977	The state of natural resources and the human environment for food and agriculture
1978	Problems and strategies in developing regions

1979	Forestry and rural development
1980	Marine fisheries in the new era of national jurisdiction
1981	Rural poverty in developing countries and means of poverty alleviation
1982	Livestock production: a world perspective
1983	Women in developing agriculture
1984	Urbanization, agriculture and food systems
1985	Energy use in agricultural production
	Environmental trends in food and agriculture
	Agricultural marketing and development
1986	Financing agricultural development 1987-88 Changing priorities for agricultural science and technology in developing countries
1989	Sustainable development and natural resource management
1990	Structural adjustment and agriculture
1991	Agricultural policies and issues: lessons from the 1980s and prospects for the 1990s
1992	Marine fisheries and the law of the sea: a decade of change
1993	Water policies and agriculture
1994	Forest development and policy dilemmas
1995	Agricultural trade: entering a new era?
1996	Food security: some macroeconomic dimensions
1997	The agroprocessing industry and economic development
1998	Rural non-farm income in developing countries
2000	World food and agriculture: lessons from the past 50 years
2001	Economic impacts of transboundary plant pests and animal diseases

FAO Agricultural Policy and Economic Development Series

AGRICULTURAL AND ECONOMIC DEVELOPMENT ANALYSIS DIVISION AND POLICY ASSISTANCE DIVISION

1 Searching for common ground – European Union enlargement and agricultural policy (K. Hathaway and D. Hathaway, eds, 1997)
2 Agricultural and rural development policy in Latin America – New directions and new challenges (A. de Janvry, N. Key and E. Sadoulet, 1997)
3 Food security strategies – The Asian experience (P. Timmer, 1997)
4 Guidelines for the integration of sustainable agriculture and rural development into agricultural policies (J.B. Hardaker, 1997)

FAO Economic and Social Development Papers

AGRICULTURAL AND ECONOMIC DEVELOPMENT ANALYSIS DIVISION

Forthcoming: The evolution of primary commodity terms of trade and the implications for developing countries (G.P. Zanias)

150 The role of agricultural taxation and anti-agriculture bias in economic growth (A.H. Sarris, 2001)
149 Two essays on socio-economic aspects of soil degradation (L. Lipper and D. Osgood, 2001)
148 Agricultural investment and productivity in developing countries (L. Zepeda, ed., 2001)
147 Undernourishment and economic growth: the efficiency cost of hunger (J.L. Arcand, 2001)
146 Applications of the contingent valuation method in developing countries – a survey (A. Albertini and J. Cooper, 2000)
145 Two essays on climate change and agriculture – a developing country perspective (R. Mendelsohn and D. Tiwari, 2000)
144 Rural poverty, risk and development (M. Fafchamps, 2000)
143 Growth, trade and agriculture: an investigative survey (P.L. Scandizzo and M. Spinedi, 1998)
142 The political economy of the Common Market in milk and dairy products in the European Union (R.E. Williams, 1997)
141 Economies in transition – Hungary and Poland (D.G. Johnson, 1997)
139 Population pressure and management of natural resources. Income-sharing and labour absorption in small-scale fisheries (J.M. Baland and J.-P. Platteau, 1996)
138 Economic development and environmental policy (S. Barret, 1996)
136 Growth theories, old and new and the role of agriculture in economic development (N. Stern, 1996)
135 The international dynamics of national sugar policies (T.C. Earley and D.W. Westfall, 1996)
134 Rural informal credit markets and the effectiveness of policy reform (A.H. Sarris, 1996)
133 Implications of regional trade arrangements for agricultural trade (T. Josling, 1997)

132 The economics of international agreements for the protection of environmental and agricultural resources (S. Barret, 1995)

131 Trade patterns, cooperation and growth (P.L. Scandizzo, 1995)

128 Agricultural taxation under structural adjustment (A.H. Sarris, 1994)

125 Transition and price stabilization policies in East European agriculture (E.M. Claassen,1994)

124 Structural adjustment and agriculture: African and Asian experiences (S. Subramian, E. Sadoulet and A. de Janvry, 1994)

121 Policies for sustainable development: four essays (A. Markandya, 1994)

115 Design of poverty alleviation strategy in rural areas (R. Gaiha, 1993)

110 Agricultural sustainability: definition and implications for agricultural and trade policy (T. Young and M.P. Burton, 1992)

107 Land reform and structural adjustment in sub-Saharan Africa: controversies and guidelines (J-P. Platteau, 1992)

105 The role of public and private agents in the food and agricultural sectors of developing countries (L.D. Smith and A.M. Thomson, 1991)

104 Structural adjustment policy sequencing in sub-Saharan Africa (N.J. Spooner and L.D. Smith, 1991)

103 The impact of structural adjustment on smallholders (J.-M. Boussard,1992)

100 Structural adjustment and household welfare in rural areas: a micro-economic perspective (R. Gaiha, 1991)

99 Agricultural labour markets and structural adjustment in sub-Saharan Africa (L.D. Smith, 1991)

98 Institutional changes in agricultural product and input markets and their impact on agricultural performance (A.M. Thomson, 1991)

Other titles

- Perspectives on agriculture in transition: analytical issues, modelling approaches and case study results (W.R. Poganietz, A. Zezza, K. Frohberg and K.G. Stamoulis, eds., 2001)
- Food, agriculture and rural development: current and emerging issues for economic analysis and policy research (K.G. Stamoulis, ed., 2001)
- Integration of sustainable agriculture and rural development issues in agricultural policy. Proceedings of FAO/Winrock Workshop, May 1995. (S.A. Breth, ed., Winrock International, 1996)
- Halting degradation of natural resources – Is there a role for rural communities? (J.-M. Baland and J.-P. Platteau, FAO-Oxford University Press, 1996)

To obtain the publications listed, please contact:

Sales and Marketing Group, Information Division
Food and Agriculture Organization of the United Nations
Viale delle Terme di Caracalla
00100 Rome, Italy

E-mail: publications-sales@fao.org
Tel.: (+39) 06 57051; Fax: (+39) 06 57053360

TIME SERIES FOR SOFA 2002 CD-ROM
Instructions for use

The State of Food and Agriculture 2002 includes a CD-ROM containing time series data for about 150 countries and the necessary software, FAOSTAT TS, to access and display these time series.

FAOSTAT TS

FAOSTAT TS software provides quick and easy access to structured annual time series databases. Even inexperienced computer users can use FAOSTAT TS, which does not require spreadsheet, graphics or database programs. FAOSTAT TS is fully menu-driven, so there are no commands to learn. Users can browse through and print graphs and tables, plot multiple-line graphs, fit trend lines and export data for use in other programs. FAOSTAT TS is trilingual (English, French, Spanish) and uses a standard menu format.

FAOSTAT TS software is in the public domain and may be freely distributed. The data files accompanying the software, however, are under FAO copyright, and users must attribute FAO as the source. FAO may provide only very limited support to users of this software and the accompanying data and cannot assist users who modify the software or data files. FAO disclaims all warrants of fitness for the software or data for a particular use.

Technical requirements

FAOSTAT TS software requires an IBM or compatible PC with a hard disk, DOS 3.0 or later version, 300 KB of available RAM and graphics capability. Graphics support is provided for all common graphics adapters (VGA, EGA, MCGA, CGA and Hercules monochrome).

FAOSTAT TS will print graphs *only* on Epson dot matrix, Hewlett-Packard and compatible laser printers. To use FAOSTAT TS with other printers, users can enable their own graphics printing utility before starting the program. One such utility is GRAPHICS.COM in DOS 2.0 or later version.

Because of its use of DOS graphics modes, if FAOSTAT TS is run under MS-Windows or OS/2, it should be set to run in a full screen DOS session.

Installation

Before running FAOSTAT TS you must install the software and data files on your hard disk.
Open a DOS session.
- To install from drive D: to drive C:
  - Insert the CD-ROM in drive D:
  - Type D: and press ENTER.
  - Type INSTALL C: and press ENTER.
  - Press any key.

A C:\SOFA02 directory is created and, after installation, you will already be in this directory.

Entering **FAOSTAT TS**

- To start the FAOSTAT TS software, if you are not already in the C:\SOFA02 directory (as after installation):
  - Change to this directory by typing CD\SOFA02 and pressing ENTER.
  - From the command prompt in the SOFA02 directory, type SOFA02 and press ENTER.

  A graphics title screen will be displayed, followed by the main menu screen.

  If FAOSTAT TS does not start, graphs do not display correctly or the menus are difficult to read, your computer may not be compatible with the default functions of FAOSTAT TS. The use of a command-line option may help. You may try to start FAOSTAT TS with the -E parameter (by typing SOFA02-E) to disable its use of expanded memory. You may also force the use of a particular graphics or text mode by typing its name as a parameter (e.g. -EGA would force the use of EGA mode graphics).

Language choices

- The initial default language for FAOSTAT TS is English. To change the default language to French or Spanish:
  - Go to the FILE menu
  - Select LANGUAGE using the ARROW key ($\downarrow$) and press ENTER.
  - Select your choice of language and press ENTER.

  The language selected will remain the default language until another is selected.

Navigating the menus

The main menu bar consists of FILE, DATA, GRAPH, TABLE and HELP menus. Most menu options are disabled until you open a data file. Navigate the menus by using the ARROW keys ($\uparrow\downarrow\leftarrow\rightarrow$) and make a selection by highlighting an item and pressing ENTER. To back out of a selection, press the ESC key.

- If you have a mouse, menu items can be selected with the mouse cursor. The left mouse button selects an item and the right mouse button acts as the ESC key.

  After you have made a menu selection, the menu will redraw and highlight a possible next choice.

- Several short-cut keys are available throughout the program:

Key	Action
F1	HELP: Displays context-sensitive help text.
ESC	ESCAPE: Backs out of the current menu choice or exits the current graph or table.
ALT+N	NOTES: Displays text notes associated with the current data file, if the text file is available. This text may be edited. Notes will not appear while a graph is displayed.
ALT+X, ALT+Q	EXIT: Exits FAOSTAT TS immediately, without prompting.

Help

- You will see context-sensitive help displayed at the bottom of each screen. Press F1 for more extensive help on a highlighted option.
- Select HELP from the main menu to access the help information. Introductory information on the software, help topics and an "About" summary screen are available from the HELP menu.
- The HELP menu options call up the same windows obtained by pressing the F1 key at any of the menu screens:
    - FAOSTAT TS displays the top-level help page.
    - TOPICS lists the help contents.
    - ABOUT shows summary program information.

Opening a data file

- To display a list of FAOSTAT TS data files:
    - Go to the FILE menu.
    - Select OPEN.

All of the FAOSTAT TS data files in the current directory are displayed. Initially, only SOFA02 will be present. Other FAOSTAT PC data files, version 3.0, can be used with FAOSTAT TS.

- Use the ARROW keys to highlight the file you wish to view and press ENTER to select it. Files are shown with the date of their last revision. You can also highlight your choice by typing the first letters of the file name. The current search string will appear in the lower left corner of the list.
- You can change the default data drive and directory from the file list by selecting the directory or drive of your choice.

If a current data file is open, loading in a new file will return FAOSTAT TS to its defaults (time trend, no trend line, no user-specified units or scalar). Only one file can be loaded at a time.

Once you have made a file selection, all the menu selections are activated.

Selecting a data series

- Use the DATA menu to select or modify a data series or to fit a statistical trend.
- Select a data series by choosing the name of a country and a data element from scrolling menus. The first entry displays a list of country names, the second entry displays a list of data item names and the third displays a list of data element names.

If you type the first letters of a name in a list, the menu selection bar will jump to the matching name. For example:

- Type NEW to skip to New Zealand.
- Press ENTER to select the highlighted name.

Displaying graphs and graph options

The GRAPH menu allows you to view the data in chart form. You can display time trends and table or column profiles. Options under the GRAPH menu change the data series shown as well as its display.

For example, to show a plot of the data selected:
- Go to the GRAPH menu.
- Select DISPLAY.

Many options to modify, save or print a graph are available only while the graph is on-screen. Remember to use the F1 help key for a reminder of your options.

Graph action keys. You have several options when a graph is displayed:

- Press ESC to exit the graph and return to the main menu.
- Press F1 for help on the graph action keys. The help box lists the choices available while a graph is on-screen. You must exit the help box before making a selection.
- Press the ARROW and (↑↓) PAGEUP, PAGEDOWN keys to change the series displayed.
- The plus key (+) allows you to add from one to three additional series to the one displayed. Press the MINUS key (-) to remove a series. To create a multiline chart:
  - Display an initial series.
  - Press the + key to add subsequent series to the chart.
- Press A to display a table of the axis data with statistics. Press T to show a table of the fitted trend data, the residuals and fit statistics (if a trend line is selected, see below).
- The INS key permits you to insert text directly on the graph. While inserting text, press F1 for help on your text options. You can type small or large, horizontal or vertical text.
- To print a graph (only with compatible printers), press P and select your choice of printer from the menu. The print output is only a screen dump of the display, so the quality is limited.
- To save a graph for later printing or viewing, press S. The graph image will be saved in the common PCX bitmap format. You can use the PRINTPCX program or other software to view or print multiple images later. PRINTPCX also permits you to convert colour PCX images into black and white images suitable for inclusion in a word processing document.

Fitting trend lines
- To fit a statistical function to a data series, select FIT from the DATA menu. The options under FIT allow you to select the type of function, data year limits to include in the fit and a final projection year for a statistical forecast.
- By fitting a trend line (selecting the option under FIT) with a projection (selecting PROJECTION under FIT), a statistical forecast can be plotted. Use the + key to add a new data series to the graph, which can be made with only a few key strokes.

Charting profiles
The options under the GRAPH menu allow you to change the year span or style

of the graph display (options LIMITS and STYLE, respectively), or to switch from a time trend to a table or column data profile (VIEWPOINT). The VIEWPOINT option is an easy means to compare data for a particular year.

Viewpoint

- If you want to change from a time series display to a country or item profile display for a given year, select VIEWPOINT from the GRAPH menu. Select DISPLAY from the GRAPH menu, and the profile will be drawn. The initial profile display is for the last year of historical data. To change the year, use the ARROW (↑↓) keys. Press F1 for help.
- For a tables profile (profile of data across countries), you can either choose the tables to be displayed or let FAOSTAT TS select the top members and array them in order.

A limit of 50 items can appear in one profile. By selecting TOP MEMBERS instead of SELECTED MEMBERS, FAOSTAT TS will sort the values in the file and display a ranking of table or column values.

Viewing tables

- The TABLE menu allows you to look at data in a tabular format and to define subset tables that may be saved and imported into other software packages.
  - Go to the TABLE menu.
  - Select BROWSE DATA to view individual data tables from the current file.
- When viewing tables, a help bar appears at the bottom of the screen. Press PAGEUP OR PAGEDOWN to change the table displayed or press ALT+1 or ALT+2 to choose from a list of tables. Use the ARROW keys (↑↓←→) to scroll the columns and rows.

Series data

- The SERIES DATA option under the TABLE menu displays the last data series selected, including summary statistics. This is the series used to plot a graph. To change the series, you must make a new choice from the DATA menu.
- The SERIES DATA screen can also be displayed while you are in a graph by pressing the letter A. If more than one series has been plotted, only the last series is shown. The range of years used for the series and statistics can be adjusted through the LIMITS option under the GRAPH menu.
- To view country or item profile lists and statistics, select VIEWPOINT from the GRAPH. You can quickly see a list of the tables with the greatest values (for example, countries with the highest commodity consumption) by choosing a table profile from VIEWPOINT and selecting the TOP MEMBERS option. Then select SERIES DATA from the TABLE menu to view the list, or select DISPLAY from the GRAPH menu to plot a chart.

Trend data

- If the FIT option has been selected (from the DATA menu) for a time trend, then the values composing the trend can be displayed with the TREND DATA option. Summary statistics for the original series and for the trend as well as residual values are included. The list scrolls with the ARROW keys, and you can toggle between the axis and trend data with the A and T keys.

Exporting data

- The EXPORT option under the FILE menu allows you to export FAOSTAT TS data into other file formats or to create custom tables for viewing or printing. By selecting EXPORT, you will jump into another set of menus.
- To select the tables and columns you want to view or save, go to the DATA menu. You must mark your choice of options with the + key. To undo all your selections quickly, select RESET MARKS.
- To arrange, view, save or print data, go to the options under EXPORT (in the FILE menu):
  - FAO TABLE creates a table with data from the last four available years.
  - VIEW displays a temporary text file of the data selected. It is a convenient way to view a subset of the tables and columns in a FAOSTAT TS file and can also be used to see the effects of the ORIENTATION or LAYOUT selections before using the SAVE or PRINT option.
  - SAVE displays a list of file formats to let you save your data choices in a file. You will be prompted for a file name. If you need to export FAOSTAT TS data for use with other software, use this menu item. The WK1 and DBF file format selections are not affected by the LAYOUT options (see below).
  - PRINT prints your current table and column selections (only with compatible printers). Many printers cannot print more than five columns of FAOSTAT TS data. Select VIEW to check the table width before printing.
  - LAYOUT allows you to display years across rows or down columns. The default direction is down columns.
- To get back to the main FAOSTAT TS menu or to clear your selections and create more tables, go the RETURN option.

Making notes

To read or edit textual information on the current data file, select NOTES from the FILE menu. You also can call up the Notes box by pressing ALT+N at any of the menus. The option NOTES allows you to read or edit text associated with the data file.

DOS shell and exit

The DOS SHELL option under the FILE menu returns you to the DOS prompt temporarily but keeps FAOSTAT TS in memory. This is not the normal way to exit the program. It is useful if you need to execute a DOS command and would like to return to the same data file. The data file itself is dropped from memory and reloaded on return, so default values will be in effect.

Exiting **FAOSTAT TS**

- To exit FAOSTAT TS:
  - Go to the FILE menu.
  - Select EXIT.

The Alt+X or Alt+Q key combinations are short cuts to exit the program from almost any screen.

Sales and Marketing Group, Information Division, FAO
Viale delle Terme di Caracalla, 00100 Rome, Italy
Tel.: +39 06 57051 – Fax: +39 06 5705 3360
E-mail: publications-sales@fao.org
www.fao.org/catalog/giphome.htm

أماكن بيع مطبوعات المنظمة
当地何处可以购买粮农组织出版物
WHERE TO PURCHASE FAO PUBLICATIONS LOCALLY
POINTS DE VENTE DES PUBLICATIONS DE LA FAO
PUNTOS DE VENTA DE PUBLICACIONES DE LA FAO

- **ANGOLA**
Empresa Nacional do Disco e de Publicações, ENDIPU-U.E.E.
Rua Cirilo da Conceição Silva, N° 7
C.P. N° 1314-C, Luanda

- **ARGENTINA**
Librería Hemisferio Sur
Pasteur 743, 1028 Buenos Aires
Correo eléctrico:
adolfop@hemisferiosur.com.ar
World Publications S.A.
Av. Córdoba 1877, 1120 Buenos Aires
Tel./Fax: (+54) 11 48158156

- **AUSTRALIA**
Tek Imaging Pty. Ltd
PO Box 404, Abbotsford, Vic. 3067
Tel.: (+61) 3 9417 5361
Fax: (+61) 3 9419 7154
E-mail: jpdavies@ozemail.com.au
or admin@tekimaging.com.au

- **BELGIQUE**
M.J. De Lannoy
202, avenue du Roi, B-1060 Bruxelles
CCP: 000-0808993-13
Mél.: jean.de.lannoy@infoboard.be

- **BOLIVIA**
Los Amigos del Libro
Av. Heroínas 311, Casilla 450
Cochabamba;
Mercado 1315, La Paz
Correo eléctrico:
gutten@amigol.bo.net

- **BOTSWANA**
Botsalo Books (Pty) Ltd
PO Box 1532, Gaborone
Tel.: (+267) 312576
Fax: (+267) 372608
E-mail: botsalo@botsnet.bw

- **BRAZIL**
Fundação Getúlio Vargas
Praia do Botafogo 190, C.P. 9052
Rio de Janeiro
Correo eléctronico: livraria@fgv.br
Núcleo Editora da Universidade Federal Fluminense
Rua Miguel de Frias 9
Icaraí-Niterói 24
220-000 Rio de Janeiro
Editora UFPR
Rua Presidente Faria s/n°
Prédio Histórico da UFPR
Curitiba, Paraná, CEP 80.020-300
Tel.: (+55) 41 310 2734
Web Site: www.editora.ufpr.br

- **CAMEROUN**
CADDES
Centre Africain de Diffusion et
Développement Social
B.P. 7317, Douala Bassa
Tél.: (+237) 43 37 83
Télécopie: (+237) 42 77 03

- **CANADA**
Renouf Publishing
5369 chemin Canotek Road, Unit 1
Ottawa, Ontario K1J 9J3
Tel.: (+1) 613 745 2665
Fax: (+1) 613 745 7660
E-mail: order.dept@renoufbooks.com
Web site: www.renoufbooks.com

- **CHILE**
Librería - Marta Caballero
c/o FAO, Oficina Regional para América
Latina y el Caribe (RLC)
Avda. Dag Hammarskjold, 3241
Vitacura, Santiago
Tel.: (+56) 2 33 72 314
Correo eléctrico:
german.rojas@field.fao.org
Correo eléctrico:
caballerocastillo@hotmail.com

- **CHINA**
**China National Publications
Import & Export Corporation**
16 Gongti East Road, Beijing 100020
Tel.: (+86) 10 6506 3070
Fax: (+86) 10 6506 3101
E-mail: serials@cnpiec.com.cn

- **COLOMBIA**
INFOENLACE LTDA
Calle 72 N° 13-23 Piso 3
Edificio Nueva Granada
Santafé de Bogotá
Tel.: (+57) 1 6009474-6009480
Fax: (+57) 1 2480808-2176435
Correo electrónico:
servicliente@infoenlace.com.co

- **CONGO**
Office national des librairies populaires
B.P. 577, Brazzaville

- **COSTA RICA**
Librería Lehmann S.A.
Av. Central, Apartado 10011
1000 San José
Correo electronico:
llehmann@solracsa.co.cr

- **CÔTE D'IVOIRE**
CEDA
04 B.P. 541, Abidjan 04
Tél.: (+225) 22 20 55
Télécopie: (+225) 21 72 62

- **CUBA**
**Ediciones Cubanas
Empresa de Comercio Exterior
de Publicaciones**
Obispo 461, Apartado 605, La Habana

- **CZECH REPUBLIC**
Myris Trade Ltd
V Stinhlach 1311/3, PO Box 2
142 01 Prague 4
Tel.: (+420) 2 34035200
Fax: (+420) 2 34035207
E-mail: myris@myris.cz
Web site: www.myris.cz

- **DENMARK**
Gad Import Booksellers
Siljangade 6-8
DK-2300 Copenhagen S
Tel.: (+45) 3254 8011
Fax: (+45) 3254 2368

- **ECUADOR**
Libri Mundi, Librería Internacional
Juan León Mera 851
Apartado Postal 3029, Quito
Correo electrónico:
librimu1@librimundi.com.ec
Web site: www.librimundi.com
**Universidad Agraria del Ecuador
Centro de Información Agraria**
Av. 23 de julio, Apartado 09-01-1248
Guayaquil
Librería Española
Murgeón 364 y Ulloa, Quito

- **EGYPT**
**MERIC
The Middle East Readers' Information
Centre**
2 Baghat Aly Street, Appt. 24
El Masry Tower D
Cairo/Zamalek
Tel.: (+20) 2 3413824/34038818
Fax: (+20) 2 3419355
E-mail: mafouda@meric-co.com

- **ESPAÑA**
Librería Agrícola
Fernando VI 2, 28004 Madrid
**Librería de la Generalitat
de Catalunya**
Rambla dels Estudis 118 (Palau Moja)
08002 Barcelona
Tel.: (+34) 93 302 6462
Fax: (+34) 93 302 1299

Mundi Prensa Libros S.A.
Castelló 37, 28001 Madrid
Tel.: +34 91 436 37 00
Fax: +34 91 575 39 98
Sitio Web: www.mundiprensa.com
Correo electrónico:
libreria@mundiprensa.es
Mundi Prensa - Barcelona
Consejo de Ciento 391
08009 Barcelona
Tel.: (+34) 93 488 34 92
Fax: (+34) 93 487 76 59

- **FINLAND**
Akateeminen Kirjakauppa
PL 23, 00381 Helsinki
(Myymälä/Shop: Keskuskatu 1
00100 Helsinki)
Tel.: (+358) 9 121 4385
Fax: (+358) 9 121 4450
E-mail: akatilaus@akateeminen.com
Web site: www.akateeminen.com/
suurasiakkaat/palvelut.htm

- **FRANCE**
Editions A. Pedone
13, rue Soufflot, 75005 Paris
Lavoisier Tec & Doc
14, rue de Provigny
94236 Cachan Cedex
Mél.: livres@lavoisier.fr
Site Web: www.lavoisier.fr
Librairie du commerce international
10, avenue d'Iéna
75783 Paris Cedex 16
Mél.: librarie@cfce.fr
Site Web: www.cfce.fr

- **GERMANY**
**Alexander Horn Internationale
Buchhandlung**
Friedrichstrasse 34
D-65185 Wiesbaden
Tel.: +49 611 9923540/9923541
Fax: +49 611 9923543
E-mail: alexhorn1@aol.com
**TRIOPS - Tropical Scientific Books
S. Toeche-Mittler
Versandbuchhandlung GmbH**
Hindenburstr. 33
D-64295 Darmstadt
Tel.: (+49) 6151 336 65
Fax: (+49) 6151 314 048
E-mail for orders: orders@net-library.de
E-mail for info.: info@net-library.de /
triops@triops.de
Web site: www.net-library.de /
www.triops.de
Uno Verlag
Am Hofgarten, 10
D-53113 Bonn
Tel.: (+49) 228 94 90 20
Fax: (+49) 228 94 90 222
E-mail: info@uno-verlag.de
Web site: www.uno-verlag.de

- **GHANA**
SEDCO Publishing Ltd
Sedco House, Tabon Street
Off Ring Road Central, North Ridge
PO Box 2051, Accra
Readwide Bookshop Ltd
PO Box 0600 Osu, Accra
Tel.: (+233) 21 22 1387
Fax: (+233) 21 66 3347
E-mail: readwide@africaonline.cpm.gh

- **GREECE**
Librairie Kauffmann SA
28, rue Stadiou, 10564 Athens
Tel.: (+30) 1 3236817
Fax: (+30) 1 3230320
E-mail: ord@otenet.gr

- **GUYANA**
**Guyana National Trading
Corporation Ltd**
45-47 Water Street, PO Box 308
Georgetown

- **HONDURAS**
**Escuela Agrícola Panamericana
Librería RTAC**
El Zamorano, Apartado 93, Tegucigalpa
Correo electrónico:
libreriazam@zamorano.edu.hn

- **HUNGARY**
Librotrade Kft.
PO Box 126, H-1656 Budapest
Tel.: (+36) 1 256 1672
Fax: (+36) 1 256 8727

- **INDIA**
Allied Publisher Ltd
751 Mount Road
Chennai 600 002
Tel.: (+91) 44 8523938/8523984
Fax: (+91) 44 8520649
E-mail:
allied.mds@smb.sprintrpg.ems.vsnl.net.in
**EWP Affiliated East-West
Press PVT, Ltd**
G-I/16, Ansari Road, Darya Gany
New Delhi 110002
Tel.: (+91) 11 3264 180
Fax: (+91) 11 3260 358
E-mail: affiliat@nda.vsnl.net.in
Oxford Book and Stationery Co.
Scindia House
New Delhi 110001
Tel.: (+91) 11 3315310
Fax: (+91) 11 3713275
E-mail: oxford@vsnl.com
Periodical Expert Book Agency
G-56, 2nd Floor, Laxmi Nagar
Vikas Marg, Delhi 110092
Tel.: (+91) 11 2215045/2150534
Fax: (+91) 11 2418599
E-mail: pebe@vsnl.net.in
Bookwell
Head Office:
2/72, Nirankari Colony, New Delhi - 110009
Tel.: (+91) 11 725 1283
Fax: (+91) 11 328 13 15
Sales Office:
24/4800, Ansari Road
Darya Ganj, New Delhi - 110002
Tel.: (+91) 11 326 8786
E-mail: bkwell@nde.vsnl.net.in

- **INDONESIA**
P.F. Book
Jl. Setia Budhi No. 274, Bandung 40143
Tel.: (+62) 22 201 1149
Fax: (+62) 22 201 2840
E-mail:
pfbook@bandung.wasantara.net.id

- **IRAN**
**The FAO Bureau, International
and Regional Specialized
Organizations Affairs**
Ministry of Agriculture of the Islamic
Republic of Iran
Keshavarz Bld, M.O.A., 17th floor
Teheran

- **ITALY**
FAO Bookshop
Viale delle Terme di Caracalla
00100 Roma
Tel.: (+39) 06 57052313
Fax: (+39) 06 57053360
E-mail: publications-sales@fao.org
**Libreria Commissionaria Sansoni
S.p.A. - Licosa**
Via Duca di Calabria 1/1
50125 Firenze
Tel.: (+39) 55 64831
Fax: (+39) 55 64 2 57
E-mail: licosa@ftbcc.it
**Libreria Scientifica Dott. Lucio de Biasio
"Aeiou"**
Via Coronelli 6, 20146 Milano

- **JAPAN**
**Far Eastern Booksellers
(Kyokuto Shoten Ltd)**
12 Kanda-Jimbocho 2 chome
Chiyoda-ku - PO Box 72
Tokyo 101-91
Tel.: (+81) 3 3265 7531
Fax: (+81) 3 3265 4656

أماكن بيع مطبوعات المنظمة
当地何处可以购买粮农组织出版物
WHERE TO PURCHASE FAO PUBLICATIONS LOCALLY
POINTS DE VENTE DES PUBLICATIONS DE LA FAO
PUNTOS DE VENTA DE PUBLICACIONES DE LA FAO

05/02

Maruzen Company Ltd
PO Box 5050
Tokyo International 100-31
Tel.: (+81) 3 3275 8582
Fax: (+81) 3 3275 9072
E-mail: o_miyakawa@maruzen.co.jp

• **KENYA**
Text Book Centre Ltd
Kijabe Street
PO Box 47540, Nairobi
Tel.: +254 2 330 342
Fax: +254 2 225 77 79
Inter Africa Book Distribution
Kencom House, Moi Avenue
PO Box 73580, Nairobi
Tel.: (+254) 2 211 184
Fax: (+254) 2 223 570
Legacy Books
Mezzanine 1, Loita House, Loita Street
Nairobi, PO Box 68077
Tel.: (+254) 2 303853
Fax: (+254) 2 330854

• **LUXEMBOURG**
M.J. De Lannoy
202, avenue du Roi
B-1060, Bruxelles (Belgique)
Mél.: jean.de.lannoy@infoboard.be

• **MADAGASCAR**
**Centre d'Information et de
Documentation Scientifique et
Technique**
Ministère de la recherche appliquée
au développement
B.P. 6224, Tsimbazaza, Antananarivo

• **MALAYSIA**
MDC Publishers Printers Sdn Bhd
MDC Building
2717 & 2718, Jalan Parmata Empat
Taman Permata, Ulu Kelang
53300 Kuala Lumpur
Tel.: (+60) 3 41086600
Fax: (+60) 3 41081506
E-mail: mdcpp@mdcpp.com.my
Web site: www.mdcpp.com.my

• **MAROC**
La Librairie Internationale
70, rue T'ssoule
B.P. 302 (RP), Rabat
Tél.: (+212) 37 75 0183
Fax: (+212) 37 75 8661

• **MÉXICO**
**Librería, Universidad Autónoma de
Chapingo**
56230 Chapingo
Libros y Editoriales S.A.
Av. Progreso N° 202-1° Piso A
Apartado Postal 18922
Col. Escandón, 11800 México D.F.
Correo electrónico: lyesa99@mail.com/
ventas@lyesa.com
Mundi Prensa Mexico, S.A.
Río Pánuco, 141 Col. Cuauhtémoc
C.P. 06500, México, DF
Tel.: (+52) 5 533 56 58
Fax: (+52) 5 514 67 99
Correo electrónico:
resavbp@data.net.mx

• **NETHERLANDS**
Roodveldt Import b.v.
Brouwersgracht 288
1013 HG Amsterdam
Tel.: (+31) 20 622 80 35
Fax: (+31) 20 625 54 93
E-mail: roodboek@euronet.nl
Swets & Zeitlinger b.v.
PO Box 830, 2160 Lisse
Heereweg 347 B, 2161 CA Lisse
E-mail: infono@swets.nl
Web site: www.swets.nl

• **NEW ZEALAND**
Legislation Direct
PO Box 12418
Bowen Street, Wellington
Tel.: (+64) 4 496 56 92
Fax: (+64) 4 496 56 98
E-mail: donna@legislationdirect.co.nz

Oasis Official
PO Box 3627, Wellington
Tel.: (+64) 4 499 1551
Fax: (+64) 4 499 1972
E-mail: sales@oasisbooks.co.nz
Web site: www.oasisbooks.co.nzl

• **NICARAGUA**
Librería HISPAMER
Costado Este Univ. Centroamericana
Apartado Postal A-221, Managua
Correo electrónico:
hispamer@munditel.com.ni

• **NIGERIA**
University Bookshop (Nigeria) Ltd
University of Ibadan, Ibadan

• **PAKISTAN**
Mirza Book Agency
65 Shahrah-e-Quaid-e-Azam
PO Box 729, Lahore 3

• **PARAGUAY**
**Librería Intercontinental
Editora e Impresora S.R.L.**
Caballero 270 c/Mcal Estigarribia
Asunción

• **PHILIPPINES**
International Booksource Center, Inc.
1127-A Antipolo St, Barangay Valenzuela
Makati City
Tel.: (+63) 2 8966501/8966505/8966507
Fax: (+63) 2 8966497
E-mail: ibcdina@pacific.net.ph

• **POLAND**
Ars Polona Joint Stock Company
Krakovwskie Przedmiescie 7
00-950 Warsaw, PO Box 1001
Tel.: (+48) 22 826 12 01
Fax: (+48) 22 826 62 40
E-mail: books119@arspolona.com.pl
Web site: www.arspolona.com.pl

• **PORTUGAL**
**Livraria Portugal, Dias e Andrade
Ltda.**
Rua do Carmo, 70-74
Apartado 2681, 1200 Lisboa Codex
Correo electrónico:
liv.portugal@mail.telepac.pt

• **REPÚBLICA DOMINICANA**
CEDAF - Centro para el Desarrollo
Agropecuario y Forestal, Inc.
Calle José Amado Soler, 50 - Urban.
Paraíso
Apartado Postal, 567-2, Santo Domingo
Tel.: (+001) 809 540 6416/
5655603
Fax: (+001) 809 5444727/5676989
Correo electrónico: fda@Codetel.net.do
Web site: www.fda.org.do

• **SINGAPORE**
Select Books Pte Ltd
Tanglin Shopping Centre
19 Tanglin Road, #03-15,
Singapore 247909
Tel.: (+65) 732 1515
Fax: (+65) 736 0855
E-mail: info@selectbooks.com.sg
Web site: www.selectbooks.com.sg

• **SLOVAK REPUBLIC**
**Institute of Scientific and Technical
Information for Agriculture**
Samova 9, 950 10 Nitra
Tel.: (+421) 87 522 185
Fax: (+421) 87 525 275
E-mail: uvtip@nr.sanet.sk

• **SOMALIA**
Samater
PO Box 936, Mogadishu

• **SOUTH AFRICA**
Preasidium Books (Pty) Ltd
810 - 4th Street, Wynberg 2090
Tel.: (+27) 11 88 75994
Fax: (+27) 11 88 78138
E-mail: pbooks@global.co.za

• **SUISSE**
UN Bookshop
Palais des Nations
CH-1211 Genève 1
Site Web: www.un.org
Adeco - Editions Van Diermen
Chemin du Lacuez, 41
CH-1807 Blonay
Tel.: (+41) (0) 21 943 2673
Fax: (+41) (0) 21 943 3605
E-mail: mvandier@ip-worldcom.ch
Münstergass Buchhandlung
Docudisp, PO Box 584
CH-3000 Berne 8
Tel.: (+41) 31 310 2321
Fax: (+41) 31 310 2324
E-mail: docudisp@muenstergass.ch
Web site: www.docudisp.ch

• **SURINAME**
Vaco n.v. in Suriname
Domineestraat 26, PO Box 1841
Paramaribo

• **SWEDEN**
Swets Blackwell AB
PO Box 1305, S-171 25 Solna
Tel.: (+46) 8 705 9750
Fax: (+46) 8 27 00 71
E-mail:
awahlquist@se.swetsblackwell.com
Web site: www.swetsblackwell.com/se/
Bokdistributören
c/o Longus Books Import
PO Box 610, S-151 27 Södertälje
Tel.: (+46) 8 55 09 49 70
Fax: (+46) 8 55 01 76 10; E-mail:
lis.ledin@hk.akademibokhandeln.se

• **THAILAND**
Suksapan Panit
Mansion 9, Rajdamnern Avenue,
Bangkok

• **TOGO**
Librairie du Bon Pasteur
B.P. 1164, Lomé

• **TRINIDAD AND TOBAGO**
Systematics Studies Limited
St Augustine Shopping Centre
Eastern Main Road, St Augustine
Tel.: (+001) 868 645 8466
Fax: (+001) 868 645 8467
E-mail: tobe@trinidad.net

• **TURKEY**
DUNYA ACTUEL A.S.
"Globus" Dunya Basinevi
100. Yil Mahallesi
34440 Bagcilar, Istanbul
Tel.: (+90) 212 629 0808
Fax: (+90) 212 629 4689
E-mail: aktuel.info@dunya.com/
Web site: www.dunyagazetesi.com.tr/

• **UNITED ARAB EMIRATES**
Al Rawdha Bookshop
PO Box 5027, Sharjah
Tel.: (+971) 6 538 7933
Fax: (+971) 6 538 4473
E-mail: alrawdha@hotmail.com

• **UNITED KINGDOM**
The Stationery Office
51 Nine Elms Lane
London SW8 5DR
Tel.: (+44) (0) 870 600 5522 (orders)
       (+44) (0) 207 873 8372 (inquiries)
Fax: (+44) (0) 870 600 5533 (orders)
       (+44) (0) 207 873 8247 (inquiries)
E-mail: ipa.enquiries@theso.co.uk
Web site: www.clicktso.com

and through The Stationery Office
Bookshops
E-mail: postmaster@theso.co.uk
Web site: www.the-stationery-
office.co.uk
Intermediate Technology Bookshop
103-105 Southampton Row
London WC1B 4HH
Tel.: (+44) 207 436 9761
Fax: (+44) 207 436 2013
E-mail: orders@itpubs.org.uk
Web site:
www.developmentbookshop.com

• **UNITED STATES**
Publications:
BERNAN Associates (ex UNIPUB)
4611/F Assembly Drive
Lanham, MD 20706-4391
Toll-free: (+1) 800 274 4447
Fax: (+1) 800 865 3450
E-mail: query@bernan.com
Web site: www.bernan.com
United Nations Publications
Two UN Plaza, Room DC2-853
New York, NY 10017
Tel.: (+1) 212 963 8302/800 253 9646
Fax: (+1) 212 963 3489
E-mail: publications@un.org
Web site: www.unog.org
UN Bookshop (direct sales)
The United Nations Bookshop
General Assembly Building Room 32
New York, NY 10017
Tel.: (+1) 212 963 7680
Fax: (+1) 212 963 4910
E-mail: bookshop@un.org
Web site: www.un.org
Periodicals:
Ebsco Subscription Services
PO Box 1943
Birmingham, AL 35201-1943
Tel.: (+1) 205 991 6600
Fax: (+1) 205 991 1449
The Faxon Company Inc.
15 Southwest Park
Westwood, MA 02090
Tel.: (+1) 617 329 3350
Telex: 95 1980
Cable: FW Faxon Wood

• **URUGUAY**
Librería Agropecuaria S.R.L.
Buenos Aires 335, Casilla 1755
Montevideo C.P. 11000

• **VENEZUELA**
Tecni-Ciencia Libros
CCCT Nivel C-2
Caracas
Tel.: (+58) 2 959 4747
Fax: (+58) 2 959 5636
Correo electrónico:
tclibros@attglobal.net
Fudeco, Librería
Avenida Libertador-Este
Ed. Fudeco, Apartado 254
Barquisimeto C.P. 3002, Ed. Lara
Tel.: (+58) 51 538 022
Fax: (+58) 51 544 394
Librería FAGRO
Universidad Central de Venezuela (UCV)
Maracay

• **YUGOSLAVIA**
Jugoslovenska Knjiga DD
Terazije 27
POB 36, 11000 Beograd
Tel.: (+381) 11 3340 025
Fax: (+381) 11 3231 079
E-mail: juknjiga@eunet.yu
  or babicmius@yahoo.com

• **ZIMBABWE**
Grassroots Books
The Book Café
Fife Avenue, Harare
Tel.: (+263) 4 79 31 82
Fax: (+263) 4 72 62 43